Techne, from Neoclassicism to Postmodernism

LAUER SERIES IN RHETORIC AND COMPOSITION
Series Editors: Catherine Hobbs, Patricia Sullivan, Thomas Rickert, and
Jennifer Bay

The Lauer Series in Rhetoric and Composition honors the contributions Janice
Lauer Hutton has made to the emergence of Rhetoric and Composition as a disciplinary study. It publishes scholarship that carries on Professor Lauer's varied
work in the history of written rhetoric, disciplinarity in composition studies,
contemporary pedagogical theory, and written literacy theory and research.

OTHER BOOKS IN THE SERIES

Rhetoric's Earthly Realm: Heidegger, Sophistry, and the Gorgian Kairos by Bernard
Alan Miller (2011)
Greek Rhetoric Before Aristotle, Revised and Expanded Edition, by Richard Leo
Enos (2011)
Walking and Talking Feminist Rhetorics: Landmark Essays and Controversies, ed-
ited by Lindal Buchanan and Kathleen J. Ryan (2010)
Transforming English Studies: New Voices in an Emerging Genre, edited by Lori
Ostergaard, Jeff Ludwig, and Jim Nugent (2009)
Ancient Non-Greek Rhetorics, edited by Carol S. Lipson and Roberta A. Binkley
(2009)
Roman Rhetoric: Revolution and the Greek Influence, Revised and Expanded
Edition, by Richard Leo Enos (2008)
Stories of Mentoring: Theory and Praxis, edited by Michelle F. Eble and Lynée
Lewis Gaillet (2008)
Writers Without Borders: Writing and Teaching in Troubled Times by Lynn Z.
Bloom (2008)
1977: A Cultural Moment in Composition, by Brent Henze, Jack Selzer, and
Wendy Sharer (2008)
The Promise and Perils of Writing Program Administration, edited by Theresa
Enos and Shane Borrowman (2008)
*Untenured Faculty as Writing Program Administrators: Institutional Practices and
Politics*, edited by Debra Frank Dew and Alice Horning (2007)
Networked Process: Dissolving Boundaries of Process and Post-Process by Helen
Foster (2007)
Composing a Community: A History of Writing Across the Curriculum, edited by
Susan H. McLeod and Margot Iris Soven (2006)
*Historical Studies of Writing Program Administration: Individuals, Communities,
and the Formation of a Discipline*, edited by Barbara L'Eplattenier and Lisa
Mastrangelo (2004). Winner of the WPA Best Book Award for 2004–2005.
Rhetorics, Poetics, and Cultures: Refiguring College English Studies (Expanded
Edition) by James A. Berlin (2003

TECHNE, FROM NEOCLASSICISM TO POSTMODERNISM

Understanding Writing as a Useful, Teachable Art

Kelly Pender

Parlor Press
Anderson, South Carolina
www.parlorpress.com

Parlor Press LLC, Anderson, South Carolina, USA

SAN: 254-8879

Library of Congress Cataloging-in-Publication Data

Pender, Kelly, 1974-
 Techne, from neoclassicism to postmodernism : understanding writing as a useful, teachable art / Kelly Pender.
    p. cm. -- (Lauer series in rhetoric and composition)
 Includes bibliographical references and index.
 ISBN 978-1-60235-207-0 (pbk. : alk. paper) -- ISBN 978-1-60235-208-7 (hardcover : alk. paper) -- ISBN 978-1-60235-209-4 (adobe ebook) -- ISBN 978-1-60235-210-0 (epub)
 1. Techne (Philosophy) 2. Composition (Language arts) I. Title.
 B105.T43P46 2011
 808.001--dc22

                          2011010084

Cover design by David Blakesley.
Printed on acid-free paper.

Parlor Press, LLC is an independent publisher of scholarly and trade titles in print and multimedia formats. This book is available in paper, cloth and Adobe eBook formats from Parlor Press on the World Wide Web at http://www.parlorpress.com or through online and brick-and-mortar bookstores. For submission information or to find out about Parlor Press publications, write to Parlor Press, 3015 Brackenberry Drive, Anderson, South Carolina, 29621, or email editor@parlorpress.com.

In Memory of My Mother,
Carolyn Whitley Pender, 1942-1989

Contents

Acknowledgments

As I was finishing up my bachelor's degree at the University of North Carolina at Chapel Hill, I had a conversation with Jane Danielewicz about what my next step would be. Knowing that I was interested in writing, Jane suggested that I consider applying to the master's program in English at North Carolina State University since they had a track in rhetoric and composition. Of course many factors affect how we've all gotten to where we are, and, in some ways, it's silly to single out one of those factors and attribute special importance to it. Nevertheless I am sure that if Jane had not made this recommendation, I would not be here, doing a job that I love in a place that I love. So, I want to thank Jane Danielewicz, a friend and mentor who understood what I wanted to do with my life before I did.

At North Carolina State, I had the good fortune of working with Steve Katz, Carolyn Miller, and Michael Carter. Although I am sure this book provides ample evidence that I have not lived up the example they set, I very much appreciate having worked with scholars whose research is as careful and rigorous as theirs is. As Chapters 4 and 6 of this book demonstrate, Mike's work has had an especially powerful impact on how I understand writing. An earlier version of Chapter 4 was published as "Negation and the Contradictory Technics of Rhetoric" in *Rhetoric Society Quarterly* 38.1 (2008): 2-24.

From NCSU, I went to Purdue, and it is to the friends and teachers I met there that I owe the greatest debt. Janice M. Lauer ignited my interest in the debates surrounding the term *"techne"* by introducing me to its long and complicated history without letting me succumb to the idea that there was nothing left to say about it. Thomas Rickert has also greatly influenced me and this book—first as a teacher, then as a friend, and finally as an editor. I am very grateful to him and to Jenny Bay, the other Lauer series editor, for their support of my work and the helpful comments they've given me along the way. I also want to thank Karen Kopelson, without whose friendship and incisive commentary (on things both academic and non-academic) my experience of graduate school and this book would have surely suffered.

I am indebted to David Blakesley for supporting this project and smoothly guiding it (and me) through the publication process. John Muckelbauer's smart, thoughtful feedback was extremely helpful, and I thank him for taking the time to work through it with me. Colleagues at Virginia Tech have also given me helpful feedback, not the least of which was Paul Heilker's (gentle) insistence that, no matter how ready I felt to "move on" from this project, I had to give it a shot by at least writing the book proposal. He deserves to stand at my door and loudly chant "I told you so." I also want to thank the members of my writing group—Kelly Belanger, Carlos Evia, Carolyn Rude, and Clare Dannenberg—for providing both feedback and a sense of community as I worked on the book's early chapters. David Radcliffe and Katy Powell read the entire manuscript and generously gave me suggestions for revision. Katy has also been a constant source of moral support (and fun) in the five years we've been at Tech. To say that I'm glad she ended up here with me is an understatement.

Last but in no way least I want to acknowledge my husband, Matthew Vollmer, and my son, Elijah Vollmer. There's really no way to adequately thank Matthew for the sacrifices he's made to get me through graduate school and the writing of this book, which, just to name a few, include working as an entomology research assistant in the cornfields of Indiana, teaching 4/4 loads as an adjunct at Purdue (while still managing to publish his own writing and give me the time I needed to work), complying with my almost insane need to split child care duties 50/50, and constantly having to attend to my learned helplessness with technology. As for Elijah, he has never known a time when I wasn't working on this book in some fashion or another, which is to say that he has never known a time when I wasn't preoccupied with something *else,* something *not him.* I am grateful to him not so much for simply tolerating my preoccupation but rather for being the perfect antidote to it.

Techne, from Neoclassicism to Postmodernism

Introduction

This is a book about *techne*. More specifically, it is a book about the relationships between *techne* and (1) the development of rhetoric and composition as an academic discipline in the mid-twentieth century, (2) the influence of postmodern theory on that development, and (3) what we often teach (or don't teach) under the rubric of "writing" in contemporary composition courses. The arguments I make about these relationships are deconstructive, which is to say—in the most general sense—that they seek to challenge some of our field's most firmly entrenched binaries about what writing is and how (or if) it should be taught. Although challenging these binaries is my primary goal here, it would be disingenuous to suggest that I am not also interested in recuperating or re-establishing the value of *techne* as a theory and pedagogy of writing for our field. In other words, it would be disingenuous *not* to acknowledge the fact that, even though I go about it in a different way, I am doing what a number of other rhetoricians have done before me: defending *techne* against charges that it is an inadequate, if not unethical, way to understand and teach writing.

Depending on your background (that is, how much you know about the field of rhetoric and composition and, importantly, where you learned what you know), the need for such defense of *techne* could either be immediately obvious or a total mystery. I've learned this from repeated attempts to answer the question, "What are you working on?" In some cases, the simple response "a book about *techne*" suffices. I elaborate a little on my particular approach to the topic, and the person who asked the question appears satisfied. More often than not, though, I have had to work harder, explaining not just what the term "*techne*" means but also why someone who studies writing would want—or need—to write a book about it. For the purposes of this introduction, I am going to assume that readers fall into this second camp. That is, I am going to assume that before I can make my argument about *techne*, I need to explain (in general terms) what *techne*

3

means and why it matters. Of course most of what I say here will be complicated by what I say later. But we have to start somewhere.

To summarize, then, "*techne*" is the Latin version of the Greek term "τέχνη," which, transliterated, is usually spelled "tekhne." The word has no equivalent in English, and so is usually understood as one of the three terms that approximate its Greek meaning: art, skill, craft. As many scholars have pointed out, however, none of these terms embrace "the whole complex structure" indicated by the term "*techne*" (Wild 255). Because the main point of chapter 1 is to explain what a phrase like "whole complex structure" means in the context of *techne*, I won't go into it here. Suffice it to say, though, that when we translate *techne* as either art *or* craft *or* skill, we're getting only a small, usually misleading piece of the puzzle. The situation isn't necessarily any better when we combine those translations since, as in the case of art and craft, they can contradict each other. The word "art" is most commonly used to refer to fine art, for instance, a painting or poem, while "craft" almost always connotes something more utilitarian like a chair or quilt. This particular contradiction has been a significant source of confusion in rhetoric and composition because "art" was the term used most frequently when *techne* reemerged in disciplinary conversations in the mid-twentieth century. Thus scholars were using a word associated with fine art to refer to a primarily instrumental understanding of rhetoric and writing. Later, as the debate about *techne* in rhetoric and composition developed, more scholars began using the term "*techne*," reducing (but not eliminating) this potential for confusion. In keeping with this trend, my choice here is to use the term "*techne*," although I do switch to "art" when it's the preferred term of the source I'm working with.

The key (for now) to understanding what *techne* means is understanding what connects it to those three related terms, "art," "craft," and "skill." Along with "*techne*," all of these words have to do with a process of making, that is, a process of producing or bringing-forth. Thus when we talk about the art of painting, for instance, we're talking about the knowledge, talent, and skill needed to bring a painting into existence. Likewise, when we talk about the craft of quilting, we're talking about the knowledge, talent, and skill needed to bring a quilt into existence. In Greek, the word that describes this process of bringing something into in existence is *poiesis*. Thus we can say that *techne* is a form of *poeisis*. As Aristotle argues in chapter 6 of *Nicoma-*

chean Ethics, however, *techne* is not just any form of *poeisis* but rather one that (1) follows a true course of reasoning, (2) has its origin in a maker, (3) is concerned with things that can either be or not be, and (4) locates its end outside the process of making in the use of the thing made. If there were such a thing as a "baseline" definition of *techne,* then arguably this would be it. Here, in these four criteria articulated by Aristotle, we can see essential features of *techne* that span across many (though not all) of its definitions, distinguishing it from other processes of making (e.g., nature) and from other kinds of knowledge (e.g., theoretical knowledge and practical knowledge). Perhaps more significantly, we can also see in these four criteria the reasons why some rhetoricians would want to argue that rhetoric (or writing)[1] is a *techne.* In the case of the first criterion, for instance, any process of making that follows a "true course of reasoning" is one that can be studied, systematized, and taught. Thus whether you're a fifth-century sophist who wants to make a living teaching rhetoric or a twentieth-century English professor who wants to make a living researching it, establishing the connection between rhetoric and *techne* is extremely important, as it legitimizes your work by allowing you to make a claim to knowledge. The second criterion has the same appeal in the sense that it directs work on rhetoric toward something knowable—the maker and the processes he goes through in order to conceive and produce his product. Acting in some ways as a counterbalance to the first two criteria, the third criterion allows rhetoricians to locate rhetoric in the world of the contingent, that is, in the world of things can come into being but don't have to and, importantly, don't do so according to any kind of universal law or principle. Thus while rhetoricians can try to explain the "true course of reasoning" that underlies the process of making, they are still able to acknowledge the limited, context-dependent nature of that reasoning. And finally, the appeal of the fourth criterion is, among other things, that it places rhetoric in a category of activities meant to accomplish something in the world, fill some need, achieve some end, or, if we want to put it in rhetorical terms, respond to some exigence. While this association of rhetoric with the instrumentality of *techne* hasn't given it a proper subject matter in the sense Socrates was after in Plato's *The Gorgias,* it has allowed contemporary scholars to align rhetoric with particular kinds of ends, thus quelling (some) concerns about its disciplinary identity and purpose.

As just this brief discussion demonstrates, there's a lot at stake in how we understand the relationship between *techne* and rhetoric. Chapter 2 (and, indeed, the whole book) will bear this point out more fully, but even here we can see that identifying rhetoric as a *techne* has important implications for what it means to be a rhetorician. If this is the case, however, then why don't more rhetoricians write about *techne?* Or, to put it differently, why would the significance of a book about *techne* be such a mystery to so many people? Of course there's no one answer to this question, but I think any complete answer would have to take into account the fact that some of *techne*'s features have become a kind of invisible foundation for the field. By that I mean that they are non-issues—premises so central to the day-to-day operations of rhetoric and composition that they usually go unnoticed and uncontested. Think, for example, of the number of teachers whose pedagogies are based on an explanation of the "true course of reasoning" underlying some aspect of the composing process (e.g., invention or revision). Although few of these teachers would refer to the criteria set out by Aristotle in *Nicomachean Ethics* to explain how they understand rhetoric, their teaching implicitly defines it is as a *techne*. As we will see later, this kind of pervasive acceptance of some of *techne*'s features is what early proponents of the term were after. In order for rhetoric and composition to become an academic discipline, they reasoned, it would need theories and pedagogies of writing based on research rather than tradition or personal preferences. By giving scholars a vocabulary and a history through which they could justify their efforts to do this research, *techne* helped fill this need, which is to say that it provided a foundation upon which the contemporary discipline of rhetoric and composition could be built.

While this foundation was, arguably, a very sturdy one, it was also a narrow one. By that I mean that while *techne* did, in fact, help to establish the research agendas necessary for improving pedagogy in first-year courses and establishing graduate programs in English departments, it also circumscribed those agendas within clear parameters, namely that rhetoric was to be understood as an instrumental form of discourse, that the point of studying it was to better understand the processes of producing it, and that the point of better understanding the processes of producing it was to create explicit methods for teaching it. For those who see these parameters as central to the identity and the day-to-day operations of rhetoric and composition—

or, more pointedly, for those who do not see them at all—it might not be clear why anyone would characterize them as narrow. But a number of scholars have done just this. Relying on the discourses of postmodernism, they have characterized the foundation provided by *techne* as narrow (and worse) because they see in rhetoric something more than the ends we can accomplish with it, the things we can know about it, and the methods we can use to teach it. Not surprisingly, other scholars have responded to these characterizations, calling upon a host of sources—postmodern and otherwise—in order to broaden our understanding of *techne* and (re)establish its relevance to a field that has outgrown many of the needs that made the term such an appealing resource for earlier researchers. Between these two sides (which are not really sides but rather conglomerations of positions that shift and evolve) there is an active debate about *techne* in rhetoric and composition, and through this debate we can see rhetoricians from all areas of the field engaging questions of epistemology, ethics, subjectivity, and disciplinarity that—though they might not have originated in the classroom—almost always have implications for it.

In short, *Techne* is a book about this debate; that is, it's a book about how scholars in rhetoric and composition have dealt with the fact that theirs is a field built on a foundation too narrow to anticipate—or perhaps even to accommodate—the changes in the English department brought on by the advent of postmodern theory. While *techne* is certainly an elastic concept, it's hard to imagine how its emphasis on reason, the maker, and instrumentality could be reconciled with a body of theory that explicitly challenges all of these things. Yet it's equally hard to imagine how that theory could be used to simply dismiss *techne* and its corollary pedagogies as inadequate or outdated. Isn't there enough subtlety and complexity within postmodern theory for us to keep some version of *techne?* If so, which version? What does a concept of *techne* that's compatible with postmodern theory look like? How does it have to change? Or does it have to change? These are the main questions that I try to answer in *Techne.* Thus while chapter 1 provides a general introduction to *techne*'s meanings across disciplines and historical periods, the majority of the book focuses on its meanings and significance in rhetoric and composition since the middle of the twentieth century. In this sense, it is fair to say that *Techne* is a history of the ways in which the concept of *techne* has changed and evolved in rhetoric and composition over the past four decades. However, because of the close connection between *techne* and disciplinarity, it is also a history of rhetoric and composition itself. Of course it is a necessarily narrow or selective history—one constructed from the perspective provided by a single concept. But as I suggested earlier, debates about *techne* cross subfields in rhetoric and composition, raising fundamental questions about what it means to study and to teach writing. In fact, I would argue that the advantage of looking at the history of rhetoric and composition through the lens of *techne* is that we are able to see the theoretical complexity and controversy surrounding some of the field's most basic claims without losing sight of the classroom. Thus if the perspective of this history is a narrow or selective one, it is also deep one. This is a tradeoff I can live with since the goal here is not to tell the whole story but instead to tell part of the story in a way that highlights both the problems and the promise of this sometimes invisible foundation upon which rhetoric and composition sits.

I begin telling this story in chapter 1, "What Is *Techne?*," which, as I explained, is a general introduction to *techne*'s meanings. Importantly, though, the point of this introduction is not broad coverage. In other words, the point is not to explain as many definitions of *techne* as possible. Rather, my goal in chapter 1 is to give readers a way of understanding how the term "*techne*" can have such variable, even contradictory meanings. To do this, I group definitions according to their epistemological and axiological features. That is, I group them according to (1) the requirements they establish in order for knowledge to qualify as "technical"[2] knowledge and (2) the kind of value they attribute to the process of making. Although no two definitions share precisely the same epistemological and axiological features, there is enough proximity among some of them to form the following five composite definitions:

1. *Techne* as a "how-to" guide or handbook
2. *Techne* as a rational ability to effect a useful result
3. *Techne* as a means of inventing new social possibilities
4. *Techne* as means of producing resources
5. *Techne* as a non-instrumental mode of bringing-forth

I draw on scholarship from across disciplines and historical periods to explain these five composite definitions in chapter 1, arguing that while there are discernible, sometimes obvious differences among them, they are better understood as relative positions on two continua than as discrete, self-contained entities.

In chapter 2, "The New Classicist Definition of Art," my focus narrows, and I explain how and why *techne* entered the professional discourse of rhetoric and composition in the mid-twentieth century. The "how" part of this explanation focuses on the new classicist definition of art, particularly on its relationships to the new romanticist definition of art, to heuristics, and to three theories of invention that became prominent around this time—tagmemic theory, Burkean theory, and pre-writing theory. The advantage of this approach is that it allows me to explain the sometimes confusing connections between terms like "art," "heuristics," and "invention" and then, through those connections, to account for some of the ways in which the new classicist definition of art influenced the development of rhetoric and composition as an academic discipline. In the second part of the chapter, I shift to the "why" part of the explanation, looking at some of what Robert J. Connors has called the "scattered and mostly rootless" conversations of rhetoric and composition's pre-disciplinary period ("Composition" 8). The point in looking back to work that predates the new classicist definition of art is to explain not only why *techne* entered the professional discourse of rhetoric and composition but also why it had the impact it had. Oftentimes we try to understand this impact in terms of its immediate context, that is, in terms of the work of those who supported the new classicist definition of art and the pedagogies associated with it. In fact, this is what I do in the first part of chapter 2. While these efforts are both necessary and productive, alone they can foster a kind of "heroes and villains" reading of history that places too much emphasis on the agency of individual scholars, thus obscuring the larger web of political, institutional, and social forces from which the new classicist definition of art emerged. Although chapter 2 is not a comprehensive account of those forces, it does help us understand how the new classicist definition art reflects changes that were happening not just in rhetoric and composition but also throughout the discipline of English at both the university and the high school levels.

In chapter 3, "Postmodern Theory and the Re-Tooling of *Techne*," I turn to scholarship written in the later twentieth century and the early twenty-first century, looking closely at what happened to *techne* once its association with heuristics weakened and once the discourses of postmodernism entered the field. Specifically, I explain how theorists used these discourses to go beyond earlier critiques of *techne* (which usually targeted the pedagogies associated with it) to challenge the theories of epistemology and subjectivity that operated within it, as well as the ethics (and sometimes the politics) of writing that were based upon it. While not all of these theorists wrote about *techne* per se, their work did raise questions about two of its most prominent and problematic features: its association with instrumentality and its emphasis on teachability. What happened to *techne* once critics began connecting composition's commitment to production to the ethical and institutional problems of instrumentality? And what happened once they began pointing out how theories of writing that privilege its teachable dimensions, which is to say, its rational dimensions, often ignore its non-rational, material dimensions? How did *techne* endure such challenges? I answer these questions in the second half of chapter 3 by reviewing work that has tried to "update" *techne*, that is, work that has revised it in order to better meet the changing needs of rhetoric and composition. In some instances, the goal of this work has been to make *techne* more compatible with postmodern theory by offering a new version of the term, while in others it has been to broaden our understanding of an existing version by recovering its forgotten features. Despite the fact that these efforts have sometimes produced conflicting accounts of *techne*'s meaning, I argue that they have all advanced the debate about *techne* in rhetoric and composition by demonstrating the concept's resistance to narrow definitions and (thus) its continuing relevance to the field.

Chapters 4 and 5 mark a shift in *Techne:* rather than focusing on how other scholars in the field have defined and valued *techne*, I begin making my own case, arguing that while the revisions and redefinitions that I review in chapter 3 have advanced the debate about *techne* in rhetoric and composition, they have also left important criticisms unanswered. By that I mean that more often than not these revisions and redefinitions have responded to critiques of *techne* by advocating a version of it that de-emphasizes its problematic features rather than by directly addressing arguments critical of them. In other words, while these revisions have shown why *techne* cannot be reduced to the features of teachablity and instrumentality, they have not shown why these features do not make *techne* an inadequate—epistemologically, ethically, or otherwise—way to understand and teach writing. I respond to this gap in *Techne* not only by explaining the larger arguments out of which the critiques of *techne* have come (chapter 3) but also by demonstrating how we can accept these critiques while still valuing *techne* as a theory and pedagogy of writing (chapters 4 and 5). To do this, I turn, in chapter 4, to Samuel Weber's understanding of *Ge-stell* in "Upsetting the Set Up: Remarks on Heidegger's Questing After Technics." "*Ge-stell,*" of course, is the term Heidegger uses in "The Question Concerning Technology" to describe how modern technology controls nature by challenging it forth and setting it in place as a ready-to-use resource. Although Lynn Worsham is (to my knowledge) the only scholar in rhetoric and composition who has critiqued *techne* explicitly because of its likeness to *Ge-stell,* others have critiqued it for similar reasons, arguing most frequently that *techne* reduces writing to rational, reproducible practices that allow us to more easily control and use language. Whereas most translators use the word "Enframing" to capture this controlling or setting-in-place function, Weber chooses "Emplacement" because it calls our attention to the "uncanny mixture of movement and stasis" that characterizes modern technics (988). He then explains how *Ge-stell,* by setting in place, gives way to new settings that require continuous re-setting, thus concluding that the "goings-on" of modern technics can "serve not just to close down but also to open up" (989). Accepting the critiques of *techne* as evidence of its ability to "close down," I use Weber's re-translation of *Ge-stell* as Emplacement in both chapters 4 and 5 to argue that it also has the ability to "open up." I demonstrate this ability in two ways. First, in chapter 4, "Closing Down and Opening Up: *Techne* and the Issue of Instrumentality," I use Maurice Blanchot's understanding of negation in "Literature and the Right to Death" to show that we can make language usable to us as an instrument only by simultaneously making it unusable to us as an object. In other words, I show that by putting language to work, we inevitably risk its ability to work. Second, in chapter 5, "Closing Down and Opening Up: *Techne* and the Issue of Teachability," I rely on Joseph Dunne's understanding of the relationship between *techne* and nature in *Back to the Rough Ground,* as well as Joseph Libertson's explanation of the non-dialectical nature of opposition in the work of Georges Bataille, to explain how the rational activity of *techne* both protects us from the possibility of losing control of writing and makes us vulnerable to that possibility. I then argue that contradictions like these explain how *techne* can create opportunities for us to experience writing as an inherently valuable, non-rational activity, despite its strong identification with instrumentality and teachability.

Relying on the arguments I make in chapters 4 and 5, I turn in chapter 6, "Why *Techne?* Why Now?," to explain why, despite its ability to "close down," we should still teach writing as a *techne.* At the heart of this explanation is the very straightforward claim that teaching writing as a *techne* encourages us to teach writing *as* writing, which is to say that it encourages us to focus our courses on writing itself as a process of textual production rather than the content that writing makes available through the processes of textual interpretation.[3] Although I recognize that this binary between producing and interpreting texts has been productively complicated by a number of scholars, I make this argument in chapter 6 because I share Susan Miller's concern that, as she puts it, "few discussions of writing pedagogy take it for granted that one of our goals is to teach how to write" (480). In other words, I make this argument because I believe that courses about writing often (and easily) slip into courses about something else, typically some form of cultural hermeneutics. Acknowledging that there are a number of explanations for this trend, I argue that it is attributable, at least in part, to the oppositions that have been created between the term "writing," which, in various ways, has come to refer to a kind of "opening up" activity—that is, an inherently valuable, sometimes unteachable activity—and the seemingly mundane, "closing down" activities that often fall under the rubrics of "composition" and "scribing." While I agree that these terms do not refer to the same thing—and while I do not advocate any kind of uncritical return to only the most teachable and instrumental of composition pedagogies and practices—I conclude chapter 6 by explaining why teaching writing *as* writing should not (and, in fact, cannot) be understood as a matter of *not* teaching composition or scribing.

1 What Is *Techne?*

technai *are means to an end or tools.*

—Barbara Warnick

Techne *is an epistemology. It is productive but not of things.*

—Ryan Moeller and Kenneth McAllister

To produce is to count, to codify, to systematize, to homogenize, to regulate via techne.

—Michelle Ballif

—techne, *or the belief that rhetoric is the practicable and perfectible art that enables one to be eloquent and persuasive.*

—Joseph Petraglia

techne *enables cultural critique and becomes the means by which new social possibilities are invented.*

—Janet M. Atwill and Janice M. Lauer

Based on the epigraphs above, it would seem that the answer to the question *what is techne?* depends entirely on whom you ask and when you ask them. In fact, I have often thought that if psychologists were to develop a Rorschach test specifically for rhetoricians, one of the cards should read "*TECHNE.*" That some scholars can look at those six letters and see the worst elements of humanism while others can look at it and see a progressive form of cultural critique or even a post-humanist means of rhetorical invention seems like clear evidence of the term's inkblot-like ambiguity. My goal in this first chapter is not to eliminate that ambiguity but rather to show how it's possible. In other words, I am less interested in defining *techne* than I am in explaining how it can be defined in such varied if not contradictory terms. Doing this allows me both to provide background for subsequent chapters and to begin, albeit in a very subtle way, my own argument about *techne*. After all, if I want to establish *techne*'s value as a theory and pedagogy of writing, then I need to demonstrate that it is *not* the semantic equivalent of an inkblot.

Before I begin this demonstration, however, I want to be very clear about *Techne*'s organization and purpose. Specifically, I want to emphasize that it should not be read as a history of *techne*'s meanings. While some portions of my discussion happen to proceed chronologically, others do not. While I try to represent the work of the scholars I review accurately, those representations are unavoidably partial. And while I provide examples of *techne*'s meaning from several historical periods, I do not believe those examples can reveal its complex history in any one particular period. What I believe they can—and do—reveal, however, is that definitions of *techne* can be usefully understood as existing on two continua: one that we could call "epistemological" since it designates the criteria that must be met in order for knowledge to attain the label of "technical" according to a particular definition; and a second that we could call "axiological" since it designates the kind of value a particular definition attributes to the activities under its purview.

There are, of course, other ways of understanding definitions of *techne*. For instance, we could map them chronologically according to historical period; we could map them according to discipline, distinguishing those definitions advocated by rhetoricians from those advocated by philosophers from those advocated by historians and so on; or we could map them around key figures like Plato, Aristotle, and Heidegger. But none of these features satisfactorily explain the variety in definitions of *techne;* that is, they do not help us to understand how *techne* can be valorized as an embodied form of creativity one minute and rejected as objectified mechanical skill another. That kind of definitional variety is better understood as the result of differences in epistemology and axiology than as the result of differences in period, discipline, or figure.

By "differences in epistemology," I am referring to the fact that definitions of *techne* establish different criteria for what kinds of knowledge can count as technical knowledge. According to one of Plato's definitions of *techne,* for instance, knowledge must be amenable to precise analysis, that is, to itemization and organization, if it is to attain the title of "*techne*" (*Phaedrus* 265–266; 270–273; 277). Thus arts based on weighing, counting, or measuring are paradigmatic in his view (*Protagoras* 356a). The writer of the Hippocratic text, "On Ancient Medicine," however, de-emphasizes this criterion in his effort to establish medicine as a bona fide *techne,* contending that even though the art of healing has "not attained exactness in every detail," readers should recognize its "discoveries as the work, not of chance, but of inquiry rightly and correctly conducted" (qtd. in Roochnik 48–9). As these examples indicate, my argument here is that definitions of *techne* can be placed on an epistemological continuum that is characterized at one end by knowledge exhibiting high degrees of precision, reliability, universality, and teachability and at the other by knowledge exhibiting the same traits but to a significantly lower degree.

The second continuum, which I described as "axiological," designates the kind of value associated with *techne.* To some this might seem like a cut-and-dried issue, one that requires no continuum since by most definitions *techne* refers to a process of making that is always instrumental. In other words, the end of a particular *techne* always resides in the use of its products, not in the activity of producing them. Aristotle makes this point very clearly in chapter 6 of *Nicomachean Ethics,* arguing that it is, in part, the instrumentality of *techne* that distinguishes it from theoretical and practical knowledge. As it turns out, though, Aristotle had a hard time maintaining a strictly instrumental understanding of *techne.* In *Magna Moralia,* for instance, he described flute-playing as an art in which the end and the activity are the same, thus giving us an instance of a *techne* whose value is intrinsic rather than instrumental (2.12.1211b26–31). Heidegger also complicates *techne*'s identification with instrumentality when, in *An Introduction to Metaphysics,* he defines it as a mode of bringing forth into unconcealment that allows the being of things to shine forth (159–60). Heidegger is actually quite emphatic about the non-instrumental value of *techne,* insisting in "The Origin of the Work of Art" that the term should not be reductively understood as the making of equipment (59). Far from being cut-and-dried, then, the issue of value and *techne*—like the issue of epistemology and *techne*—is a complex one that allows for a number of different positions.

While it's probably obvious that no two definitions of *techne* occupy exactly the same axiological or epistemological position, I would argue that there is enough proximity among some of them (or among some elements of them) for distinct groups of definitions to emerge. More specifically, I would argue that if we mapped as many definitions of *techne* as possible on these continua, we would see that they cluster around the epistemological and axiological positions represented by the following five composite definitions:

1. *Techne* as a "how-to" guide or handbook
2. *Techne* as a rational ability to effect a useful result
3. *Techne* as a means of inventing new social possibilities
4. *Techne* as a means of producing resources
5. *Techne* as a non-instrumental mode of bringing-forth

My goal in the rest of the chapter is to explain and illustrate these definitions through the work of scholars from a variety of historical periods and a variety of disciplines. It is very important to note that by using a particular scholar's work to explain or illustrate one of these definitions, I am not necessarily mapping him or her in the epistemological and/or axiological position of that definition. While it's true that some writers do advocate one definition of *techne* in particular, it is more often the case that they define and/or use the term in a variety of ways. As the brief discussion of Aristotle above demonstrated, sometimes not even the most systematic of thinkers manages to produce a totally unified or consistent understanding of the term. This inconsistency explains my reluctance to map individual scholars on the graph. As a final caveat, I also want to acknowledge that I do not believe this list of five definitions is exhaustive or that their positions on these continua are immutable. Both the book in general and the following discussion in particular will bear this qualification out, while still demonstrating the heuristic value of viewing *techne*'s meanings through the lens of these five definitions and their epistemological and axiological positions.

TECHNE AS A "HOW-TO" GUIDE OR HANDBOOK

When rhetoric is the activity at issue, we usually refer to this definition of *techne* simply as the "handbook tradition," imagining classical treatises such as the *Rhetorica ad Herennium,* early twentieth-century books such as Edwin C. Woolley's *Handbook of Composition: A Compendium of Rules,* or perhaps most readily, a contemporary guide to grammar like *The Brief Penguin Handbook* (Faigley). While there's plenty of disagreement about when texts like these came into existence, there's little disagreement about the features that characterize them. Most are highly (if not obsessively) organized collections of rules, techniques, or stock examples designed to give readers basic knowledge about some aspect of rhetoric. To that end, they often use prescriptive language and, unlike classical rhetorics such as Aristotle's or contemporary rhetorics such as *Everything's An Argument* (Lunsford and Ruszkiewicz), tend not to embed their prescriptions in the context of richer theoretical discussion.

For classical philosophers like Plato and Aristotle, this absence of theoretical discussion marks the primary deficiency of handbooks. Whereas a handbook offers techniques to be applied or examples to be mimicked, a real *techne* tries to impart a more comprehensive understanding of what causes rhetorical success and failure. In Plato's view, art without an understanding of causes is no art at all but rather "merely the preliminaries of the art" (*Phaedrus* 269). In his attempt to teach Phaedrus what a genuine *techne* of rhetoric would require, Socrates argues that the rhetorician would have to understand (through rigorous analysis) which kinds of discourse affect which kinds of souls so that he could "give an account of causation"—that is, so he could explain why some speeches succeed and why some fail (271). Aristotle agrees with his teacher on this point, arguing in *On Sophistical Refutations* that teaching rhetoric with a handbook is like offering a man with foot pain many kinds of shoes without teaching him the *techne* of shoemaking: his pain might disappear for a while, but he lacks the knowledge necessary to find a long-term solution to the problem (184a10–b4).

According to Quintilian, it was the status associated with established arts like shoemaking that some classical rhetoricians were after when they first included "*techne*" in the titles of their rhetorical handbooks. In other words, they were hoping the term would lend their treatises "an additional title of respect" (*Institutio of Oratoria* 2.17.2–3). From a contemporary perspective, however, it seems that the lending may have also gone the other way, inadvertently producing a conception of *techne* that is easily de-legitimized because of its association with handbooks or "how-to" guides. After all, underlying the production of any handbook is the assumption that knowledge of its subject matter can be expressed and taught through rules, precepts, and examples. Such knowledge would have to be knowable, reliable, transferable, and teachable to the extreme.

When it comes to rhetoric, however, only its most superficial elements fit this epistemological bill. Thus to understand rhetoric as a *techne* with this definition in mind is either an act of simplification (i.e., of reducing rhetoric to grammar or mechanics) or, as George Kennedy argues, one of ossification since a handbook that attempts to treat more complex elements like invention would almost surely turn them into rigid rules. In either case, the result would be not only the devaluation of rhetoric but also the devaluation of teaching since reading rules from a manual doesn't exactly warrant the intervention (or payment) of a teacher. It is no wonder, then, that Isocrates rejected the "hard and fast rules" of the handbook conception of *techne,* contending that it was a paradigm of knowledge more compatible with spelling than speechwriting (*Against* 171). Unlike Plato, Isocrates considered himself a teacher of the discursive arts, and so he had a stake in differentiating the content of his courses from the superficial content of the handbooks. In addition, Isocrates's emphasis on the situational nature of rhetoric, that is, the premium he put on a discourse's "fitness for the occasion, propriety of style, and originality of treatment," made the idea of a handbook of rhetoric seem inappropriate if not somewhat oxymoronic (171). After all, how do you codify and teach knowledge about a situation-dependent activity in advance of an actual situation?

Contemporary critics of the handbook definition of *techne* have focused on difficult epistemological questions like this one, typically paying less attention to any problems that might arise from its axiological position. Take, for example, Hans-Georg Gadamer's critique of *techne* in *Truth and Method,* his major philosophical work. To cut to the chase, Gadamer's answer to the question of how you teach knowledge about a situation-dependent activity in advance of the actual situation is that you don't—or rather, that you can't. The activity at issue for Gadamer is interpretation, and his project can be described as a refutation of what most nineteenth-century theorists had to say about it. Gadamer was particularly troubled by the belief that the interpreter's prejudices were some kind of barrier between the reader and the real meaning of the text. Developing methods for overcoming such prejudice became the central focus of nineteenth-century hermeneutics, revealing what Gadamer saw as an ongoing commitment to Enlightenment prejudices, namely the prejudice against prejudice itself (270).

Opposed to the rationalism that he saw operating in this commitment to Enlightenment thinking, Gadamer argued that no technique could fully liberate an interpreter from her prejudices. Thus the goal of interpretation wasn't somehow to access a text unobstructed by those prejudices but instead to use them as ways of interacting with the text in order to reveal new meanings. Such interaction, however, required that the interpreter gain some awareness of "effective history"; that is, she had to understand that understanding itself is a thoroughly historical event (300). Gadamer highlighted the challenge of gaining this awareness by pointing to the difficulty of gaining awareness of any situation, including a hermeneutical situation:

> The very idea of a situation means that we are not standing outside of it and hence are unable to have any objective knowledge of it. We always find ourselves within a situation, and throwing light on it is a task that is never entirely finished. This is also true of the hermeneutic situation—i.e., the situation in which we find ourselves with regard to the tradition that we are trying to understand. The illumination of this situation—reflection on effective history—can never be completely achieved; yet the fact that it cannot be is due not to a deficiency in reflection but the essence of the historical being that we are. *To be historical means that knowledge of oneself can never be complete.* (301–2)

It is this emphasis on the limited and incomplete nature of self-knowledge (or any knowledge) that led Gadamer to critique *techne* as the kind of objectifying, decontextualized skill found in handbooks. Although he was careful to point out that the hermeneutical awareness described above is not a form of ethical knowledge, Gadamer nevertheless compared it to Aristotle's concept of *phronesis* (i.e., ethical knowledge) in order to stress its situation-bound, non-objectifiable nature. But of course Aristotle contrasted *phronesis* to *techne* in his *Nicomachean Ethics*, and it seems as though Gadamer picked up on this contrast, suggesting not only a link between *phronesis* and hermeneutical consciousness but also one between *techne* and nineteenth-century interpretive methods. Like those interpretive methods, "the skill [. . .] of the craftsman" is something that can be developed and acquired independently of the situation in which it is to be applied (314, 317). Moreover, it can be applied to many different situations, providing the craftsman (or interpreter) with a "pregiven universal" that, according to Gadamer, risks obscuring the demands of particular situation (313, 324). Thus it is probably more accurate to say that for Gadamer the problem with *techne* is that it is a de-contextualiz*ing* (as opposed to just decontextualiz*ed*) form of knowledge. The problem, in other words, isn't simply that technical knowledge has been taken out of context but that in applying that knowledge one actually loses sight of the context.

Joseph Petraglia made a very similar argument about *techne* in "Is There Life After Process? The Role of Social Scientism in a Changing Discipline," claiming that if compositionists remained committed to improving students' writing by creating technical knowledge (i.e., by creating generic writing skills), then they were sure to lose sight of the "web of cultural practices, social interaction, power differentials, and discursive conventions governing the production of text" (54). According to Petraglia, this commitment—what he later called the "tether to *techne*"—has serious consequences for the field both professionally and pedagogically ("Shaping" 90–1). Echoing Isocrates's complaint about the sophists' handbooks, he argued that when compositionists understand writing as a *techne,* they threaten to return their work to "the realm of scribal skill" where their job consists of "conveying how-tos, reciting rules of thumb, passing out essay assignments, and correcting exercises" (60). And perhaps worse, they fail to teach students the important receptive skills they need in order to understand how members of discursive communities write (61–2). Again like Isocrates, Petraglia doesn't believe that students can be taught to communicate "irrespective of the actual situations in which rhetoric is used" ("Shaping" 90–1). Thus he maintained that they need thick descriptions of how writers learn to write "within specialized domains outside the composition classroom"—not the generic writing skills offered by the *techne* tradition (56–7).

Clearly both Petraglia and Gadamer understand the "*techne* tradition" in rather narrow terms. While it is true that Gadamer never explicitly connects *techne* to rhetorical handbooks, I would argue that his emphasis on the problems of de-contextualization and objectification suggests that he had something like a handbook or manual in mind when used the term.[4] Petraglia, on the other hand, does explicitly idenitify *techne* with the handbook tradition, arguing that even though students learn valuable "mechanical skills and academic conventions" in the "*techne*-centric classroom," such a "palliative" approach to writing is an impediment to a "richer rhetorical education" ("Shaping" 90–1). Because their understanding of *techne* is, indeed, so narrow, we can easily understand why Petraglia and Gadamer would reject it as an approach to the production and interpretation of discourse. As I have tried to demonstrate, the epistemological requirements established by this definition of *techne* make it all but incompatible with activities that depend as much (or more) on responding to the demands of a situation as they do on following the rules of a manual.

TECHNE AS A RATIONAL ABILITY TO EFFECT A USEFUL RESULT

This second definition of *techne* is a paraphrase of Aristotle's claim in chapter 6 of *Nicomachean Ethics* that an art is "a state of capacity to make, involving a true course of reasoning" (1140a10–12). It is here in *Nicomachean Ethics* that Aristotle presents his tripartite theory of knowledge, explaining the differences among *episteme* (theoretical knowledge), *techne* (productive knowledge), and *praxis* (practical knowledge). Like *praxis*, the reasoned state of capacity to *act, techne* is concerned with the variable, that is, with those things not governed by nature or necessity. But whereas the end of *praxis*—*eudaimonia* or "the good life"—is inherently valuable, the end of *techne* is instrumentally valuable, abiding in the use made of its product. This instrumentality distinguishes *techne* not only from *praxis* but also from *episteme,* which Aristotle understands as an unchanging knowledge of "universal and necessary" first principles that cannot be applied in order to accomplish or produce anything (1140b31). In sharp contrast, *techne* is knowledge about things "capable of either being or not being" that exists *only* in order to accomplish or produce something (1140a10–12).

In the introduction, I described this understanding of *techne* from *Nicomachean Ethics* as a kind of baseline definition, arguing that in it we can see the raw material for a number of the other definitions. This is certainly true in the case of the one we just looked at—*techne* as a "how-to" guide. At the heart of this definition lies the method, technique, or skill that the artist uses in order to produce. As even a cursory review of Aristotle's *On Rhetoric* (or, for that matter, any rhetoric) will show, methods, techniques, and skills are an important part of *techne* understood as a rational ability to effect a useful result. But, as I explained earlier, those methods, techniques, and skills must be accompanied by a deeper, more comprehensive understanding of the causes of success and failure if one is to claim possession of a genuine *techne* according to this definition. Such an understanding endows the artist with the ability to teach his art and removes him from dependence on habit and chance. Thus he is distinguished from the practitioner who possesses only a knack, that is, an unreflective (or unreflected-upon) habit attained through practice.

In Plato's *The Gorgias,* Socrates unambiguously labels rhetoric a knack, claiming that it has no proper subject matter about which a rational account of causes could be given (463b). Throughout the dialogue Socrates subordinates knacks to real *technai,* focusing primarily on their ethical and epistemological differences. A knack is ethically inferior, he argues, because it aims for the pleasurable, while *techne* aims for the good, which is to say, the useful (464d, 465a, 501a). And a knack is epistemologically inferior because it is irrational, while a *techne* is rational (465a, 501a). To say that a *techne* is rational is to say that it is knowable, which in turn means that the one who practices it can "itemize" its component parts and understand how they work together to produce a specific result (501a). According to Socrates, this understanding grants the artist the power of forethought, meaning he "doesn't select and apply his materials aimlessly, but [instead] with the purpose of getting the object he's making to acquire a certain form" (503e-504a). Based on his study of *techne*'s meanings in all of the Platonic dialogues, philosopher John Wild argues that such foresight is paramount for Plato because it's the only thing that can give the artist "genuine technical control" over the process of making. Summarizing Plato's understanding of *techne,* Wild writes:

> The aim of *techne* is the *complete* permeation of action by plan. Where events are within our power, nothing must be left to chance; where they are not, we must work out the various possibilities, and take account of them. The whole complex sequence in all its relations must first be grasped as a whole. Then, in light of this, a course of technical action must be charted which will really bring us to the end. (263)

Although Aristotle does not emphasize the all-important power of forethought and control to the degree his teacher does, his explanation of the difference between a *techne* and a knack is cut from the essentially same cloth as Plato's. In his *Metaphysics,* for example, Aristotle argues that one has an art when, based on a number of experiences with a particular object or activity, she can form a universal judgment about that object or activity. In the case of medicine, for example, a practitioner has an art if, rather than making judgments about the effect of a treatment in individual cases, she can "judge that it has done good to all persons of a certain constitution, marked off in one class, when they were ill" (I.1.5–12). In order to make this judgment, however, she must understand "the 'why' and cause" of the treatment's effect on that kind of patient. In Aristotle's view, such knowledge makes her "more honorable" and "wiser" than those who can heal but do so "without knowing what they do, as fire burns" (I.1.24–35).

Aristotle applies the same understanding of *techne* in the *Rhetoric,* arguing that because particulars are "limitless and not knowable," rhetoric does not "theorize about each person—what may seem so to Socrates or Hippias—but about what seems true to people of a certain sort" (1356b). The underlying assumption here, of course, is that there is something to theorize, that rhetors who can successfully persuade an audience use similar strategies that can be observed, described, taught, and then applied across a number of situations. We can clearly see this assumption at work through Aristotle's explanation of many teachable, transferable strategies for finding and applying the available means of persuasion, (e.g., using the topics as a means of invention, creating enthymemes and paradigms, preparing audiences emotionally, constructing appropriate forms of ethos, etc.)

We can also clearly see this assumption at work in the scholarship of the so-called new classicist rhetoricians who, in the 1960s, 1970s, and 1980s, argued that writing should be understood and taught as a *techne.* Because this work is the subject of chapter 2, I won't describe it in detail here. But a detailed review isn't necessary to reveal the continued emphasis on the importance of teachable, transferable strategies. No one articulated this emphasis more explicitly than Richard E. Young when, in "Arts, Crafts, Gifts, and Knacks: Some Disharmonies in the New Rhetoric," he wrote that for the new classicists, an art is "the result of an effort to isolate and generalize what those who have knacks do when they are successful" (56). More often than not

those efforts to isolate and generalize were directed at invention since
it was widely considered to be the most neglected canon of rhetoric
and—not incidentally—the one upon which the future of the field
depended.[5] Concerned that novice writers ended inquiry before reach-
ing genuine insight, for instance, teachers like E. M. Jennings inves-
tigated how expert writers remained open to seemingly incongruous
ideas in order to discover new relationships among them. In his 1968
essay, "A Paradigm for Discovery," Jennings offered students what he
called "a method for 'stopping to think,' for deliberately seeking jux-
tapositions of apparently unrelated contexts" (193). In essence, this
method asked students to manipulate three factors related to context:
(1) items sensed, (2) relationships perceived, and (3) their own view-
point (195). Like other inventional heuristics of the era (perhaps most
notably Young, Becker, and Pike's nine-celled tagmemic discovery procedure), Jennings's method was somewhat cumbersome or, as he put it,
"[c]lumsy when articulated." Despite that, however, he firmly believed
in its ability to get students out of "familiar ruts" and push them toward "innovative thinking" (197). Importantly, he also firmly believed
in its teachability, arguing that while audiences might perceive the
writer's effort at "mental manipulation" as a kind of magic, "to the
practitioner it is an explainable skill developed, after analysis, by conscious control and practice" (197).

To some, it might appear as though this definition of *techne* establishes the same epistemological requirements as the first definition
(*techne* as a "how-to" guide) and, as a result, is subject to the same criticism, namely that it represents a decontextualizing form of knowledge.
The emphasis on transferring strategies from one situation to another
would certainly seem to support this conclusion. Again Young makes
this emphasis clear in "Arts, Crafts, Gifts, and Knacks" when he writes
that for the new classicists, the use of heuristics "implies a generic
conception of the [writing] process." If writers regard each situation
they encounter as "unique," he elaborates, then they have no reason
to think that a formerly effective strategy will be effective again (57).
Importantly, though, Young qualified this emphasis, pointing out that
a heuristic is developed for a particular "*kind* of situation" and that the
writer must see a match between his current situation and that *kind* of
situation in order for the heuristic to be effective (57).

In acknowledging this limitation of heuristics, Young is following in the footsteps of Aristotle and Plato, both of whom recognized

(to different degrees) that the universal judgments that distinguish a *techne* from a knack are not unlimited in their scope but instead apply to a group of "similar objects" (*Metaphysics* I.1.7); to persons of "a similar constitution, marked off in one class" (*Metaphysics* I.1.10); or to "types of soul [. . . and] their affections" (*Phaedrus* 271). Because of this recognition, it's harder to make the charge of decontextualization stick. That is, it's harder to argue that applying this kind of knowledge causes the artist to lose sight of the specific situation in which she works. In fact, some would counter-argue that without an understanding of causation, the artist has no way of deciding which strategy to apply in a particular situation. If a doctor didn't understand how different chemotherapies affect cancer cells, for instance, she wouldn't know which medicine to prescribe to a particular patient with a particular kind of cancer. In this sense, then, we could say (somewhat paradoxically) that it is the artist's ability to make universal judgments that allows her to take a specific situation into account.

Importantly, though, what it actually means to "take a specific situation into account" will vary across different kinds of *technai* according to this definition, undermining the idea that we can locate its epistemological requirements at just one point on a continuum. In other words, while all arts here are distinguished from the "hard and fast rules" of handbooks by the need to respond to the specifics of situation, success in some arts will depend on that response more than others. This variation has everything to do with the ambiguity of the word "result" in the phrase "useful result." All results are instrumentally valuable according to this definition of *techne*. But those results can either be products (e.g., tables, chalices, or boats), or they can be conditions (e.g., health, peace, or safe passage). While those *technai* that result in products work with relatively stable materials, those that result in conditions work with relatively unstable materials. In "Failure and Expertise in the Ancient Conception of Art" James Allen explains that these latter *techne*, which are commonly referred to as the "stochastic *technai*," differ from the traditional (or nonstochastic) *technai* in that their end and function are not coextensive. The end of medicine, for instance, is to heal patients; but its function is to do everything possible to heal patients (87). This distinction between an end and a function legitimizes not only the greater likelihood that an artist will fail at one of the stochastic arts, according to Allen, but also the increased need for that artist to develop a sensitivity to situation if he wants any chance at succeeding (88). In *The Fragility of Goodness,* Martha Nussbaum places even more emphasis on the power of situation in the stochastic *technai*, arguing that because their ends are not entirely "antecedently specifiable," part of the artist's job is to discover his end as he carries out his art (98–99). For example, a politician might try to persuade the leaders of a war-torn region to negotiate a peace agreement, but what counts as peace for those leaders and in that region will depend on the situation. As a result, the politician cannot know exactly what end he is aiming for in advance of the negotiations but instead will have to discover it as those negotiations occur.

In cases like these, "taking the situation into account" requires not only the ability to modify one's plans for achieving a particular end but also the ability to redefine that end as the situation dictates. Because of these requirements, most scholars agree that the stochastic *technai* cannot be held to the same epistemological requirements of the nonstochastic *technai*, much less those established by the handbook tradition. However, this is not to say that artists involved in stochastic *technai* can't provide accounts of causation—they can. And they can turn those accounts into teachable strategies, but as Allen points out, those strategies will be characterized by "a certain roughness and imprecision," and they will need to be supplemented by "practice and hands-on experience" if the artist is to succeed (88).[6] We can see this "roughness and imprecision" in heuristics like Jennings's, as well as those associated with the tagmemic, Burkean, and pre-writing theories of invention developed and promoted by rhetoricians of the 1960s, 1970s, and 1980s.

TECHNE AS A MEANS OF INVENTING NEW SOCIAL POSSIBILITIES

As I have tried to demonstrate, the primary difference between the first two definitions of *techne* is an epistemological difference. When understood as a "how to" guide or handbook, *techne* establishes very strict epistemological requirements that can be met by only the most static, decontextualized kinds of knowledge. When understood as a rational ability to affect a useful result, however, *techne* becomes more responsive to the demands of particular situations, and, as a result, its epistemological requirements become less strict. This third definition of *techne*—*techne* as a means of inventing new social possibilities—

continues the trend of weakening epistemological requirements, but, importantly, that weakening corresponds to a more significant change on the axiological continuum: instead of producing a "useful result," we are now talking about *techne* as a way of inventing "new social possibilities." Both of these ends are instrumental; but, as I will explain, the latter is characterized by a capacity to challenge the status quo not directly associated with the former. Of course many useful results have the potential to upset dominant power relations. But whereas that potential remains unarticulated in the second definition of *techne,* it is brought front and center in the third.

Arguably, no one in rhetoric studies has done more to bring this potential front and center than Janet M. Atwill. It's true other writers have indirectly acknowledged *techne*'s ability to invent new social possibilities (and a few have done so directly), but none have explicitly defined *techne* as an art of invention and intervention and connected its ability to challenge the status quo to specific traits of productive knowledge the way Atwill has. Citing its dependence on time and circumstance, for instance, Atwill and Lauer argue that productive knowledge cannot claim to be a disinterested representation of truth or a means to whatever "unexamined social or political end" a particular culture (or a particular group within a culture) associates with eudaimonia, or "the good life" ("Refiguring" 27). Thus rather than "securing the borders" of what already exists—that is, dominant versions of "the true" and "the good"—Atwill concludes that *techne* is more likely to "mark the shifting and contestable borders of what is possible" ("Instituting" 113–4). In other words, *techne* is more likely to intervene into the indeterminacies of those borders in order to invent new social possibilities (*Rhetoric Reclaimed* 48).

Generally speaking, these new social possibilities can be grouped into two categories: those that happen as the result of an exchange of power and those that happen as a result of cultural critique. Of these two kinds of possibilities, the first is the most obvious since *techne*'s instrumentality automatically implies an exchange between the maker and the user of an artistic product. A carpenter doesn't build a table for the sake of the table, for example, but rather for the capital (monetary or otherwise) it will bring when a user buys it. From a contemporary Western perspective, the potential for social mobility created by such an exchange might seem relatively limited, but, as Atwill points out, in ancient Greek society it "played a powerful role in displacing the aristocratic social order, which distributed privileges according to birth" (*Rhetoric Reclaimed* 110). Arts like navigation, metallurgy, and rhetoric could not only redistribute power and wealth, she argues, but they could also form new modes of social identification (103). S. Cuomo takes this argument a step further in *Technology and Culture in Greek and Roman Antiquity*, suggesting that *techne* actually made the act of recognizing social identities more difficult. In other words, the social mobility created by *techne* helped blur the lines between previously distinct social classes, producing problems for those who wanted to evaluate others according to provenance rather than performance. *Techne* "changes people," Cuomo writes; it "produces mutants, people born as one thing and transmogrified into another" (37). For many in power, then, *technai* were a dangerous necessity—key to human survival but a threat to the established social order (38, 40).

According to French historians Marcel Detienne and Jean-Pierre Vernant, the threat associated with *techne* also came from its ability to trick, deceive, or create illusions. This ability is perhaps best illustrated by the phrase "dolie *techne*," which means "trap art." In *Cunning Intelligence in Ancient Greek Culture and Society*, Detienne and Vernant explain that "dolie *techne*" was often used in antiquity to refer to the special capability of figures like Proteus and animals like the fox to wriggle out of inextricable situations by creating cheating schemes or transforming their appearances (58, 115). Describing Oppian's second century A.D. text, *Treatise on Fishing*, they provide the following example of *techne*'s deceptive nature:

> The sea is like a world full of snares, inhabited like it is by ambiguous creatures whose harmless appearance belies their true, deadly nature. A rock looks like a grayish mass, unalarming and still. But all the time it is an octopus. Oppian says that it is by *techne* that the octopus merges with the rock to which it clings. In this way, thanks to the illusion (*apate*) which they create, they have no difficulty in eluding the pursuit of the fisherman as well as that of the fish whose strength they fear. (29)

While the octopus's illusion doesn't produce new social possibilities in the way that the carpenter's table does, it is still a means of exchanging power—or, to put it more accurately, it is a means of changing the source and nature of power. Through cunning intelligence and visual deception, the octopus is able to compensate for its lack of physical power and thereby protect itself from predators. Atwill recounts similar instances of trickery in the work of Homer, Hesiod, and Aeschylus, highlighting the ways in which *techne* allowed figures like Prometheus to "seize the advantage" over powerful adversaries who had "nature, force, and experience" on their side (*Rhetoric Reclaimed* 103–4).

As one might imagine, being able to "seize the advantage" over an adversary or deceive a predator isn't exactly a matter of knowing a set of pre-established rules or principles. In fact, according to rhetoricians Ryan Moeller and Ken McAllister, it's not really a matter of knowing at all—at least not if we understand knowing as a purely intellectual activity. In their 2002 essay, "Playing with *Techne*: A Propaedeutic for Technical Communication," Moeller and McAllister directly address the issue of epistemology, claiming that when *techne* is understood as a force in the "transformation of social orders," it requires a more experiential kind of knowledge, one that resides in the artist's "muscles and nerves" as much as it does in any information she learns (194, 201). Atwill argues that this experiential, embodied knowledge is particularly crucial for responding to the *kairos* of a situation. According to her, successfully deploying an art is largely dependent on the artist's ability to recognize the opportune moment. However, that ability cannot be taught through explicit precepts but instead must be ingrained in the artist's being and body (*Rhetoric* 59). Similarly, Atwill argues that the reasoning involved in *techne*—*metis,* or what Detienne and Vernant call "cunning intelligence"—cannot be taught as a set of precepts or identified with the "timeless principles" of philosophical reasoning (*Rhetoric* 56). Typically associated with qualities like resourcefulness and wily thought, *metis* operates in contingent situations where, according to Detienne and Vernant, "there are no ready-made rules for success, no established methods" (21). Importantly, this absence of rules does not mean that *techne* has now moved into the realm of mysterious genius or unteachable talent. To the contrary, Atwill argues that "it is [still] the character of an art to make its principles explicit and to systematize those principles in order to make them more transferable" ("Bodies and Art" 165). But now there is an acknowledgment that those principles must work in concert with not only the demands of a particular situation but also the experiential knowledge of a particular body.[7]

If *techne* had moved into the realm of unteachable talent—that is, if its principles could *not* be known and taught—then the second category of new social possibilities would not exist. As I explained earlier, *techne* leads to new social possibilities in two ways according to this definition: those that happen as the result of an exchange and those that happen as the result of cultural critique. Typically, *techne* and cultural critique are not associated with one another. In fact, many would argue that they represent (or enact) different kinds of knowledge—inventive knowledge (*techne*) versus interpretative knowledge (cultural critique). But in their 1995 essay, "Refiguring Rhetoric as an Art," Janet M. Atwill and Janice M. Lauer argue that *techne* creates opportunities for cultural critique by making tacit social practices explicit. To support this argument, Atwill and Lauer turn to Pierre Bordieu's notion of the "habitus"—a set of first- and second-order strategies used in social situations to secure the regularity of both subjects and circumstances (35). According to the authors, first-order strategies, which are acquired with language, function tacitly and appear to be natural as long as the social conditions that produced them remain in tact. However, when a social formation is no longer homogenous and its relationships are threatened, first-order strategies are formalized into explicit principles, or second-order strategies, in order to maintain those relationships. Atwill elaborates this point in her 2006 essay, "Bodies and Art," arguing that *technai* often arise "when a boundary between insider and outsider is marked—when agents who have not been socialized into the practices of certain rhetorical situations must learn by art what those who have long been in those situations have done by habit" (169).

Despite the regulatory function of these second-order strategies (or arts), Atwill and Lauer argue that they expose the arbitrary, indeterminate nature of social conditions since they come about only when the first-order strategies are jeopardized by change. In the case of rhetoric, for example, some have suggested that no matter how much flexibility one tries to incorporate into teachable strategies, the result is always the kind of regulation and ossification associated with handbooks. But Atwill and Lauer would counter that it's only when practices have been made explicit in teachable strategies that the values, subjectivities, and ideologies operating in them can be examined and critiqued. And once they've been critiqued, they can be revised or replaced to better serve the goals of the literacy education and democratic participation. If the practices were to remain tacit, however, then those values, subjectivities, and ideologies would continue to appear natural, as though they represented "immutable structures of reality and truth" rather than a particular construction of reality and truth (Atwill, "Instituting" 113). Thus Atwill and Lauer argue that while *techne* is, in fact, explicit and teachable, it "calls into question what it makes explicit and what it teaches" ("Refiguring" 37). And in doing that, they conclude, it "enables cultural critique and becomes the means by which new social possibilities are invented" ("Refiguring" 38).

TECHNE AS A MEANS OF PRODUCING RESOURCES

This definition represents another shift on the axiological axis, but this time the shift is in the opposite direction, locating *techne* in a position of extreme instrumentality. We can see this positioning reflected in the word "resources," which indicates that there is no end to the production process. The significance of this absence becomes clear when we compare the meaning of "resources" here to the meaning of "useful result" in the second definition of *techne*. When understood as a rational ability to effect a useful result, *techne* is deemed instrumental because the value of that result lies in its use. But there is no suggestion that this result (e.g., a chair if we are talking about nonstochastic arts or health if we are talking about stochastic arts) will automatically become the means for another round of production. To the contrary, once that result is achieved, that round of production is finished. When *techne* is understood as a way to produce resources, however, production never ends, which is to say that every product is or has the potential to become a means in future rounds of production.

Perhaps the most well known explanation (and critique) of this form of production is Heidegger's 1954 essay, "The Question Concerning Technology." Importantly, Heidegger himself does not believe that *techne* is a means of producing resources. However, he does believe that the tendency to view everything as raw material for production, a tendency he identifies with modern technology and refers to as *Ge-stell*, is related to *techne* in that both are ways of revealing, that is, ways of moving what is concealed into unconcealment (11–12, 21). But whereas *techne*, a form of poiesis, reveals by "bringing-forth" those things that cannot come into existence on their own, modern technology reveals by "challenging-forth" nature into resources, or what Heidegger calls "standing-reserve" (13, 20). To illustrate this difference, Heidegger compares two ways of creating energy: using a windmill and mining coal. A windmill uses the earth's resources to create energy, but it does not fundamentally transform, exhaust, or dominate those resources (14). In other words, the windmill "lets the wind be wind" (Zimmerman 216). Coal mining, on the other hand, dominates a tract of land, transforming it into a "coal mining district" so that the soil's resources can be "stockpiled" or placed "on call, ready to deliver the sun's warmth that is stored in it." The sun's warmth, in turn, is "ordered to deliver steam whose pressure turns the wheels that keep a factory running" (15). While this process of producing resources is endless, it does not proceed haphazardly or uncontrollably according to Heidegger. To the contrary, control—that is, "regulating and securing" the standing-reserve—becomes its trademark and primary objective (16, 27).

For some scholars, the distinction between *techne* and modern technology is not as clear as Heidegger's comparison of a windmill and a coal mine portrays it to be. In fact, they see in *techne* a mode of unconcealment more akin to the challenging-forth of *Ge-stell* than to the bringing-forth of *poiesis*. Thus they also see in *techne* the dangers Heidegger associates with *Ge-stell,* particularly its tendency to drive out those forms of bringing-forth that allow what is unconcealed to actually come into appearance (27). Once this happens, Heidegger warns, we face the related danger that everything brought-forth will concern us only as standing-reserve; that is, we will be unaware of and uninterested in the existence of artifacts as objects, as things in the world that have value in and of themselves (27). In her 1987 essay, "The Question Concerning Invention: Hermeneutics and the Genesis of Writing," Lynn Worsham applies this warning to work in rhetoric and composition, arguing that the new classicist version of *techne* threatens writing in much the same way *Ge-stell* threatens other forms of bringing-forth. Specifically, she argues that when scholars like Richard E. Young and Janice M. Lauer understand writing as a *techne,* they reduce it to a mere "instrument of knowledge," that is, "a set of techniques or methods for achieving certain goals or ends established by human beings" (208–9). According to Worsham, this oversimplified understanding of writing corresponds to an oversimplified understanding of causality in which the efficient cause, that is, the maker, is assumed to be a subject who independently brings products into being in order to achieve predetermined goals (207). Echoing Heidegger, Worsham claims that such a reduction is symptomatic of a kind of "technological thinking" in which human being sees itself as a subject whose primary task is the control and regulation of the earth's resources (205).

Not surprisingly, we also hear echoes of Heidegger in Hannah Arendt's critique of "*homo faber*" in *The Human Condition,* the 1958 book in which she argues for a return to a *vita activa* (active life) guided by civic and political participation rather than labor or work. For Arendt, the phrase *homo faber* corresponds to work, referring to the man who uses the materials of nature in order to fabricate the "human artifice," that is, the physical and cultural realm that separates humans from nature (136). Arendt's larger argument about the work of fabrication is that it isolates *homo faber* from the public world of politics and threatens to degrade that world by turning it into a means to an end (162, 220–30). To make this argument, Arendt links the technological thinking described by Worsham (and Heidegger) to what she sees as the fundamental inability within a "society of craftsmen" to understand the difference between utility and meaningfulness (154). Importantly, by "society of craftsmen," Arendt is referring specifically to a society dedicated to the fabrication of resources, that is, objects that will go on to become means in other rounds of production (157). In such a society, she argues, utility and usefulness become the standards by which all activities are judged (157). As a result, members of that society can no longer distinguish "in order to" (utility) from "for the sake of" (meaning) (154). In fact, utility becomes the content of "for the sake of," generating what Arendt sees as a state of meaninglessness (154). The solution to this problem, she writes, is to shift attention away from "the objective world of things" and toward "the subjectivity of use." The solution, in other words, is to think technologically by making "man the user" the ultimate cause and end of all production (155).

Of course, making "man the user" the cause and end of all production creates more problems than it solves. Chief among those problems is what Robert Meagher describes in his 1988 article "Techne" as "a new metaphysics contemptuous of contemplation and faith, celebrative of human being as the defining center of existence" (163). Within this new metaphysics—or, what many would simply call "humanism"—the goal of society is to re-create the world according to human will and ideas (160). Thus what the maker needs before he begins the production process is not only a rational understanding of causation but also a rational understanding of the idea or model upon which his re-creation will be based. Both Heidegger and Arendt connect this reliance on ideas and models to Plato's eternal forms, arguing that here production becomes more like a means of representation, that is, a means of generating copies that strive for resemblance to an ideal original (Arendt 140–3; Heidegger, *An Introduction to Metaphysics* 180–6).

From this claim about representation, it is but a small step to the charge that *techne* is an epistemologically foundationalist form of knowledge, one that assumes that in order for something "to be" it must first be produced according to a "permanently present foundation" (Zimmerman xv). Michelle Ballif critiques this epistemology in her 2001 *Seduction, Sophistry, and the Woman with the Rhetorical Figure,* arguing that it fuels the metaphysical drive to make everything (e.g. every identity and every phenomena) representable through the process of negation. Not only has this process allowed philosophy to sustain its "hegemonic dualisms," she argues, but it has also fostered a tremendous amount of violence "by insisting on the absence [i.e., the denigration, exclusion, and potential annihilation] of the other" (72). Arendt and Meagher also regard the negation involved in production as inherently violent. Thus Arendt describes *homo faber* as a "destroyer of nature" whose work consists in activities like "killing a life process" or "interrupting one of nature's [. . .] processes" (139); and Meagher writes, ironically, that the "genius" of human being is to "look at the forest and see not the trees but a village of houses [. . .], to look at a deer and see not a deer but a shirt, a pair of shoes, and a week's meals" (160). As arguments like these make clear, when *techne* is understood as a means of producing resources, it becomes vulnerable to charges of instigating extreme, even apocalyptic forms of violence. Meagher concludes his argument with such a charge, claiming that "modern *techne* has amassed primarily destructive power, power perversely suited to uttering the last word, the word which would send the world into the void instead of summoning it therefrom" (164).

Techne as a Non-Instrumental Mode of Bringing-Forth

If, as Meagher writes, *techne* is capable of sending the world into the void when understood as a means of producing resources, then it is also capable of the opposite—summoning the world from the void—when understood as a non-instrumental mode of bringing-forth. For reasons that will become clear later, it would be a mistake to over-emphasize the distance between these definitions. However, it should be noted that, more than any other two discussed here, they represent differing views on the meaning of *techne*. This difference, of course, is reflected in the word "non-instrumental," which indicates that *techne* has clearly moved away from the extreme instrumentality associated with the production of resources. Importantly, this is not to say that *techne* is at the other end of the spectrum, defined exclusively as the ability to produce fine art. To the contrary, *techne* can still produce useful objects according to this definition. But that process of production is now understood as a bringing-forth of something (e.g., being, nature, or relationships) from concealment into unconcealment.

The idea of production as bringing-forth from concealment into unconcealment is a characteristically Heideggerian idea. Or, perhaps it is more accurate to say that the vocabulary used to express that idea is characteristically Heideggerian vocabulary. That doesn't mean, however, that we should view this last definition of *techne* exclusively as Heidegger's. In fact, I want to stress that my goal here is not to provide a comprehensive account of Heidegger's understanding of *techne*. Still, there would be no way to explain *techne* as a non-instrumental mode of bringing-forth without recourse to Heidegger's work, particularly his published lecture series, *An Introduction to Metaphysics* and the two essays, "The Origin of the Work of Art" and "The Question Concerning Technology." In these three texts, Heidegger argues that *techne* is a kind of knowledge that, contrary to modern interpretations of the term, has nothing to do with technique or skill. In fact, Heidegger repeatedly claims that *techne* cannot be reduced to any kind of action or practical performance that results in a product ("The Question" 13; "The Origin" 59; "Building" 159). In contrast, he understands *techne* as knowledge that provides an opening through which the being of a work can come into appearance in the world. Key to this understanding of *techne* is Heidegger's identification of being with *physis,* a Greek word that was translated into Latin as "natura" and then into English as "nature." Once this translation occurred, Heidegger argues, the original meaning of *physis* as a "self-blossoming emergence" that encompasses both the earthly and the heavenly, both the organic and the inorganic was lost, replaced by the more restricted idea of nature as the natural world (*An Introduction* 14–15). Whereas *techne* is usually opposed to nature defined as the natural world, Heidegger sees it as complicit with nature defined as *physis*. Thus to produce something in the sense of *techne* is, for him, to allow it's own way of presencing, its "emerging power," to shine forth (*An Introduction* 159).

As I mentioned earlier, in defining *techne* as the bringing-forth of being, Heidegger is not suggesting its products are incapable of fulfilling a predetermined end or telos. In fact, according to Heidegger, a product's telos (what Aristotle called its "final cause") plays a key role in how it comes into appearance. In the case of a chalice, for instance, he argues that its telos circumscribes it within the "realm of consecration and bestowal." Rather than limiting the chalice, this circumscription allows it to become "what, after production, it will be" ("The Question" 8). What Heidegger stresses, however, is that telos combines with the other three Aristotelian causes (material, formal, and efficient), which he prefers to call "modes of occasioning," in order to set that chalice "on its way into arrival" (11). As he makes clear, then, it is not the rejection of predetermined purpose that distinguishes *techne* from instrumentality but rather the idea of a kind of co-responsibility among the four modes of occasioning. This emphasis on co-responsibility (as well as the shift from "causing" to "occasioning") stands in contrast to the maker-centered "technological thinking" critiqued by Worsham, Arendt, and Meagher. According to Heidegger, the maker is important because he "considers carefully and gathers together" the other three modes of occasioning, but this does not mean he controls them or positions himself as the standard for all causality (7–8). Rather the four modes of occasioning together "hold sway" in the process of bringing-forth, allowing "the growing things of nature as well as whatever is completed through the crafts and arts [to] come at any given time into their appearance" (11).

In rhetoric and composition, Byron Hawk has done more than any other scholar to promote this non-instrumental definition of *techne*—a definition that he refers to with the term "post-*techne*."[8] While his work is heavily influenced by Heidegger, Hawk also relies on more contemporary sources, for instance, Mark C. Taylor's work on complexity and Katherine N. Hayles's work on posthumanism, in order to shift the field's understanding of *techne* from an instrumental means of production to a non-instrumental mode of bringing-forth. Such a shift, he argues, would require that rhetoricians see the specific writing techniques they teach not only as transferable tools that allow writers to produce texts but also as ways of locating writers within complex, ambient situations that reveal "constellations" and thus allow them to invent or to "see something as something else" ("Toward a Post-*Techne*" 379, 384). Whereas the former view assumes writers are independent subjects who work through the power of their own agency to act *on* nature, the latter view, according to Hawk, assumes they are embedded elements of complex situations who work through the power of that embeddedness to act *with* nature (379, 381).

What's significant about Hawk's argument here is what it reveals about the epistemological requirements of this last definition of *techne*. As just this brief review of his work indicates, Hawk's efforts to re-understand *techne* are, in large part, driven by his interest in the complexity of situations, particularly the ways in which that complexity resists rational prediction and control by a human subject (377). For him, then, successfully bringing forth something from concealment into unconcealment depends more on how a subject is situated within a situation than it does on the precision or reliability of the knowledge she brings to that situation (382, 388). In other words, what counts here, that is, what determines the outcome of particular instance of bringing-forth, are the relationships among the elements of a situation, not the accuracy of the writer's understanding of causation (377). In this sense, Hawk, like Moeller, McAllister, and Atwill before him, recognizes the sometimes embodied, intuitive nature of technical knowledge. But, whereas scholars like Atwill still insist on the importance of making that knowledge as transferable as possible, Hawk worries that too much emphasis on transferability will result in generalized writing strategies that do not take the particularities of situation into account. Thus he argues that while technical knowledge may, in fact, need to be transferable across situations, it will also need to undergo modifications when enacted within a particular situation in order to produce specialized rather than generic strategies for writing (383, 388).

Not an Inkblot But . . .

As I said at the outset of this chapter, there are a number of ways to understand the differences among *techne*'s many meanings. It would have no doubt been helpful to have charted the changes in definitions of *techne* through history, to have connected those definitions to the disciplinary contexts from which they emerged, or to have placed them within the larger philosophies or rhetorics of the figures who espoused them. What I've done here, however, is describe the epistemological and axiological features of the five composite definitions of *techne* that are most common in the disciplinary discourses of rhetoric and composition. The advantage to this approach is that it explains how *techne* can be defined in such different, sometimes contradictory ways, while simultaneously highlighting the fact that those differences exist on a continuum. Too often, we fail to take this continuum into account when we make arguments about *techne*. This failure leads not only to confusion (since we use the same term to refer to quite different meanings) but also to a certain kind of limitation, that is, a tendency within work that promotes *techne* to define it almost exclusively in positive terms (e.g., as a means of solving problems or inventing new social possibilities) and a corresponding tendency within work that critiques *techne* to define it almost exclusively in negative terms (e.g., set of inflexible rules or a means of producing resources). On the one hand, these tendencies are understandable, which is to say it makes sense to use (or develop) whatever definition of *techne* we need in order to support the point we're making. On the other hand and as I will argue later, if we want to establish *techne*'s value as a theory and pedagogy of writing for rhetoric and composition in the twenty-first century, then we have to consider the ways in which definitions from across the continuum I've described here contaminate each other, making it almost impossible to understand this protean concept in purely positive or negative terms. Before I can make that argument, however, I need to explain the definition that got us here in the first place, that is, the definition that made *techne* an issue in the modern field of rhetoric and composition—the new classicist definition of art.

2 The New Classicist Definition of Art

In the previous chapter, I purposefully avoided introducing *techne*'s many meanings by way of chronological review. My goal there wasn't to tell a story about *techne*'s development over time but rather to introduce composite definitions of the term in a way capable of accounting for their similarities and differences. In other words, I was more concerned with giving readers a way to think about *techne*'s definitions in general than I was with explaining any one definition in detail. In this chapter, however, explaining a particular definition is precisely my goal, and the one at issue is the new classicist definition of art articulated most clearly by Richard E. Young in his 1980 essay, "Arts, Crafts, Gifts, and Knacks: Some Disharmonies in the New Rhetoric." As many readers already know, Young's goal in this essay was to uncover the contradictory conceptions of art at work in the new rhetoric. According to him, one faction of the new rhetoric, the new romanticists, understood art from the perspective of vitalism as a mysterious gift, something unknowable and, therefore, unteachable. In this sense, art contrasts with craft, those mechanical skills that can be easily taught but do not actually confer the ability to write well (55–6). Young argued that the other faction, the new classicists, understood art as a conscious, rational ability to effect preconceived results (56). As I explained in chapter 1, this definition of art contrasts with knack, an unreflective and unteachable habit acquired through experience.

Although Young was careful to acknowledge the overlap between these two definitions of art, he strongly preferred the one advocated by the new classicists. And, as subsequent chapters will demonstrate, that preference had important consequences for rhetoric and composition. Perhaps most obviously, it rekindled the debate about rhetoric and *techne* Plato had begun over 2,500 years earlier when Socrates asked if rhetoric was a real *techne* in *The Gorgias*. Whether their answer was affirmative, negative, or something in between, most major rhetoricians of the classical era responded to Socrates's question. For some, rhetoric was a specious form of knowledge that posed a serious moral threat; for others, it was a way to make a living through teaching, entertaining, or both; and for still others, it was the cornerstone of a good government and a healthy polis. Much was at stake, then, in whether it was legitimized as a *techne* or denounced as a knack. As rhetoric's importance and reputation waned after the classical period, however, so did the imperative to answer Socrates's question. If rhetoric didn't matter, in other words, then its status as a *techne* was either a foregone conclusion (*it doesn't matter because it's not a techne*) or a moot point (*why answer the question? rhetoric doesn't matter*).

But as rhetoric slowly began coming back to life in the mid-twentieth century, so did the debate about *techne*. And the stakes of this debate, like those of its historical antecedent, had much to do with legitimacy, in particular the legitimacy that comes from being a bona fide academic discipline. If rhetoric was understood as a *techne* in the new classicist sense of the term advocated by Young in "Art, Crafts, Gifts, and Knacks," then explanations of causation (i.e., theories of why some writers succeed and some fail) could be identified; those explanations could then be tested; and the ones that stood up to testing could eventually be developed into theoretically sound pedagogies. More than a theory of writing, then, this definition provided the outlines of a research agenda that, in the view of Young and others, could help substantiate rhetoric and composition's claim to disciplinarity. And, by some accounts, that is exactly what it did. This isn't to say Young's work unified the field around a common commitment to the goals and ideals of new classicism. To the contrary, just a handful of scholars explicitly identified themselves or their work in those terms. But many implicitly accepted the basic premises of the new classicist definition of art, thus opening up avenues for the kinds of research needed to demonstrate that rhetoric and composition was becoming a bona fide academic discipline.

However, as I explained earlier in the introduction, accepting the basic premises of the new classicist definition of art meant closing some avenues for research in order to open others. In his 1987 *The Making of Knowledge in Composition: Portrait of an Emerging Field*, for instance, Stephen North argued that Young's research agenda, which he described as an "investigative assault" on invention designed to "unlock its secrets," was part of a "scramble" within the field to claim territory and establish professional power (339, 317). According to North, this "scramble" had disenfranchised rhetoric and composition's "indigenous population"—the practitioners—by de-legitimizing practice as a form of inquiry (21, 33). Byron Hawk made a similar but much more thorough argument in his 2007 *A Counter-History of Composition: Toward Methodologies of Complexity,* claiming that research on vitalism had been de-legitimized in rhetoric and composition because of its misidentification in the work of Young and others' with a watered-down, stereotypical version of romanticism (19). The result of this "widespread and unnoticed confusion" was not only a misunderstanding of the figures who supposedly espoused vitalist views (e.g., Samuel Coleridge) but also a more general and long-term inability to recognize vitalism's connections to *techne,* invention, and rhetoric (21). From the perspectives of North and Hawk, then, Young might have managed to help secure rhetoric and composition's disciplinary status, but he did so at the expense of any methodology, theory, or pedagogy that appeared to be at odds with the new classicist definition of art.

Obviously Young's explanation of that definition in "Arts, Crafts, Gifts, and Knacks" will figure prominently in the story I tell in this chapter. In fact, it marks the place where I begin that story. Somewhat ironically, though, one of my main goals here will be to demonstrate why we shouldn't understand this explanation as a beginning. On the one hand, the problem with such an understanding is that it isn't chronologically accurate. While it's true "Arts, Crafts, Gifts, and Knacks" provides the clearest articulation of the new classicist definition of art, it does not provide the first articulation of that definition. As Janet M. Atwill points out in her 2006 "Bodies and Art," Young's characterizations of art in 1980 were the culmination of discussions about heuristics that had been going on since the 1960s (167). Thus it becomes necessary take a step back, that is, to explain those characterizations but then turn to earlier discussions about heuristics, looking at how they were defined and how they shaped the new classicist definition of art. On the other hand, the problem with understanding Young's argument in "Arts, Crafts, Gifts, and Knacks" as a beginning is about more than chronology. It's also about focus—about how identifying a particular text as the beginning of any story narrows our focus to the degree that we can't help but to attribute more agency to its author than we should. Identifying a particular text as a beginning, in other words, separates that text from the ecology from which it emerged, leaving us with a kind of *creatio ex nihilo* explanation of its existence that inevitably points to the power of an autonomous creator. In order to avoid such an explanation here, we have to step back even further, considering what—besides (and before) those 1960s discussions of heuristics—made the new classicist definition of art and its impact on the field possible.

Jenny Edbauer helps us to understand why such a wide view is necessary in her 2005 essay, "Unframing Models of Public Distribution: From Rhetorical Situation to Rhetorical Ecology." There she argues that as rhetors we are always part of a "networked interconnection of forces, energies, rhetorics, moods, and experiences" (10). "In other words," she writes "our practical consciousness is never outside the prior and ongoing structures of feeling that shape the social field" (10). For Edbauer, this emphasis on rhetoric's connected, distributed nature raises questions about the value and efficacy of trying to understand it through the lens of the rhetorical situation. When we look at rhetoric through this lens, she explains, our view is limited to set of discrete elements, that is, to a *rhetor* who responds to an *exigence* for an *audience* according to a set of *constraints*. As a result, we fail to see not only how those elements bleed into one another but also—and more important for my purposes here—the fact that when they emerge, they are "*already* infected by the viral intensities that are circulating in the social field" (14, emphasis added). To put it in the terms of Edbauer's argument, then, one of my goals here is to describe some of the "viral intensities" that "infected" the new classicist definition of art *before* it emerged in the work of Young and others. In other words, I want to move to "a wider social field of distribution" than a discussion of the new classicist definition of art would normally occupy in order to look at a series of arguments and events that share with that definition not a rhetorical situation but rather a rhetorical ecology. Before I move into that "wider social field of distribution," however, I want to explain the new classicist definition of art, focusing specifically on its relationship to the new romanticist definition of art, to heuristics, and to the three theories of invention that became dominant during this time.

New Classicism Versus New Romanticism

Despite the amount of attention Young has received (and will continue to receive) here, it would be misleading to suggest that the new classicist definition of art was *his* definition or that he was the only scholar who promoted it. As he and others have recounted, those first few decades of research in rhetoric and composition were characterized by a very strong sense of community and collaboration. Ideas were more freely shared and borrowed than they tend to be now because, as Young put it, there wasn't enough "turf" to provoke a real sense of defensiveness ("Working" 327). Thus the new classicist definition of art should be understood as a crystallization of ideas and attitudes that characterized the work of many rhetoricians—for instance, Virginia Burke, Francis Christensen, Janice M. Lauer, W. Ross Winterowd, and David Harrington, among others—rather than as Young's personal achievement. However, Young did explain that definition more clearly than anyone else writing at the time. In fact, reading through his work gives one the sense that he believed if he could just explain the new classicist definition of art clearly *enough*, then its eminent reasonableness and appeal would be realized by everyone who encountered it. We can see this belief in Young's reliance on categories, that is, in his dissection of the new rhetoric into two camps: the new classicists and the new romanticists. Young often explained new or confusing ideas by dividing them into contrasting categories. The clearest way to say what something *is*, after all, is to say what it *is not*. But the interesting thing about Young's categories is the fact that he often tried to blur the lines between them. After carefully sorting some body of knowledge into groups, he would remind readers that those groups were not mutually exclusive. Such reminders, however, never had the same impact as the lines they were meant to blur. In other words, Young's habit of attaching a caveat to a set of categories did little to undermine his initial act of categorization. This was certainly the case with "Arts, Crafts, Gifts, and Knacks," where, after making the distinction between the new classicist and new romanticist conceptions of art, Young issued a call for rhetoricians to develop the kind of Keatsian negative capability that would allow them to accept the idea—and here he was quoting Neils Bohr—that the opposite of a deep truth may very well be another deep truth (59–60). Despite the apparent incompatibility between the two camps, Young did not want to leave readers with the impression that the new classicist conception of art was a repudiation of its new romanticist counterpart.

Yet many would argue that this is precisely what happened—that Young's argument in "Arts, Crafts, Gifts, and Knacks" portrayed the new classicist conception of art more or less as a foil to the new romanticist conception. For instance, Young argued that whereas the new romanticists believed writing was essentially an individual, imaginative process that should be relatively free of deliberate control, the new classicists believed that because some of its phases were rational and generic, it could be "consciously directed" (55, 57). Thus while the new romanticists identified art with "mysterious powers which may be enhanced but which are, finally, unteachable," the new classicists identified it with "the knowledge necessary for producing preconceived results by conscious, directed action (55, 56). Out of these contrasting definitions of art grew contrasting roles for composition teachers. Young characterized the new romanticist teacher as someone who believes the creative elements of writing are unteachable but does not use that belief as an excuse to turn the composition course into a study of mechanics. Rather than becoming a "purveyor of information about the craft of writing," Young wrote, the new romanticist teacher becomes "a designer of occasions that stimulate the creative process" (55). In other words, she avoids directly teaching writing, preferring instead create situations in which it can be learned (56). He argued that, contrary to popular belief, such situations are not "devoid of rigor" since they often require students to imitate the teacher's "tough-minded" intellectual and stylistic habits (56). The new classicist classroom is also "not devoid of rigor," according to Young, but for different reasons. In this case, the teacher is someone who believes that knowledge about writing can be turned into "knowledgeable practice" that can be directly taught to students in order to give them more control over the creative elements of writing ("Recent" 22). Thus she looks to the work of successful writers, trying to "isolate and generalize" the strategies that help them go beyond the known to new ideas and associations (56).

As if to make this already sharp contrast even sharper, Young portrayed the new classicist and new romanticist conceptions of art as representatives of very different philosophical systems. According to him, the new romanticist understanding of art and its corollary pedagogy were based on "the vitalist philosophy of an old romanticism enriched by modern psychology," while the new classicist understanding and its pedagogy had their origin in Aristotelian philosophy ("Arts, Crafts, Gifts, and Knacks" 55). Citing the field's lack of historical studies on vitalism, Young didn't explain the nature of the connection between vitalism and new romanticism. He did, however, elaborate on the connection between new classicism and Aristotelianism, turning to Aristotle's claim in *On Rhetoric* that it is possible—and, in fact, the function of an art—to systematize rhetoric by observing how those who have knacks achieve their goals. Young also turned to Aristotle's *Metaphysics,* again relying on the distinction between an art and a knack in order to emphasize the importance of trying to understand the causes of success and failure in writing. Although Young clearly considered Aristotle to be "the most appropriate spokesman" for the new classicist position, he did not believe those who subscribed to it must teach classical rhetoric in the writing classroom (57). In fact, Young found many aspects of classical rhetoric theoretically and pedagogically unsuitable for the modern writing classroom.[9] What he did find suitable, however, were heuristics.

Heuristics as "Knowledgeable Practice": The Influence of New Classicism on Rhetorical Invention

To be sure, heuristics were a definitive part of the new classicist conception of art. More specifically, they were its pedagogical manifestation, that is, the "knowledgeable practice" that could be taught to students in order to give them more control over writing. As I explained earlier, though, the idea of using heuristics in the classroom didn't grow out of the new classicist conception of art. In fact, it would be more accurate to describe their relationship the other way around, that is, to say the new classicist definition of art grew out of the idea of using heuristics in the classroom. For instance, if we look at Young's 1965 "Toward a Modern Theory of Rhetoric: A Tagmemic Contribution," an essay he co-authored with Alton L. Becker fifteen years before "Arts, Crafts, Gifts, and Knacks," we see that he was already thinking in the terms he would later use to characterize the new classicist definition of art. Most notably, we see that Young thought a new rhetoric would need "systematic methods of inquiry" or "an explicit practical method" if it were to avoid becoming "a superficial and marginal concern" (453,

455). Referring to such methods as both heuristics and "discovery procedures," Young explained that they imply a writing process that, while not mechanical, is subject to guidance and control (457). More specifically, he explained that heuristics could guide the writing process by providing a series of steps or questions writers could use across a number of different situations to find a probable solution to problem (457). Young described his process of problem solving as "broad, flexible, and intuitive" and argued that it could help to create a rhetoric that "stands somewhere between the rigorous theories of science and the almost purely intuitive theories of the humanities" (460, 468).

Despite the fact that many of these features became core components of the new classicist definition of art—namely, a systematic and explicit method, transferability from one situation to another, and a kind of middle positioning between reason and intuition—Young didn't discuss heuristics and that definition together until his 1976 "Invention: A Topographical Survey," a widely read bibliographic essay that stressed the need to understand and teach invention as an art. Although Young had not explicitly named the new classicist definition of art or opposed it to the new romanticist definition at this time, he did argue that a writer possesses an art of writing (as opposed to a knack) when "what he does is made explicit in the form of reusable heuristic procedures" (2). When this transformation happens, Young believed, aspects of the writing process can be taught as well as learned (2). From this perspective, heuristics provided an elegant solution to a very old and difficult problem: how to make writing, particularly invention, teachable without reducing it to a mechanical process. But of course not everyone understood heuristics from Young's perspective. As he admitted in "Arts, Crafts, Gifts, and Knacks," their introduction into disciplinary discourse of rhetoric and composition fifteen years earlier had created a considerable amount of confusion and debate (57). Even a brief review of the term's various definitions will bear this point out.

In the same year Young and Becker first defined heuristics in "Toward A Modern Theory of Rhetoric," D. Gordon Rohman described them in "Pre-Writing: The Stage of Discovery in the Writing Process" as a models that were designed to give students both "a sense of direction to their groping, and an actual 'puzzle' to impose on their writing" (110). Two years later in 1967, Janice M. Lauer wrote that a heuristic was "a conscious and non-rigorous search model which explores a creative problem for seminal elements of a solution" ("Invention" 4). She reiterated this definition five years later in "Heuristics and Composition," the extensive bibliography on problem solving research that started her famous exchange with Ann E. Berthoff. Also in 1970, Young, Becker, and Pike published *Rhetoric: Discovery and Change,* the textbook where they defined "heuristic" as a "systematic art of inquiry [. . . that] provides a method for gathering information about a problem and asking fruitful questions" (120). In 1975, W. Ross Winterowd tried to quell concerns that heuristics were too scientific by pointing out that they were "nothing more than ways the writer can 'walk around' a subject, viewing it from different angles, taking it apart in various ways, probing it" (*Contemporary* 90). One year later Young wrote that heuristics were "explicit plans for analyzing and searching" ("Invention" 2), while Lauer suggested that they were guides to inquiry that could lead a student "into the cave of his deepest self where insight might be hoped for" ("The Teacher" 342). In her 1979 "Toward a Metatheory of Heuristics," Lauer again defined heuristics, proposing that they were models meant to help writers "retrieve past meanings and to symbolize new associations" (268). Young then described them as "explicit strategies for effective guessing" in "Arts, Crafts, Gifts, and Knacks" and as "promising paths through the large number of choices open to the writer during the process of origination" in his 1987 "Recent Developments in Rhetorical Invention" (25).

In this list of definitions (which is not exhaustive), heuristics are variously identified as methods, models, plans, guides, strategies, and paths. They are touted as ways of helping writers solve problems, gain direction, gather information, ask questions, probe subjects, analyze and search data, access their deepest selves, and symbolize new associations. It is no wonder, then, that their introduction was met with confusion. Simply put, scholars who tried to explain and promote them rarely did so with the same language. On the one hand, this inconsistency in language reflects the fact that these scholars were often trying to explain and promote different heuristics; thus while one might be better described as a series of questions designed to broaden a student's perspective on a subject, another might be better described as strategy for generating support for an idea. On the other hand, the inconsistency reflects something more fundamental about the nature of heuristics, namely the fact that they embodied an inexact, contingent, and productive form of knowledge meant to help writers *do* something rather than *know* something. In other words, they were not based on an airtight theory of what writing was or how one produced it but rather on the more general belief that some aspects of it were amenable to conscious control and that others could be stimulated by that control. Thus there was plenty of room for interpretation, that is, plenty of room for scholars to offer varying, even competing, explanations of what heuristics were and what they could help writers do.

As we saw earlier, it is this underlying belief in the writer's ability to control some aspects of writing that connects heuristics to the new classicist understanding of art.[10] Young made this connection explicit in "Methodizing Nature," the 1982 essay where he argued that researchers should be concerned not only with how we engage in intellectual exploration but also what we can do to better control it, "to make it more deliberate, efficient, and complete" (127). For Young, the way to gain this control was to develop "an explicit plan, a heuristic procedure, for exploring the problematic data" (128). Again, the basic assumption here is that by engaging in deliberate, "more or less systematic" exploration, a writer increases her chances of generating and communicating a genuine insight through writing ("Arts, Crafts, Gifts, and Knacks" 57). Many of those who were working on heuristics at the time found support for this assumption in the field of psychology, particularly in work on creativity and problem solving. For example, in "A Paradigm for Discovery," an essay I discussed in chapter 1, E. M. Jennings drew on Arthur Koestler's *The Act of Creation* to explain how writers could juxtapose seemingly unrelated concepts and contexts in order to move their writing out of what he called "the rut of familiarity" (192). Others like D. Gordon Rohman and Richard Larson also drew on Koestler's work, in addition to that of Erich Fromm, Jerome Bruner, and Rollo May, to demonstrate how students could use journaling, meditation, analogies, and lists of questions to discover both the exigency and the content necessary for successfully writing about their own experiences. Of all the attempts to explain the effectiveness of heuristics through work in psychology, though, the most comprehensive was Lauer's 1967 dissertation, "Invention in Contemporary Rhetoric: Heuristic Procedures." There she surveyed the work of almost two hundred psychologists to explain heuristics and the role they could play in the process of writing. Relying on the work of British social psychologist Graham Wallas, for instance, Lauer argued that the conscious striving associated with heuristics acted as a way to stimulate or instruct the unconscious activity necessary for discovery (16). As Lauer explained, Wallas believed the creative process could be understood as the combination of four stages: (1) preparation, a time when one explores the subject; (2) incubation, a period of unconscious activity; (3) illumination, the time when insight appears; and (4) verification, the time when one validates the insight by putting it into a final form (16). According to Wallas (and others like Brewster Ghiselin, a poet who studied creativity in artists), if one could sufficiently explore a subject in the preparation stage, then subsequent unconscious activity was more likely to produce insight in the illumination stage. Lauer applied this reasoning to writing, arguing that writers could use heuristics during invention to actively encourage inspiration rather than passively "bit[ing] their pencils" for it (154).

While much of the psychological research Lauer reviewed in her dissertation helped to explain heuristics and establish their applicability to writing, Wallas's work was particularly significant because it located the use of heuristics within a larger process of inquiry that confirmed rather than denied the role of non-rational activity in invention. Lauer used this process of inquiry to structure *Four Worlds of Writing,* the 1981 composition textbook she wrote with Andrea Lunsford, Gene Montague, and Janet Emig. In each unit (or world) of writing, students were reminded that while they can prepare their unconscious for insight by thoroughly exploring their subjects, that insight was more likely to appear *after* they had taken a break from conscious, rational activity (42). Young, Becker, and Pike also structured their textbook, *Rhetoric: Discovery and Change,* around Wallas's process of inquiry; and although a primary object of the text was to teach students how to use heuristics during the preparation stage, the authors made a point of acknowledging the necessity and inaccessibility of the incubation stage.[11] "People tend to ignore its importance," they argued, "placing undo emphasis on conscious, analytical procedures as if these alone were sufficient for solving problems. But each of us has a subconscious intelligence, a strong and vital force in our mental life that seems to have a greater capacity than reason for dealing with the complex and the unfamiliar" (73–4). In "Arts, Crafts, Gifts, and Knacks," Young reiterated this point, drawing on the work of psychologist Jerome Bruner to argue that while heuristics could help prepare the writer's mind for discovery, the "imaginative act" could not be directly controlled (57, 59). A heuristic isn't an algorithm for writing, he emphasized, but rather "a way of moving the mind out of its habitual grooves, of shaking it loose from a stereotypic past that wants to be retrieved [. . .] " (59).

Tagmemic Invention

As most readers already know, the heuristic Young considered particularly well-suited for moving writers out of their habitual grooves was the one he helped create, the tagmemic discovery procedure. Closely if not sometimes synonymously associated with the new classicist definition of art, this heuristic was the result of a larger collaborative effort between Young and Alton L. Becker that began in the early 1960s to apply Kenneth L. Pike's principles of tagmemic linguistics to rhetoric. Pike developed tagmemics, a branch of structural linguistics, in the 1950s to help linguistics researchers identify the phonological, grammatical, and semantic features of languages that had no alphabet, dictionary, or written grammar ("Methodizing" 128). Although he explained all eight of its principles (and corresponding writing exercises) in his 1964 *College Composition and Communication* article, "A Linguistic Contribution to Composition," the heuristic Young and Becker introduced a year later in "Toward a Modern Theory of Rhetoric: A Tagmemic Contribution" was based on only two: (1) the etic/emic distinction, which contrasts culture-neutral accounts of behavior to culture-specific accounts; and (2) the principle of trimodalism, which asserts that a complete analysis of any unit of experience requires it be understood as a particle (a discrete, contrastive bit), a wave (an unsegmentable physical continuum), and a field (a system of relationships). As they explained, the goals of this heuristic were to prod writers to recognize that their worldviews were not objective views and to provide a safeguard against too narrowly understanding the subject at hand (458–9). Thus it asked writers three relatively straightforward sets of questions (460).

1. What are the distinctive features of the reader's conception of the topic? What characteristics does it have that lead him to contrast with similar things? (Particle view)
2. How are the reader's views on this topic part of a mental process, a phase in the continual development of his system of values and assumptions? (Wave view)
3. How does the reader partition the topic? What are its functional elements for him? How does he classify it? (Field view)

By the time *Rhetoric: Discovery and Change* appeared in 1970, how-ever, the tagmemic discovery procedure had become somewhat less straightforward if arguably more powerful as an aid to invention. Here Young, Becker, and Pike combined the principles of tagmemic linguis-tics with the psychology of Carl Rogers to produce a modern rhetoric that, according to them, could meet the needs of contemporary writ-ers better than classical rhetoric (8). At the heart of this rhetoric was the newly revised discovery procedure, a nine-celled matrix of exer-cises that combined the principle of trimodalism with the another of the tagmemic principles—the idea that at any level of focus (particle, wave, or field), a unit of experience can only be adequately understood if one determines its contrastive features, its range of variation, and its distribution in larger context (55–6). In effect, then, Young, Becker, and Pike's new heuristic was based on two principles of trimodalism since it asked writers to identify three sets of characteristics about their topic from three different perspectives or levels of focus. For instance, in order to understand their topic as a field, the third level of focus, writers were asked to view it as a complex system and identify (1) the relationships among its components; (2) the ways in which particu-lar instances of the system varied; and (3) the position of the system within a larger system (127).

Somewhat ironically, Young, Becker, and Pike believed that togeth-er with the other strategies and principles advocated in the book, their tagmemic discovery procedure could help writers gain control over the difficult and messy process of writing (xiii). "The book's struc-ture," they wrote, "is a consequence of our belief that the discipline of rhetoric is primarily concerned with the control of a process. Master-ing rhetoric means not only mastering a theory of how and why one communicates but mastering the process of communication as well" (9). According to them, learning to use the tagmemic discovery pro-cedure was a, if not *the*, key step toward mastering that process. As it turns out, though, relatively few students learned to use the procedure because many teachers found it too complicated for the composition classroom. Hence the irony of Young, Becker, and Pike's belief: what they perceived as a systematic, orderly way to explore an experience or problem was, in the eyes of many, "too abstract, complex, or sophis-ticated for students to understand" (Kneupper, "Revising" 160). In other words, when put into practice, the tagmemic discovery procedure seemed to confuse many students, giving them less rather than more control over writing.

Burkean Invention

While the tagmemic discovery procedure was arguably the most discussed heuristic to emerge from this era of composition research, it was by no means the only one. By the mid-1980s, heuristics had been developed for everything from discovering rhetorical situations and composing abstracts to producing expressive discourse and analyzing audience.[12] For the most part, though, heuristics like these came and went unnoticed, making relatively little impact on composition scholarship and pedagogy. The heuristics that did make an impact tended to be those that grew out of one of the major new theories of invention, which, in addition to tagmemic theory, included Burkean theory and pre-writing theory. Along with classical theory (which, though neglected, had been around for a couple of millennia), these were the three theories Young included in his 1976 "Invention: A Topographical Survey." Although when Young wrote this essay he was four years away from the fully articulated new classicist definition of art featured in "Arts, Crafts, Gifts, and Knacks," he used elements of that definition—namely, the art/knack distinction and the art/heuristics connection—to determine what counted as "a principal development" in research on invention (3). In other words, it was from a nascent new classicist perspective that Young surveyed current research and decided to focus his (and the field's) attention on tagmemic, Burkean, and pre-writing theory. While he acknowledged that those theories embodied different, sometimes conflicting ideas about creativity, language, and writing, he saw in each a promising approach to invention that, if thoroughly studied, could mean significant advancements in both classroom pedagogy and disciplinary status.

Like the tagmemic theory that emerged from Kenneth L. Pike's research in linguistics, Burkean theory was based on the work of one scholar—philosopher, literary critic, and rhetorician Kenneth Burke. Although just about every rhetorician writing at the time agreed that Burke's theory of language as symbolic action could contribute to the formation of a new rhetoric, few knew exactly how to apply it to perceived pedagogical needs. As W. Ross Winterowd remarked in his 1968 *Composition/Rhetoric: A Synthesis,* the field needed someone to do for Burke's work what linguists Paul Roberts and Owen Thomas had done for Chomsky's: make it relevant to the teaching of English (79). Winterowd himself tried to be that "someone," that is, he tried to translate Burke's thinking into rhetorical theory and pedagogy that could be understood and used by college writers. In his 1975 textbook, *The Contemporary Writer,* for instance, he offered readers a heuristic based on the pentad, Burke's tool for analyzing motive in human relations.[13] When transformed into the following five questions, Winterowd argued, the terms of the pentad (act, agent, agency, scene, and purpose) could help students generate ideas about written and spoken discourse (82).

1. What does it say?
2. Who wrote it?
3. In what source was it published?
4. When and where was it published?
5. What is its purpose?

Burke's work was made accessible to students in other textbooks (e.g., William Irmscher's *The Holt Guide to English* and Lauer et al.'s *Four Worlds of Writing*) through similar redactions of the pentad; but as Young remarked in "Invention," the price for such accessibility was the loss of the pentad's philosophical context and thus some of "its power, intelligibility, and reason for being" (16). Not surprisingly, what Young and others wanted from Burke's work wasn't just a heuristic based on the pentad but rather "a full-fledged method of invention that could be used in the teaching of writing" ("Recent Developments" 30).

As Young himself acknowledged, a major obstacle to developing such a method was Burke's insistence that the pentad was designed as way to help readers analyze motive in existing discourse rather than a way to help writers generate new discourse.[14] In other words, the pentad was meant to aid interpretation not invention. In light of this distinction, some rhetoricians looked beyond the pentad for elements of Burke's work that could inform composition theory and pedagogy. In both "Burke for the Composition Class" and "Burkeian Invention, from Pentad to Dialectic," for instance, Philip M. Keith turned to Burke's understanding of dialectic to offer a set of five exercises that, according to him, could help writers develop an argument without relying on the oversimplified methods found in most handbooks ("Burke for the Composition Class" 348). Others, however, still per-

sisted in using the pentad as a heuristic for invention. In fact, Charles
Kneupper argued that the pentad was Burke's most important meth-
odological contribution and that the philosopher's training as a literary critic had blinded him to its value as technique for the invention of
discourse (Kneupper, "Dramatistic Invention" 133; Harrington et al.
201). For Young, this persistence was a good sign—an indication that
despite a slow pace, the field was "moving toward a theory of invention
based on Burke's work that could serve as both an art of reading and
an art of writing" ("Recent" 31).

Invention as Pre-Writing

While the theory of invention associated with pre-writing didn't
emerge from the work of one scholar in the way that tagmemic and
Burkean theories did, most accounts of its history do begin with a particular figure, D. Gordan Rohman. Funded by the US government,
Rohman worked with other researchers at Michigan State University
in the mid-1960s to determine how students could learn to engage in
the kind of creative thinking necessary for producing good writing.
Rohman termed this thinking "pre-writing" and argued that it aided
writers by allowing them to assimilate their subjects to themselves
(106). Pre-writing, in other words, was that stage of writing when an
external event was converted into an internal experience worth communicating to others (108). Rohman described this conversion as a
form of self-actualization and, in order to encourage it, asked students
in the experimental group of his study do three things: (1) keep a journal; (2) meditate; and (3) create analogies (108–9). Compared to the
writing produced by those in the control group, he reported, the experimental writing "showed statistically significant superiority," which
is to say it was based on "the discovery of fresh insight" and grounded
in "the principle of personal transformation" (112). Rohman acknowledged that such writing wasn't appropriate for all rhetorical situations
but argued that it "ought to be the *basic* writing experience for all
students at all levels, the propaedeutic to all subsequent and more specialized forms of writing" (112).

Like others, Young found some aspects of pre-writing theory problematic, namely its linear, think-then-write conception of composing
and its failure to address the role of audience in writing ("Invention"
17–8). Despite these problems, however, Young believed that because
Rohman's work had roots in psychological research, it made a signifi-

cant contribution to efforts to understand and teach invention as an art. As I explained earlier, Rohman's ideas about creativity were influenced by the research of scholars like Arthur Koestler, Erich Fromm, and Jerome Bruner. Generally speaking, it was from their work that he culled the idea of assimilation, that is, the idea that a writer must make a topic his own before he can write meaningfully about it. For Young, this connection between pre-writing and creativity research was paramount; it meant the heuristics associated with pre-writing, like those that grew out of Pike's tagmemics and Burke's dramatism, advanced the understanding of writing as an art. In other words, they were not just another of the rapidly proliferating "ad hoc and arbitrary" methods of invention but rather part of a theory that explained how teachers could foster creative behavior in students (20–1). Young anticipated that without such theories, composition pedagogy would become susceptible to the idea that the creative act was unteachable and, as a result, writing would "dwindle to an art of editing" (21).

What Young didn't anticipate, however, was how Rohman's work on pre-writing was influencing a group of scholars who, in a clear departure from the principles of new classicism, not only embraced the idea of writing as mysterious and unteachable but also used that idea as the foundation of composition textbooks. David Harrington, Philip M. Keith, Charles Kneupper, Janice Tripp, and William Woods reviewed these and other textbooks in their 1979 "A Critical Survey of Resources for Teaching Rhetorical Invention." Written as a complement to Young's 1976 bibliographic essay, Harrington et al.'s survey was meant to help teachers who wanted to emphasize invention in the classroom find the materials necessary to do so (188). To that end, they reviewed available textbooks, looking specifically at how (or if) they applied the four methods of invention previously identified by Young—classical, Burkean, tagmemic, and pre-writing. When they examined the textbooks associated with pre-writing, they saw that while Rohman's heuristics were featured in many, the "more significant principle" connecting them was the fundamental assumption that writing is successful when based on personal discovery and transformation (192–3). Thus the primary aim of these textbooks wasn't to teach explicit methods of invention (in the spirit of new classicism) but rather to bring about "the self-actualization of the writer, to make the student more aware of the power of creative discovery within her or him" (192–3).

Although differences among the texts that share this assumption are often masked by reductive labels like "expressivist," it's clear to see that Rohman's emphasis on personal discovery was a definitive feature of some of their most well known representatives, for instance, Donald C. Stewart's *The Authentic Voice,* Peter Elbow's *Writing Without Teachers,* and Ken Macrorie's *Telling Writing.* Echoing Rohman's idea of assimilation, the authors of these texts all argued that in order for writing to be successful, it had to be based on truth—not what we would call objective or "capital T" truth but rather what Macrorie described as the kind truth that reflects a connection between the writer's experience and her words (5). But what distinguished the work of writers like Stewart, Elbow, and Macrorie from that of Rohman was their association of this truth with the development of voice in writing. In other words, they all believed that when writing emerged from personal discovery and transformation, it had an "authentic" or "real" voice. When it simply fulfilled the requirements of an assignment or reiterated the ideas of others, on the other hand, it was the voiceless, "phony" writing that Macrorie called "Engfish" (1). Stewart made this connection between discovery and voice most explicit in the preface to *The Authentic Voice,* explaining that the book "proceeds from the conviction that the primary goal of any writing course is self-discovery for the student and that the most visible indication of that self-discovery is the appearance, in the student's writing, of an authentic voice" (xii). To develop voice, all three scholars promoted freewriting, a practice that, according to Elbow, required writers to turn off their automatic editors, thus allowing their "natural way of producing words," that is the "sound, texture, and rhythm" of their voice, to come through to the page (6). As Elbow made clear in *Writing Without Teachers,* however, freewriting wasn't a formula for good writing; in fact, it often produced bad writing (7). But if writers practiced long and often enough, he believed they could learn to produce meaningful prose in their own unique voice. Importantly, this doesn't mean Elbow believed they could be *taught* to produce meaningful prose in their own unique voice, however (ix). To the contrary, he claimed that writing was ultimately unteachable, that it "obey[ed] inscrutable laws" that put writers under its power, not vice versa (13). Macrorie expressed a similar position in *Telling Writing,* arguing that during freewriting, a writer often finds herself "watching the words go down on paper," as her pen or typewriter takes over the job of writing (148). A writer should do whatever she can to "bring about this state," Macrorie advised. It doesn't happen all of the time, but she "would be foolish not to try to set up the conditions which welcome this spirit, this Muse" (184).

New Classicism Versus New Romanticism—Again

As we already know, eventually Young did recognize the nature of Rohman's influence in composition, identifying it in "Arts, Crafts, Gifts, and Knacks" as new romanticism and contrasting it to new classicism. What he had initially perceived as a significant contribution to the effort to understand and teach invention as an art (in the new classicist sense of the term) had become something quite different: an affirmation of the fundamentally unteachable nature of writing. Young acknowledged this shift in his second bibliographic essay on invention research, "Recent Developments in Rhetorical Invention," by renaming the pre-writing theory of invention the romantic theory. There Young explained that because his earlier survey focused on Rohman's three heuristics (journaling, meditation, and creating analogies), it had masked the fact that most pedagogies and textbooks influenced by pre-writing included no formal method of invention (29). He identified this lack of a formal method as a defining feature of the romantic theory of invention, arguing that those who subscribed to it tended to portray writing as "organic, essentially mysterious, and hence inaccessible to analysis and resistant to deliberate control" (29). Yet their work was still very valuable, Young insisted. Although romantic rhetoric included "no characteristic method of invention," he wrote, "it has nevertheless encouraged the development of pedagogical practices designed to foster the ability to invent, and it has clearly contributed to a critical self-consciousness in the discipline that has encouraged theoretical work and research on the processes that concern us here" (29).

Young's affirmation of new romanticism here may seem like an afterthought, like something tacked on once he had made his real point, which was that new romanticism had no formal method of invention and was therefore at odds with the new classicist definition of art. After all, he didn't provide examples of what he meant by "critical self-consciousness," and he directed readers who wanted more explanation to his own work, a revised version of "Arts, Crafts, Gifts, and Knacks." Moreover, as Hawk demonstrates in *A Counter-History of Composition*, new classicists like Young did little to investigate the origins of romanticism or the figures who supposedly espoused it. Thus it was understood monolithically as a subjectivist, anti-mechanistic theory of creativity when, in fact, there are many forms of romanticism, some of which do not reject the value of rules and reason. Young acknowledged this gap in research in "Arts, Crafts, Gifts, and Knacks" when he admitted the field lacked the historical studies necessary to explain the connection between romanticism and vitalism. Yet he and others assumed one existed, and, as a result, vitalism was also understood monolithically as a subjectivist and anti-mechanistic theory. Hawk responds to this misunderstanding in *A Counter-History* by recuperating vitalism through the philosophies of Nietzsche, Bergson, Deleuze and Guattari, among others, in order to disentangle it from this narrow definition of romanticism. Thus the "counter-history" he provides is the one he believes composition could have had if new classicists like Young would have truly affirmed romantic rhetoric by studying its contributions rather than simply acknowledging it had made some.

Although I agree with Hawk that new classicists could have done more to understand the complex nature of romanticism, I don't think we should read Young's affirmation of romantic rhetoric as just a footnote to his broader effort to advance the new classicist definition of art. Such a reading, I would argue, obscures the ways in which Young tried to cultivate and apply the Keatsian negative capability he had asked others in the field to cultivate. Young knew writing was too complex to assume that any one theory could explain it or that any one pedagogy was best for teaching it. In other words, he knew that when it came to writing, Neils Bohr was right: the opposite of a deep truth is another deep truth. Thus I think it's more accurate (and certainly more generous) to read his affirmation of romanticism as an attempt to be inclusive by acknowledging the value of ideas that appeared to contradict his own. We see this kind of acknowledgement in Young's use of the terms "grammar" and "glamour" in "Arts, Crafts, Gifts, and Knacks" to refer (respectively) to the new classicist and new romanticist definitions of art. Following Jacqueline de Romily in *Magic and Rhetoric in Ancient Greece,* Young used these terms because they are etymologically related and thus, he reasoned, capable of highlighting the connection between the teachable and unteachable elements of writing (53). Young made a similar point in his first bibliographic essay, where, after explaining the differences among several invention pedagogies, he urged readers to "acknowledge the truths in disparate approaches" rather than assuming that if some were true, others must be false. "One need not repudiate classical invention or any other formal procedure to embrace less formal methods which rely more heavily on the student's intuitive ability," he wrote ("Invention" 42). And, as we saw earlier in this chapter, Young rejected the idea that a lack of explicit teaching methods in the new romanticist classroom entailed a lack of rigor ("Arts, Crafts, Gifts, and Knacks"). Did Young prefer the explicit teaching methods of the new classicist classroom? *Yes.* And he tried very hard to justify that preference. But I think he also tried to acknowledge the legitimacy of other preferences, even if, as Hawk shows us, he didn't exactly encourage the kinds of research needed to support them.

If this reading of Young's affirmation of new romanticism is, in fact, more accurate (and not just more generous), then it raises some important questions about the new classicist conception of art. Chiefly, why did Young define it against the new romanticist conception if he knew the two were not mutually exclusive? Or, more generally, why was it so important for him to distinguish pedagogies of writing that offered an explanation of causation from those that did not? Or formal methods of invention from informal methods? Why not accept any method that worked in the classroom rather than trying to single out the ones that could be taught explicitly? In short, why not fully embrace the complementarity expressed in Keats's notion of negative capability by supporting the development of pedagogies based on *both* new classicism and new romanticism?

Hawk provides an answer to these questions in *A Counter-History of Composition,* arguing that because of his "drive to disciplinarity," Young was more focused on establishing "specific disciplinary roots" for rhetoric and composition than he was on improving classroom practice (13, 16, 25). In order to establish these roots, Hawk explains, Young had to create scapegoat categories, that is, sets of theories, pedagogies, and histories against which he could define new classicism and demonstrate its superiority (16). Lumped together under the broad rubric of "anti-mechanism," romanticism and vitalism became one of these scapegoat categories and were thus sacrificed by Young and others for the sake of rhetoric and composition's disciplinary legitimacy (19).[15] According to this explanation, we could say that while Young might have been philosophically committed to Keats's idea of negative capability, he was pragmatically committed to establishing rhetoric and composition as a discipline. And, as Hawk points out, it was easier to achieve this pragmatic goal if researchers were studying formal methods of writing (and the theories they came from) than if they were studying informal methods (25).

On the one hand, I think Hawk's answer to our questions about the new classicist definition of art has obvious merit. Young's "drive to disciplinarity" is clear to see in the way he characterized that definition and used it to advance particular approaches to writing and invention over others. On the other hand, I wonder—or rather, worry about—what this answer actually tells us about that definition. Admittedly, Hawk's goal in *A Counter-History* is not to provide a detailed explanation of the new classicist definition of art. Because that is my goal here, however, I think we have to go beyond the observation that Young had a "drive to disciplinarity" to ask where that drive came from. If we don't ask this question, then we are implicitly accepting the idea it was the product of his personal beliefs and desires. As I argued earlier, this idea not only perpetuates a problematic theory of agency, but—more troubling for my purposes here—it also leaves us with an ahistorical understanding of the new classicist definition of art. In other words, it blinds us to the fact that the new classicist definition didn't just *have consequences* for the development of rhetoric and composition as a field but also that it *was a consequence* of that development. In the abstract, this is a fairly obvious point. In practice, however, it has been obscured by the fact that most disciplinary histories identify the mid-1960s or early 1970s as rhetoric and composition's birthdate.[16] As a result, most of us don't really start paying attention to the field's modern history until the time when scholars like Young and Lauer were already articulating elements of the new classicist definition of art. In other words, we more or less skip over the period before their work, characterizing it as a conflicted and directionless pre-history that should be separated from rhetoric and composition's history. Take, for example, the following passage from Robert J. Connors's "Composition History and Disciplinarity":

> Examine an issue of CCC from 1960 and contrast it to an issue from 1970 and the difference will immediately become apparent to you. I think we can trace the possibility of the field of composition studies from this point; what had been scattered and mostly rootless conversations was evolving into a dialogical and culminating scholarly literature. The rebirth of classical rhetoric, the development of tagmemic rhetoric,

the prewriting movement, sentence combining, the writing-process movement, Christensen rhetoric, and the entire new seriousness of the research strand in composition [. . .] all date to the middle and late 1960s. Disparate as these ideas and movements look to us in retrospect, collectively they were the New Rhetoric, and they represent a huge leap forward for the discourse of the field. (9)

To be clear, I don't disagree with Connors's argument here. As anyone who has read issues of *College Composition and Communication* from 1950 through the early 1960s knows, there was no discipline to speak of at that time. Yet that is precisely why this period warrants our attention here. As we have seen, the new classicist definition of art did not appear *ex nihilo* in 1980 but instead was the product of a process of emergence that began before rhetoric and composition reached the point (or the possibility) of disciplinarity. In an effort to historicize that definition, then, I want to turn to rhetoric and composition's pre-disciplinary period, looking to some of the "rootless and scattered conversations" that created the ecology from which Young's "drive to disciplinarity" emerged. As I explained at the outset of this chapter, my goal in doing this isn't to identify the particular rhetorical situation to which the new classicist definition responded but instead to describe some of the "viral intensities" that "infected" it before it emerged in the work of Young and others.

The Drive to Disciplinarity

We know so little about so much.

—Herbert Hackett

Bluntly, the fault is our own low level of competence. Too many teachers are not teaching composition; too many teachers do not even know what composition is.

—Thomas S. Kane

What's interesting about Connors's claim that early issues of *CCC* were filled with "scattered and mostly rootless conversations" is the fact the scholars who actually participated in those conversations made similar claims themselves. Frequently in those first ten or fifteen years of scholarship, contributors to *CCC* would itemize the "bewildering variety" of approaches used to teach first-year writing, bemoaning the fact that decisions about what to teach and how to teach it were being made according to individual preferences or the "personal theories" of administrators rather than any communally determined body of knowledge (Kitzhaber, *Themes* 12–13). The need for such a body of knowledge was identified as early as 1949, the year before the first issue of *CCC* appeared, when George S. Wykoff published "Toward Achieving the Objectives of Freshman Composition" in *College English*. Dissatisfied with the frequent use of "I think," "I believe," and "we feel" in articles about composition, Wykoff argued that teachers would need to "adopt a more scientific attitude" about their work and apply "much more of the experimental method" than they were accustomed to if they were going to prove their value to the rest of the English department (320). According to Wykoff, the goal for composition teachers was both to conduct new studies and to verify previous ones "until the mass of information" could justify the "indisputable conclusions" required for making sound recommendations (320).

It didn't take long for calls like Wykoff's to show up in issues of *CCC* and, eventually, to raise the issue of disciplinarity. A 1953 workshop report, "Status in the Profession of the Composition Teacher," argued that instructors should be "encouraged to write [. . .] and to investigate problems in composition teaching, and that such work should be regarded as highly as literary research and, for purposes of promotion, should be considered as equivalent in worth" (90). In a 1954 issue, Henry W. Sams identified pressing research needs in the history of rhetoric, while Harold B. Allen urged composition teachers to investigate questions in linguistics if they wanted "scientifically collected and verified data" to guide their decisions about course content. For Herbert Hackett, the pertinent questions for composition couldn't be limited to just one area of inquiry, and the problems plaguing those who taught it couldn't be solved simply by choosing better course content. What was needed, he argued in a 1955 *CCC* article, was a discipline, "not a narrowing one like traditional philology or rhetorical history or whatever, but a broadening one which ranges through many other disciplines, borrowing, adapting, creating, combining" (11). Hackett believed that without such a discipline, composition teachers were destined to "remain at the bottom of the teaching profession, cheek to jowl with teachers of typing" (10). To sway readers who thought he might be "overstating the case," Hackett continued his bleak characterization of the status quo in composition, arguing that while the teaching of skills is a job,

> it is not a profession based on a discipline; it does not have, as we will hear, a rigorous graduate program, it does not have a coherent methodology; it does not have any substantial body of data based on controlled observation or experiment. It does have several philosophies, a notoriety, a jargon . . . and it does have its schools or 'camps,' at one extreme those who have plunged into General Semantics, personality development, group dynamics, listening or 'practical' communication, at the other those who spend their time with workbook exercises in the thirteen kinds of adverbial phrases, poetry and themes on nothing at all. (10)

Although Hackett's argument for disciplinarity was a strong one, it did not garner across-the-board support from members of the College Composition and Communication Conference (CCCC) in the mid-1950s. In fact, as Maureen Daly Goggin points out, during this time most teachers argued against the idea of establishing a discipline since, by virtue of their graduate training in literature, they already belonged to one—English. To them, teaching composition was simply the steppingstone to full membership in that discipline (58).[17] Ironically, though, forces within the discipline of English—that is, within literary studies—and within educational culture at large, were creating a situation in which the option of disciplinarity appeared not just more attractive to members of the CCCC but also more necessary. Among these forces, one of the strongest and most widespread was the growing rejection of progressivism in American education. Closely connected to the educational philosophy of John Dewey, the progressive movement began in the early 1900s with the broad goal of focusing education on the needs of children and their development as cooperating members of a democratic society. To that end, progressive educators tried to create informal classrooms where learning happened through group discussion, collaboration, and experimentation as much as it did through more formal means like lectures. As David Olson explains, this effort represented a significant departure from the commonly held idea that the purpose of education was to "shape" children to meet the "pre-existing needs of society" (66). In the case of English, progressive goals often led to a focus on literature as experience or exploration (Applebee 80). Thus, in addition to (or sometimes instead of) teaching the "objective" cultural value of a particular set of texts, English teachers used literature to foster personality development and "life adjustment" strategies in students. This broader goal resulted in a wider definition of "literature," with modern texts, including magazines and newspapers, often supplementing or replacing the usual cannon of classical works (Applebee 58).

Obviously I've painted this portrait of progressivism in very broad brushstrokes; however, we don't need a very detailed picture to envisage what the real and/or imagined "excesses" of progressivism might have been and the kinds of critiques they produced. Educators and scholars worried that the curriculum in English was becoming too diluted, too disparate from one institution to another, and too much of what one scholar would later describe as "the wastebasket of the total curriculum" (Allen, "Will" 228). As Arthur Applebee explains in *Tradition and Reform in the Teaching of English,* these problems with progressivism united a host of unlikely allies around the charge that English curricula lacked rigor and that those children subjected to it would not be the "intellectual equal[s]" of their parents (188). Between the early 1940s and mid-50s, books with titles like *Crisis in Education, Educational Wastelands* and *Let's Talk Sense About Our Schools* made this argument, signaling a "changing tone" and the beginning of an intellectual intensification in American education (Applebee 188). The need for such an intensification was cemented, Applebee argues, when Russia launched Sputnik into orbit in October of 1957, taking the lead in the "space race" and raising doubts about America's ability to remain a technological leader in the world (188). In response to these doubts, the US Congress and the Eisenhower administration passed the 1958 National Defense Education Act (NDEA), which provided an unprecedented $887 million for improvements in teacher training and curricula at all levels of education for those subjects deemed relevant to national defense. For these subjects—namely math and science—the NDEA funded in-service programs, summer institutes, workshops, research fellowships, and leave-of-absence support in the hopes of producing more rigorous curricula, that is, of making course content better reflect the actual research of mathematicians and scientists.

While it may have been Sputnik that initiated government-led educational reform in math and science, it was being excluded from that reform that initiated an era of intense self-reflection and change within the discipline of English. H. A. Gleason, Jr. captured the insecurity and fear created by this exclusion in his 1962 address, "What Is English?" After describing what he called the "new seriousness in education," Gleason challenged his readers to consider whether or not they could "build a new curriculum worthy to take place alongside the work of [. . . their] colleagues in other disciplines—a curriculum worthy of the subject matter, and, above all, a curriculum worthy of the coming generations of young people" (10). At stake for English educators in this challenge was the legitimacy of calling themselves members of an academic discipline at a time when many segments of the American population were just as likely to consider them skill providers whose primary responsibility was either helping students become well-adjusted citizens or preparing them to excel in the subjects that really mattered. (Sounds familiar, doesn't it?) Through a series of events and publications in the late 1950s and early 60s, leaders in English tried to dispel these notions and initiate substantial curricular reform. Although most of them did not see the need for a discipline of rhetoric and composition at this time, their efforts to secure the government funding necessary for reform drew attention to that need, thus creating a situation in which the future of English rested, at least in part, on improvements in composition. Take, for example, the 1958 "Basic Issues" conferences and the 1959 report they produced. Organized by the executive secretaries of the MLA (George Winchester Stone) and the NCTE (J. N. Hook), the "Basic Issues" conferences brought together twenty-eight participants to provide "an accurate diagnosis" for the problems in English (Counciletter 52). The report of these conferences, which was published in *PMLA*, acknowledged that members of the profession were "expressing real concern about the *quality* of the work in English," but urged readers to believe that "given the right approaches to the problems and sufficient magnitude and strength," improvements in their subject matter and the teaching of it could be made as easily as they were being made in math and science (MLA 2). Such improvement should begin, the report argued, with an examination of the thirty-five "basic issues" in English studies. Articulated as questions, these basic issues ranged from the very broad (e.g., "What is English?") to the more narrow (e.g., "Should the basic program in English be modified for students primarily interested in science, technology, or related fields?") (4). Not surprisingly, literature received the most attention in the report, with six questions addressed specifically to issues such as sequencing and coverage. What is surprising, though, is that almost the same number of questions—five—focused exclusively on issues in composition. Of those five, the following two directly acknowledged the problems created by not having a discipline of rhetoric and composition.

- *"Can the teaching of composition be raised to the same level of academic respectability as the teaching of literature?* The teaching of composition is regarded as drudgery, is paid badly, and offers little opportunity for advancement in rank. Typically it is thought to be only a steppingstone to the teaching of literature. Teachers who share this attitude are not likely to inspire a love of English in their students. The morale of the freshman course is one of the most complex and important issues which confronts the profession" (10).

- *"How much graduate training in writing, rhetoric, criticism, linguistics, and the history of language is desirable for the prospective college teacher?* It appears that our teaching-assistants and young Ph.D.s may expect ninety per cent of their first six years of teaching to be in freshman and sophomore composition. Yet the typical Ph.D. program is void of courses dealing primarily with language and rhetoric. Is it right to assume that a beginning teacher can teach well something he has not studied directly since he was an undergraduate, something that is at best peripheral to his own current training and interests?" (10–11).

While the "Basic Issues" conferences and report got the ball rolling, so to speak, they didn't gain much attention beyond the halls of English departments. As a next step toward curricular reform, the NCTE passed a resolution in 1960 to pressure Congress to fund research in English. To achieve this end, they commissioned and produced *The National Interest and the Teaching of English*, a book-length argument for reform in English that was given to every member of Congress before the 1961 Senate and House hearings on proposed revisions and expansions of NDEA (Allen, "Counciletter" 265; Donlan 3). Convinced that significant improvement could not be achieved by local institutions, authors of *The National Interest and the Teaching of English* argued for a nationally supported program committed to the following six goals:

1. To focus instruction in English upon the study of language, literature, and composition;
2. To educate teachers of English to the developmental and sequential nature of the study and institute a national program for encouraging articulation of English studies throughout the school years;
3. To improve present preparatory programs for teachers of English;
4. To improve the services and supplies available to teachers of English;
5. To encourage significant research about the teaching of English;
6. To recruit and prepare more teachers of English (3).

Despite considerable effort in *The National Interest and the Teaching of English* to link these goals to the success of American education at all levels, Congress remained unconvinced of NCTE's argument and declined to expand funding to English. However, one government official, then-Commissioner of Education, Sterling McMurrin, was persuaded by the report of the need for reform in English. His subsequent testimony before Congress about that need secured limited funding for English *not* under the provisions of NDEA but instead under Public Law 531, a law that had been passed seven years earlier in 1954 to allow "collaborative arrangements" between the Office of Education and colleges, universities, and other educational institutions (Donlan 4). Thus was born Project English, an ambitious curriculum improvement program that, at the time of its inception, represented the most significant and concerted effort on the part of college professors to improve the quality of English instruction in grades K–12.

I could easily spend a whole chapter describing the aims and outcomes of Project English, but I am sure it seems as though I have already strayed too far from the subject of this chapter, the new classicist definition of art.[18] To summarize then, over the course of the seven years between 1961 and 1968, Project English received close to four million dollars of federal money, supported twenty-three curriculum centers across the country, financed numerous small grant projects, and produced almost half a million pages of published and unpublished materials (Donlan 3). As Dan Donlan explains in "Project English (1961–1968)," while the programs funded by Project English tackled a variety of problems across different levels of education, all were required by Public Law 531 to focus on research (4). In distinction to NDEA, Public Law 531 allowed collaboration between the government and educational institutions *only* for purposes of research. To meet this requirement, Project English administrators met at a 1962 conference at Carnegie Institute of Technology to establish the research areas that would guide their efforts to improve English education. They agreed on the following four:

1. Sequence of the curriculum from the standpoints of content and individual differences in learning ability;
2. Interrelationships among various parts of content, (e.g., relationship of linguistics knowledge to reading, literature, and composition);
3. Longitudinal investigation of how ability to speak, read, and write develops;
4. Relationship of logic and the reasoning process to composition and the reading of literary and non-literary materials. (Donlan 6)

Although literature was by no means ignored by Project English programs, the studies that emerged from efforts to address these research areas focused primarily on composition and linguistics. For example, of the thirty studies conducted in the first year of Project English, ten were about issues in composition and five were about issues in linguistics, while none were about issues in literature (although six did address issues in reading ability) (Hook 34). As Applebee explains, this trend continued in subsequent years because of both "congressional restriction" and the fact that "literature remained a difficult and intractable area of research" (202). In other words, together the stipulations of Public Law 531 and the perceived difficulty of conducting research studies on literature increased the amount of attention given to composition and linguistics.[19] Among the most successful and prolific curriculum development centers, for instance, was the one established at the University of Nebraska (Donlan 8–10). Under the leadership of Paul Olson, participants at the Nebraska Center worked to produce an articulated K–12 program in language and literature. However, as Erwin Steinberg reported in a 1964 update on the progress of Project English, almost all of the topics they addressed were topics in composition.[20] In fact, the only topic that explicitly mentioned literature did so within the context of composition, suggesting that literary texts could be used as rhetorical or structural models for writing (69).

While it would be an overstatement to say the option of disciplinarity gained more traction within the CCCC *because* of the increased focus on composition within Project English, that attention—and the political and educational events that precipitated it—did make the need for change more urgent in the minds of some teachers. We can see this urgency reflected in the titles of early 1960s articles like Albert K. Kitzhaber's "Death—Or Transfiguration," Gordon Wilson's "College Freshman Composition: How Can We Improve It?" and Harold B. Allen's "Will Project English Kill Freshmen English?" In his 1961 essay, "What Are Colleges and Universities Doing in Written Communication?" Glenn Leggett summed up the sentiment expressed in articles like these by noting that while Sputnik had "landed with a bang" on public schools and initiated reform, it had "sailed noiselessly over many a college campus" (41). Citing the "pedestrian, almost paleolithic quality" of most college composition syllabi, he lamented the fact that what could be the English department's most challenging course "has frequently become a departmental embarrassment, a status symbol in reverse, a poor and guilt-inspiring step-child" (41). When they considered the changes happening in other subjects at all levels of education (but particularly at the secondary level), teachers like Leggett worried college composition was going to be rendered obsolete. In other words, they worried students would come to their courses and find them pointless and outmoded. Some expressed this worry in a kind of shape-up-or-ship-out argument, suggesting that if scholars didn't make serious, curriculum-changing improvements in both their understanding of composition and ability to teach it, then the course didn't deserve to remain on the books.[21] One of the strongest arguments for such improvements came from Albert K. Kitzhaber's "4C, Freshman English, and the Future," which was published in the 1963 "Toward a New Rhetoric" issue of *College Composition and Communication*. After surveying the changes happening elsewhere in the discipline of English, Kitzhaber argued that he and his colleagues had done "little or nothing to improve the freshman course on a wide scale—to think through its assumptions, to agree on its aims and content, to take full advantage of knowledge available in fields such as language, logic, rhetoric, [and] psychology" (132). Making necessary improvements, he continued, would require that they "start asking fundamental questions about the act of writing, and asking them in a way that will make it possible to get answers based on more hunches and personal theories and long-established custom" (133). Among the questions he had in mind were:

> How does a person actually set about composing a paper? What preliminary steps, if any, does he go through before he sets anything down in writing? As he writes, what guides him in the choices he makes? How does a writer (or speaker) actually generate the sentences he uses in discourse? How is he able to make up sentences that he has never seen or heard before? What are the exact relations between writing and speaking? What is the relation of knowledge of grammar to the development of skill in writing? Does it matter what kind of grammar is studied, or how much of it is studied, or the age at which one studies it? What is the relation between the study of standard literature and the ability to write well? Between the habit of wide reading and skill in writing? Between the study of semantics or logic and writing ability? How much effect, if any, does the systematic study of rhetoric have on the development of writing skill, and what aspects of rhetorical theory are most useful? What is the relation between class size and frequency of class meeting or frequency of writing or intensiveness of paper correction and the development of skill in composition? Are there concepts underlying the writing process that can be identified and used as the organizing principles for a sequential curriculum in composition? (133)

I've quoted Kitzhaber at length here to demonstrate just how vast the territory of the unknown appeared to some composition teachers at this time. From our perspective, which (in most cases) is informed by an epistemology much different than Kitzhaber's, it seems optimistic at best and naïve at worst to think any of those questions—save the one about class size—could be answered unequivocally. But that is what Kitzhaber and others like him were after. They believed that in order for composition to exist—let alone flourish—in the second half of the twentieth century, it would finally have to accumulate the "mass of information" called for by George S. Wykoff almost fifteen years earlier. To accumulate that information, though, they would have do research, and to do research, they would have to establish a discipline since teaching four or five classes a semester with little to no job security provided neither the time nor the motivation necessary for such work.[22]

As I acknowledged earlier, members of the CCCC did not unanimously support this movement toward disciplinarity. In fact, when the 1960 Committee on Future Directions proposed that the organization had outgrown its original mission and should focus its efforts "upon a discipline rather than upon a course or a particular group of teachers," they were met with such disagreement over the nature of a new mission that CCCC members simply opted to retain the old one (Bailey, et al. 3; Goggin 60). But, as Maureen Daly Goggin argues in *Authoring a Discipline,* even though early efforts like this one failed to unite the field around the idea of disciplinarity, they demonstrate that it was in a position for a transition (60). What I have tried to do here is describe some of the forces that put the field in this position so that we can better understand the ecology from which Young's "drive to disciplinarity" and the new classicist definition of art emerged. Like Hawk, I believe the new classicist definition of art cannot be separated from this drive. But, as I said earlier, for me this belief means we have to ask where the drive to disciplinarity came from. While I don't claim to have definitively answered such a complex question in this chapter, I have demonstrated that forces much larger and more powerful than Richard E. Young's personal ambitions were pushing rhetoric and composition toward disciplinarity, creating a need for firm foundations that preexisted the new classicist definition of art and, importantly, would have been fulfilled with or without it. For many in the English department—not just those in rhetoric and composition—the stakes were too high to be satisfied with the status quo. College-level educators were justifiably worried they were being left behind—and not just by their counterparts in math and science who had received funding from NDEA but also by their "subordinates," that is, by the high school English teachers whose curricula, thanks to efforts like Project English, were suddenly looking more sophisticated and more rigorous than their own. If English was going to matter in the second half of the twentieth century, these educators reasoned, then things were going to have to change. English was going to have to have an identifiable subject matter, clearly defined ways of studying that subject matter, and proven pedagogies for teaching it. It's true, as

Hawk notes in *A Counter-History of Composition,* that for rhetoric and composition these changes often meant a turn away from some of the traditional concerns of the humanities toward those more closely associated with the sciences (23–4).[23] But this same turn was happening throughout the discipline of English, where new criticism was giving way to the much more interdisciplinary methods of literary analysis afforded by structural linguistics and psychology. Of course these changes weren't permanent, and they weren't the only force at work in the development of rhetoric and composition as a discipline, but they were a pervasive, widely distributed, and widely felt force—one we can readily see at work in the new classicist definition of art.

To bring this chapter to a close, I want to emphasize that my objective in locating the new classicist definition of art among these forces has not been to minimize its impact on the field of rhetoric and composition. *Rather, my objective has been to explain that definition and account for its ability to have any impact at all.* Hawk is right, I think, to point out that the new classicist definition of art helped rhetoric and composition become a discipline by marginalizing the theories, methods, and pedagogies that appeared incompatible with its epistemological criteria. Thus we need his counter-history to help us to "remember the past differently"—that is, "to open a line of thought" from the work of misrepresented writers like Coleridge to the more ecological perspective on rhetoric that he develops through figures like Heidegger, Delueze, Bergson, and Neitzsche (262, 272). But we also need to apply that ecological perspective to our understanding of the new classicist definition of art. Otherwise, we have no way to explain its impact—either negative or positive—except by recourse to the agency of an autonomous creator/rhetor. As Hawk himself would argue however, such an explanation is inadequate because it focuses too narrowly on efficient cause, thus obscuring the fact that, as he puts it, expression is possible only as an "internal function" of a rhetorical ecology (165).

In the next chapter, I explain Hawk's argument about rhetorical ecologies more thoroughly, looking not only at his re-understanding of *techne* as "post-*techne*" but also at other revisions and redefinitions of the term. As we will see, these revisions and redefinitions responded (in both direct and indirect ways) to a series of arguments that began in the late 1980s and challenged the new classicist definition of art, particularly its characterization of writing as a knowable, teachable, and useful process.

3 Postmodern Theory and the Re-Tooling of *Techne*

In their 2002 collection *Perspectives on Rhetorical Invention,* both Janice M. Lauer and Janet M. Atwill observe that interest in heuristics has waned considerably since the 1970s and 1980s (Atwill, "Introduction" xi; Lauer, "Rhetorical" 2). I doubt anyone would disagree with this observation. For many the term "heuristics" is a relic of rhetoric and composition's past—that is, at least when it is used as a noun. Yes, we still talk about heuristic thinking, or we suggest that a concept or theory has heuristic value. But few in the field are developing or teaching strategies for writing that they would explicitly call "heuristics." Atwill attributes this lack of interest in heuristics to the friction between invention and postmodernism, citing in particular the propensity within certain versions of postmodernism to value theory over practice, the subjective over the empirical, and the aesthetic over the utilitarian (xii). Because the canon of invention exists in the "ill-defined space" between these binaries, she writes, it has never been able to find a home in American institutions of higher learning (xii). Importantly, though, Atwill argues that it is invention's status as a *techne* that locates it in this ill-defined space (xi-xii). In other words, the problem for invention is its identification with *techne.* Thus the real source of friction here—and, I would add, a major source of friction in many quarters of rhetoric and composition—is the incompatibility between *techne* and postmodernism.

In this chapter, I explain the incompatibility between *techne* and postmodernism by reviewing a series of arguments that, as early as the late 1980s, began challenging the axiological and epistemological features of the new classicist definition of art—features I will refer to here in shorthand as *instrumentality* and *teachability.* We encountered these features earlier in chapter 1 when I explained what it means to define *techne* as a rational ability to effect a useful result (as the new classicist definition of art does). Axiologically speaking, this definition means that the value of possessing a *techne* lies in the use made of its product rather than in the act of making that product. Epistemologically speaking, it means that the artist can produce a rational explanation of causation and that this explanation can be taught to others (in the form of heuristics, for example) and used across a variety of situations in order to give them more control over the process of making. In the first part of this chapter I explain how, over the course of thirteen years or so, arguments about these two features created—or, depending on your perspective, illuminated—a gap between *techne* and postmodern theory. While some of these arguments were aimed specifically at the new classicist definition of art, others took issue with the features of teachability and instrumentality in more general terms. In the second part of the chapter, I turn to efforts to bridge this gap, looking at how (and in what forms) *techne* endured the challenges posed by these arguments. Specifically, I argue that *techne*'s proponents responded to the critiques of instrumentality and teachability in one of two ways— either by recovering overlooked versions of *techne* in which the weight of those two problematic features is counter-balanced by other features (e.g., *metis* or *kairos*), or by offering new versions of *techne* in which those two problematic features play little to no definitional role.

Before I move on to these critiques and the responses they generated, however, I need to point out that the new classicist definition of art and heuristics drew serious criticism before the advent of postmodern theory in the English department. Most notably, Ann E. Berthoff vigorously criticized Janice M. Lauer's work on heuristics and creative problem solving in her 1971 "The Problem of Problem-Solving" and 1972 "Response to Janice Lauer." Berthoff's argument in these two pieces grew out of her rejection of Lauer's claim that writing teachers needed to move outside of English in order to solve the "composition problem" (Lauer, "Heuristics" 396). Berthoff was particularly offended by the idea that the expertise of psychologists—whom she called the "technologists of learning"—might be relevant to teaching writing. Their methods were complicit with the "institutional biases" of our "bureaucratized society," she argued, and if teachers borrowed those methods (that is, heuristics) then they were guilty of "preparing students for life in a technological society" ("Problem" 93). With claims like these, Berthoff managed to both draw a very clear line between the sciences and the humanities and suggest that anyone who

crossed it was incapable of valuing more traditionally humanistic interests, (e.g., the imagination and the symbolic nature of language)
(93). In her view, English teachers needed to be "playing on their home
ice," not that of the psychologists and linguistic scientists [who were]
operating outside their field of competence" (92, 93).

As damaging as this critique was, I would argue that it appears
both predictable and somewhat superficial when we compare it to the
critiques that were to come later. Berthoff's argument was predictable simply because others had made similar arguments before her,
and, as in the case of Louis C. Schaedler's 1966 *CCC* essay, "Call Me
Scientist," they had made them with even more vigor.[24] Unhappy
with efforts to apply structural linguistics to the teaching of writing,
Schaedler, who taught composition at New Mexico State University,
decided to parody the yearning for acceptance and authority that, according to him, drove composition teachers outside of their own discipline into the foreign land of science. Thanks to linguistics, he wrote,
the time has come for the "scientific fraternity" to make room for the
humanities; thus English teachers "are henceforth to be known as linguistic scientists and to be accorded full rights and privileges of the
brotherhood" (110). Schaedler addressed those rights and privileges
(e.g., conducting experiments, publishing research, developing axioms,
and extrapolating pedagogies), lauding each with more than enough
sarcasm to make his point perfectly clear: borrowing from the sciences
was at best unnecessary and at worst inimical to the values and goals of
the humanities. Like Berthoff's, Schaedler's argument stemmed from
the long-standing (and thus predictable) concern that collaboration
between English and the sciences would weaken the identity and authority of the humanities. Such a concern makes sense if one views the
humanities as the opposite of the sciences. From such a perspective,
any overlap or sharing between the two would necessarily entail a loss
of identity and authority.

The degree to which Berthoff's argument was driven by this concern for identity and authority accounts for what I see as its superficial nature. In other words, I think Berthoff's fear that the values of
humanists were going to be "gobbled up" by the scientists limited
her ability to offer a more substantive critique of heuristics (Lauer,
"Response" 100). This isn't to say her critique of heuristics wasn't powerful. As Janet M. Atwill has pointed out, it "had a chilling effect"
on the research Young and others called for under the rubric of new

classicism (*Rhetorical* xiv). But in Berthoff's argument, the potentially problematic epistemological and axiological features of heuristics and the new classicist definition of art were left untouched in favor of the more general claim that borrowing from the social sciences was philosophically and politically dangerous. It is true some have read her argument as a critique of instrumentality, citing her objection to the way heuristics turn writing into a means of solving problems. What's important to note, however, is that Berthoff never objected to the idea that writers are subjects who can and do put writing in the service of predetermined ends. She simply rejected the particular end at issue. Language isn't a means of solving problems, she argued, but rather "a speculative instrument, our means of creating and discovering those forms which are the bearers of meaning" ("Response" 101). Similarly, Berthoff never challenged the assumption that knowledge about writing could be observed, generalized, and taught. For her, the issue was where that knowledge—and the methods used to obtain it—came from. If English teachers turned to admired writers, to the journals of famous thinkers, and to the practices of present-day artists and artisans, she argued, then they would find plenty of appropriate strategies for teaching invention.

THE POSTMODERN CHALLENGE

My point in reviewing Berthoff's critique here isn't simply to highlight its weaknesses (even though I do find her defensiveness striking). I recognize, of course, that her argument reflects the historical context in which it was made. My point, then, is to establish a contrast, that is, to illuminate just how substantive critiques of *techne* became once postmodern theory became part of the conversation in English departments. Whereas Berthoff didn't (or couldn't) notice the potentially problematic epistemological and axiological features of heuristics and the new classicist definition of art, the critics who followed her zeroed in on them, raising questions that tapped into issues much more substantial than those associated with diminished disciplinary territory and authority. For these critics, the questions were no longer about *which* external ends language should serve or *where* we should look for theories and teachable practices. Now they were asking *if* language should serve external ends and *if* we should look for theories and teachable practices. In what follows, I review some of the arguments in which these questions were raised, looking first at those concerned with instrumentality and then at those concerned with teachability. Although I am addressing them separately here, I want to point out that these features are not entirely distinct, nor are the problems they create. Perhaps the best way to describe the connection between them is to say that teachability is a precondition of instrumentality in that we must gain some control over an activity by making it knowable (and therefore teachable) before we can put it in the service of an external end. This overlap is evident in some of the arguments below, particularly in those made by Lynn Worhsam and D. Diane Davis.

The Postmodern Challenge to Instrumentality

The critique of instrumentality at issue here is aimed at two main problems, the first of which is the subject/object dualism. As we saw in chapter 1, Lynn Worsham critiqued this split in her 1987 essay, "The Question Concerning Invention," arguing that the new classicist definition of art privileges the efficient cause, that is, the maker who independently brings products (or conditions) into being in order to achieve predetermined goals (207). Following Heidegger, she claimed that this reduction of causality is symptomatic of a kind of technological thinking or an aggressive "will-to-mastery" in which human being sees itself as a subject whose primary task is the control and regulation of the earth through objectification (205, 209). For Worsham, such thinking was plain to see in the language of new classicism, particularly in the opening chapter of *Rhetoric: Discovery and Change* where authors Young, Becker, and Pike claimed that rhetoric's primary concern was with the control of a process, that is, with mastering not only a theory of how and why one communicates but "mastering the process of communication as well" (9). Worsham also identified technological thinking in the pedagogies and practices associated with new classicism, arguing, for instance, that heuristic procedures were similar to scientific procedures in that they projected onto the world "subjective categories of the mind and thereby secur[ed] the certainty of an objective world that coincides with human subjectivity" (211). In other words, Worsham saw in heuristics a means of imposing order on the world through language, of making it "representable, calculable, and useable" for the writer who needs to solve a problem or answer a question (209).

The second problem with instrumentality according to this cri-tique is closely related to the first, though in a seemingly counter-intuitive way since, as I just explained, language becomes an object when our thinking about writing is dominated by the subject/object dualism. As Worsham argues, however, this dualism "gives way to a means-ends relationship" in which everything that falls under the cat-egory of "object" is understood only in terms of its potential to become a resource. As a result, objects actually lose their "objectness," that is, they lose their inherent or internal value in order to help the subject accomplish a predetermined goal. In the case of new classicism and its corollary pedagogies, Worsham argued, this means that language itself is no longer recognized as a principle of genesis. Instead, it becomes the merely "the instrument by which the writer articulates, explores, and solves problems" and "the means by which to impose order and arrangement on data" (211). Thus reduced, it no longer shines forth in the product but instead recedes into the product's function. Not only does this change sacrifice the rigor of "genuine questioning" for the ease and efficiency of "pre-selected answer[s]," but it also deprives the writer of the opportunity to "undergo" an experience with lan-guage. Drawing on Heidegger's *On the Way to Language*, Worsham distinguished having an experience of language from undergoing an experience with it: while the former refers to the activity of subjects who possess the experience as their own, the latter refers to activity in which "language strikes us, befalls us, overcomes us, overwhelms us, and, most importantly, transforms us" (227). "To undergo an experi-ence with language," she elaborated, "is to enter into it, to submit to it, yield to it, be owned and possessed and appropriated by it" (227). In other words, it is to engage in a kind of writing that "brings to pass an awareness of the limits of literacy, an awareness of the non-discursive elements in the event of signification" (236).

Throughout the 1990s and into the 2000s, concern for the "ob-jectness" and the agency of language remained a—if not the—driving force in critiques of instrumental approaches to writing. However, rath-er than relying on Heidegger, these critiques called on post-structural-ist and postmodernist theorists to explain what is at risk when writing is brought forth as an instrument. In "Three Countertheses: Or, A Critical In(ter)vention into Composition Theories and Pedagogies," for instance, Victor Vitanza used the work of Jean-Francois Lyotard to expose the ways in which composition tries to eliminate language's "perversity" and its "noncongruent, nonisomorphic nature" in order to achieve the common end of both traditional and modern rhetoric: community (141). As an alternative to this end and the strategies used to achieve it, Vitanza advocated paralogy, the term Lyotard uses to describe the method of creating new rules for postmodern language games through dissensus rather than consensus.[25] While the inventional strategies of traditional and modern rhetoric are "controlled or accounted for by a system or paradigm of knowledge," and are, in turn, "used to promote the capitalistic, socialistic, scientific 'efficiency' of that system or paradigm," Vitanza argued, paralogy "(re)turns—that is, radically tropes—against the system, or paradigm of knowledge" (147). In other words, whereas traditional rhetorics encourage the efficient production and consumption of systems of knowledge, paralogy works against those systems, "bear[ing] witness to the unintelligible or to disputes or differences of opinion that are systematically disallowed by the dominant language game" (147).

D. Diane Davis also highlighted composition's efforts to turn language into a means to an end, arguing in *Breaking Up [at] Totality: A Rhetoric of Laughter* that writing teachers have sacrificed genuine writing (i.e., "writing for the sake of writing") for composition: a watered-down, utilitarian knock-off that serves the consumerist agendas of the university by equipping students with the basic, transferable skills needed to help them perform well in other courses and/or jobs (229). By "pumping out *literate* citizens," that is citizens who are proficient users of language, she wrote, composition courses have come to "complete a very particular service for the university and/or society's economic structure" (228–9). To this end, composition has had to turn writing into a tool, a "set of 'teachable practices'" students can easily wield in order to produce and transfer meaning. Thus the course not only "manages to perpetually reinstate the humanist subject, in the name of *the competitive edge*" but also over-emphasizes teaching to the detriment of learning (229). Academia isn't about learning at all, Davis claimed, but instead about "protecting what has already been established, codified, and made 'teachable' from anything that might call it all into question," that is, " the excess, the noise/static that gets 'let by' (silenced) in the name of a reproducible practice" (224).

For Davis, the consequences of silencing language for the sake of external goals extend well beyond the realm of pedagogy. Drawing on Jean-Luc Nancy's work on community and Avtial Ronell's on writing,

she argued that in order to respond ethically to the posthumanist paradox—that is, to the fact that "we both make and/but are also (more
so) *made by History*"—we must celebrate the excesses of language (23).
To this end, Davis suggested using metaphors of heterogeneity and
excess (106), using parataxis rather than hypotaxis (108), and lightly
manipulating the appearance of text with diacritical marks and deliberate grammar errors (108, 111). As she pointed out, it's not that
language needs help being excessive, but rather that we need help noticing its excessiveness. By taking the time to listen to the excesses of
language (rather than devoting so much of it to muzzling them), she
argued, we create opportunities for the exposure of the "unsharable
loose ends" that provide the basis for ethical communities in a posthumanist world (191).

Offering one of the most stringent critiques of instrumentality
in our field, Geoffrey Sirc used the work of Georges Bataille in his
1995 "Godless Composition, Tormented Writing" to argue that composition is dominated by a "curriculum of writing-as-servility" (558).
While this isn't the place for a lengthy explanation of Bataille's work,
a brief description some of his key concepts will help us to see where
Sirc is coming from. Among those key concepts, one of the most important is inner experience, which Bataille describes his 1954 book
Inner Experience as an ecstatic state achieved through sacrifice or the
non-productive expenditure of energy. Bataille's work on inner experience is part of his larger critique of the utilitarianism and servility that
dominate human experience through a restricted economy that measures value only in terms of accumulation and profit. A central claim
of this critique is that humans, in an effort to evade anxiety and anguish, invest their energy into projects guided by "discursive thought"
or "discursive reason." In other words, as humans, we invest ourselves
in project through language, sacrificing it to the world of production
for the sake of the knowledge and power that it helps us acquire. Thus
for Bataille, through language, we live our entire lives as a means to
an end: the attainment of absolute knowledge, professional success, or
anything capable of quelling our apprehensions about life and death.
Yet no matter how completely we invest ourselves in project, Bataille
argues that there is always a surplus of energy that remains—something that cannot be employed toward the attainment of knowledge
or success. And it is through this unemployable energy, this "accursed
share" (which Bataille commonly associates with eroticism and laugh-

ter), that one begins to become aware of the possibility of an alternative kind of experience (inner experience) in which one becomes sovereign not through knowledge but instead through a contestation or rupture of knowledge that leads to what Bataille calls "non-knowledge" or "non-savoir." In the following, Bataille contrasts inner experience to the utilitarianism of project:

> I come to this conclusion: inner experience is the opposite of project. Nothing more. 'Action' is utterly dependent on project. And what is serious, is that discursive thought itself is engaged in the mode of existence of project. Discursive thought is evinced by an individual engaged in action: it takes place within him beginning with his projects, on the level of reflexion upon projects. Project is not only the mode of existence implied by action, necessary to action—it is a way of being paradoxical in time: *it is the putting off of existence to a later point.* (*Inner Experience* 46)

If project is characterized by action, then by contrast, inner experience is marked by passivity. In fact, the subject in inner experience is not only passive, she is no longer a subject as such because the subject-object split has disappeared. In *Inner Experience* Bataille writes: "There is no longer subject-object, but a 'yawning gap' between the one and the other and, in the gap, the subject and object are dissolved; there is passage, communication, but not from one to the other: the one and other have lost their separate existence . . . the subject is no longer there . . ." (59–60).

This description of inner experience as subject (and object)-less highlights the specific meaning of another key term for Bataille, sovereignty. Sovereignty is power but not power exercised by a subject. It is the power of pure expenditure that arises at the moment when the subject's knowledge and authority—indeed its subjectivity—have been ruptured, when energy that was previously invested in the future through project is sacrificed for the present through laughter, ecstasy, terror, intoxication, anguish, or nausea: anything capable of causing a radical loss of self and "a return to *what is there*, a return to that which one evades in discursive activity and work" (Boldt xix).

Based on this short description of inner experience, it is easy to see how Bataille's work could provide the material for a damning critique of conventional writing theories and pedagogies. In most composition classes, writing is taught as a means to an end: expressive assignments are taught as a means to self-discovery or the development of voice; arguments such as proposals are taught as a means to fixing problems; research papers are used to teach students how to understand and synthesize multiple sources. The list could go on, but the point is that all of these assignments are based on an instrumental understanding of language. This observation is the starting point of "Godless Composition, Tormented Writing," the 1995 essay in which Geoffrey Sirc argued that composition is a utilitarian enterprise in which anything and everything that doesn't serve some predetermined, edifying end is excised and relegated, heartlessly, to the dustbin of the "not useful." What we are left with after this purging, Sirc argued, is a "curriculum of writing-as-servility," that is, a "world of disciplined projects" where all that matters is results. As Sirc put it, "[c]omposition is endlessly standards, formulae, ways, methods, techniques . . . It wants no part of what escapes its ways, of the supplement, the allegory, the remainder, the doomed part, the accident, the perversion, the error, which is poetry" (547).

By "poetry" Sirc wasn't referring to poetry per se but rather to language that, because it isn't put in the service of a project or exchanged like currency in the "marketplace of ideas," is capable of disturbing "the servile economy of meaning" (i.e., the restricted economy) that produces and structures composition.[26] Contrasting this poetic form of language to the "calculated writing" of composition, that is, "the degraded utilitarianism of successfully ordering a hamburger at a fast-food restaurant," he argued that it doesn't try to accomplish or solve anything: "it simply becomes a rupture, cracks the mirror so that it can reflect the heart-breaking reality of humanity" (549).[27] For Sirc, this "useless" form of writing finds its apotheosis in Bataille, in his insistence on the fundamental inability of writing to deliver us from anything. According to Bataille, no matter what we seek to attain through writing (e.g., the exchange of information, a synthesis of ideas, a new form of self-expression) we succeed only in evading real existence. Only when we stop trying to do things with words, then, will we potentially have access to what he describes as the "silent, elusive, ungraspable" region of language that "subsists safe from verbal servilities" (*Inner* 14–15).

THE POSTMODERN CHALLENGE TO TEACHABILITY

On the surface, teachability doesn't seem like such a bad thing, or at least it doesn't seem as problematic as instrumentality. After all, underpinning almost any pedagogy in almost any discipline is the assumption that its subject matter is to some degree teachable. As I have already explained, though, when we claim something is teachable, we are making an epistemological claim. In the case of *techne,* or, more specifically, in the case of the new classicist definition of art, we are claiming that we can know writing through rational explanations of causation and that these explanations can be used to create transferable strategies that will give writers more control over writing. While many would argue that this claim is true in that transferable strategies do, in fact, give writers more control over writing, others would counter that we gain this control at the cost of anything that can't be included in a rational explanation of causation. Still others would counter that it simply isn't possible to know and teach writing through rational explanations of causation and the transferable strategies they yield. This latter claim is the thesis at the heart of post-process theory, which, as its name suggests, is a body of theory that rejects the idea that writing can be taught as a process comprised of a series of knowable, repeatable steps (e.g., pre-writing, writing, and rewriting). Associated most directly with the work of Thomas Kent, post-process theory rejects process theory on the grounds that writing is (1) a radically situated activity and (2) a fundamentally interpretive act. Understanding writing as radically situated, Kent argued in the introduction to *Post-Process Theory: Beyond the Writing-Process Paradigm,* means understanding that it happens at such specific historical moments and in such specific relations that no theory of a repeatable process could usefully describe it (2). To shore up this claim, Kent relied on Donald Davidson's concepts of prior and passing theories. Everyone enters a communicative situation with prior theories, or beliefs about how others use language. These prior theories allow communication to begin but, because no two interlocutors share prior theories, they have to create passing theories to actually decode each other's language. As Kent explained, Davidson refers to these theories as "passing" because they don't exist long enough to be codified for reuse in other situations (5).

In *Paralogic Rhetoric: A Theory of Communicative Interaction,* Kent again turned to Davidson, in addition to Jacques Derrida, to explain why writing is fundamentally interpretive. Although Davidson and

Derrida come from different philosophical traditions, Kent noted, they both believe that because of the split between signifier and signified, there is no way to predict the effect of a sign in the world. More specifically, they both believe that no "identifiable conventional element exists that links a written sign to its context, because a context can never be absolutely determinable" (28, 32). Using this claim as his major premise, Kent argued that writing must start with the writer's effort to interpret her interlocutor's code and match it to her own (26). He thus concluded that it is not the writer's inventive act of discovering her intentions or subject matter but rather the "hermeneutic guesswork" she does in order to interpret another's code that constitutes the fundamental event of writing (26–7).

Whereas post-process theorists like Kent challenged the epistemological claims inherent in the idea of teachability by flat-out rejecting them, others focused on the limits teachability imposes on writing, often arguing that those limits lead to unethical theories and pedagogies. Versions of this argument first appeared in 1987—one in Worsham's "The Questioning Concerning Invention" and the other in Vitanza's "Invention, Serendipity, Catastrophe, and a Unified, Ironic Theory of Change." Although they were working from different theoretical sources (Worsham from Heidegger and Vitanza from Paul Feyerabend and Hayden White), both writers argued that heuristics represented a teleological—and therefore "conceptually closed"—approach to invention and writing (Vitanza 136). As Worsham explained it, heuristics develop "meaning and knowledge in terms of a pre-selected answer that is always, already given by the particular methodology" (213). In other words, the problems and/or questions heuristics pose to writers are "all leading problems or questions" because they automatically limit the field of inventional possibilities to a relatively small set of corresponding solutions and answers (Vitanza 136). For Worsham, this kind of limitation inherent in a heuristics-based approach precludes the more open, radical, and creative form of questioning embodied in the act of writing itself. "Once we enter the question that brings writing into being *as writing*," she wrote, "we leave behind any adherence to system or technique, which are the guarantors of safe passage, and we risk the on-going transformation of ourselves and our world" (235, emphasis added). Vitanza similarly advocated for a more creative, transformative approach to invention, one that would "openly favor an anachronistic and sophistic bias" by beginning with solutions and then moving backward to problems. According to him, such an approach, which is based more on a theory of chance or serendipity than on a theory of probability, implies that "anything goes and that change does not begin with a problem, and that its components cannot be known and therefore codified" (137).[28]

Vitanza twice returned to this argument about the epistemological restrictiveness of heuristics, once in his 1991 "Three Countertheses" and again in his 2000 "From Heuristics to Aleatory Procedures; or, Toward Writing the Accident." Like the earlier critique, these two essays were built around the claim that when we make writing teachable through heuristics, we limit how we can experience it and what we can accomplish with it. In "Three Countertheses," for instance, Vitanza argued that the differences between the inventional strategies associated with rhetoric and those associated with paralogy reflect the differences between the larger language games of which they are a part: the language game of knowledge (which he identified with *techne*) and Lyotard's postmodern language game of art.[29] The former is distinguished from the latter, Vitanza explained, by its commitment to the grand narrative of teachability, which maintains that in order for something to be knowledge, it must be generic enough to be codified, and once codified, easily transferred from person to person (162). The problem with this narrative is that any activity too idiosyncratic or non-rational to be codified "simply falls by the wayside" or, worse, is negatively associated with vitalism (162). Thus for Vitanza, the language game of knowledge—and any writing strategy based upon it—can't help but to become a means of "fostering the dominant discourse" and is "in no way revolutionary" (152).

Relying on Bataille's theory of the restricted economy and its counterpart, the general economy,[30] Vitanza took this critique of teachability a step further in "From Heuristics to Aleatory Procedures" to argue that heuristics not only reduce knowledge about writing to what can be codified and transferred but that they also limit the ways in which writing actually produces knowledge. According to Vitanza, heuristics are a product of the restricted economy, which he described as a classical economy based on negation, while aleatory procedures are a product of the general economy, which he described an "ever-new" post-structuralist economy "baseless" on excess and "non-positive affirmation" (186). Thus heuristics generate meaning through a limiting and negative process of definition in which what something *is* is determined by what it is not (in other words, inclusion through exclusion) (186). And they do this, Vitanza argued, in accordance with Aristotle's three laws of logic: the law of identity (A must be A), the law of non-contradiction (A and not-A cannot both be true), and the law of the excluded middle (A can be only A or not-A). Aleatory procedures, on the other hand, are not beholden to the "logical categorization" at work in heuristics and therefore invent by "recalling to mind what heretofore had been excluded by the principle of the excluded middle" (186). In other words, aleatory procedures invent by seeking out and embracing what heuristics exclude: the third alternatives or "monsters of thought" that don't fit within binaries like male/female, organic/inorganic, fact/fiction, etc. (193). For example, Vitanza claimed that aleatory procedures such as Greg Ulmer's "heuretic" CATTt (contrast, analogy, theory, target, tale) are capable of inventing "para-arguments" that work by way of associational networks rather than "conventional argumentative thinking" (195). Such an approach to invention, Vitanza added, "stands diametrically opposed to the academic protocol of writing (linear, hierarchical, cause/effect writing), which is bolstered by heuristics" (195).

By linking heuristics to the restricted economy—and through it, to the laws of formal logic and conventional forms and features of academic discourse—Vitanza definitely widened the gulf between *techne* and postmodern theory. More specifically, he suggested that there is an epistemological disjunct between the two: whereas postmodern theory (in its various incarnations and manifestations) emphasizes the unstable, discontinuous, and thus unknowable nature of activities like writing, heuristics, as they are characterized here, suggest a much more stable, continuous, and thus knowable nature for such activities. For Vitanza, this difference isn't merely academic or theoretical; it has important ethical implications. If we want to "understand the often misunderstood," he argues, then we must "set aside classical, Aristotelian logic," attending instead to "the writing of the accident(s) and the accident(s) of writing" (196, 202).

One year after Vitanza made this argument in "From Heuristics to Aleatory Procedures," Michelle Ballif published *Seduction, Sophistry, and the Woman with the Rhetorical Figure,* a book that, as I briefly explained in chapter 1, critiques what we might call the epistemology of production. Although Ballif's critique of this epistemology was not aimed directly at the new classicist definition of art, it certainly implicated *techne* in the kind of epistemic violence that arises from the metaphysical drive to make everything knowable and representable. We see this connection between metaphysical violence and *techne* most clearly in Ballif's characterizations of *techne* as a method of controlling language (62, 138, 192); her association of it with mastery, negation, and systematization (89,184); and her dissociation of it from postmodernism and sophistry (64, 176). Taking issue with the idea that Gorgias understood rhetoric as an art, for example, Ballif argued that any attempt to associate sophistry with *techne* is really a form of Platonic "sophist-baiting," or in other words, an attempt to legitimate, codify, and control sophistry—"to make it something [by] giv[ing] it being and presence" (64). Instead of redeeming the sophists by trying to turn their work into a "true *techne*," Ballif urged us to read Gorgias rhetorically as a "proto-postmodernist" who wants to be taken neither seriously nor lightheartedly (70). To this end, she read "On the Non-Existent" as Gorgias's effort to prove that not being exists just as easily as Parmenides proved that being exists. "Gorgias's assertion that 'nothing is'" she claimed, "is an assertion that dividedness is, that incoherency is, that contradiction is, that change is, that irrationality is, that chaos is (all without being, however), and that *tuche* laughs at *techne*" (70). Ballif explained that in this assertion, Gorgias is criticizing the Eleatics's denial of the multiplicity of possibilities, as well as their "overarching faith in *techne* and *logos* to reflect being." Rather than advocating being or order, she wrote, Gorgias is "positing not being as the order of the day." That is, he's trying to undo the order that has been imposed on the "polyverse of phenomena" via *techne* (71).

BRIDGING THE GAP: *TECHNE* RECOVERED AND *TECHNE* REDEFINED

If, taking a cue from Vitanza, we define a postmodern approach to writing as one that requires us to attend to the writing of accidents and the accidents of writing, and, taking a cue from Young, we define *techne* as the knowledge necessary for producing preconceived results by conscious, directed action, then it would appear that these two things—postmodernism and *techne*—are exact opposites. According to Young's defintion, *techne* is about preventing accidents, not attending to them. It's about being prepared with rational knowledge and transferable strategies so that predetermined ends can be achieved as effectively as possible. As we already know from chapter 1, however, other scholars have defined *techne* in much broader, sometimes quite different terms. While not all of these other definitions are postmodern in the sense that they are explicitly based on postmodern theory, they have helped to bridge the gap between that theory and *techne* by complicating, de-emphasizing, or rejecting its identification with instrumentality and teachability. As I explained earlier, some have done this by recovering overlooked features of the term, while others have done it by offering new versions.

TECHNE RECOVERED

Of the efforts to recover *techne,* none has been more comprehensive than Janet M. Atwill's 1998 *Rhetoric Reclaimed: Aristotle and the Liberal Arts Tradition.* As its title indicates, however, Atwill's primary concern in this book is rhetoric, not *techne.* Rhetoric needs reclaiming, she argues, because historically it has been read through the theory/practice binary that dominates Western understandings of knowledge. Thus we have usually understood rhetoric as either as a form of theoretical knowledge (e.g., a of philosophy of language) or as a form of practical knowledge (e.g., a form of political action) when it is, in fact, a form of productive knowledge. Simply pointing out this fact doesn't actually solve the problem because after Aristotle, the unique features of productive knowledge were obscured by the very same theory/practice binary that has troubled interpretations of rhetoric. In order to reclaim rhetoric, then, Atwill must first reclaim *techne,* which she does by investigating its meanings in pre-Aristotelian texts like the Prometheus narratives, as well as ancient medical, rhetorical, and technical treatises.

To be clear, Atwill does not offer the version of *techne* that emerges from her investigation as a direct response to postmodern critiques of the new classicist definition of art. In fact, her engagement of twentieth-century work on *techne* in rhetoric and composition is limited to about a paragraph, and in that paragraph she makes no mention of critiques like Worsham's or Vitanza's. This does not mean, however, that Atwill's only goal in recovering *techne* (and thus rhetoric) is to set the historical record straight. While she does indeed do that, which is to say she meticulously documents the forgotten features of *techne,* she also positions those features in direct opposition to "the normalizing

tendencies of the Western tradition of humanism" (7). By "normalizing tendencies," Atwill is referring to the ways in which humanism has
historically been used to perpetuate universal notions of subjectivity,
knowledge, and value, as though these things transcend the particularities of time and place rather than derive from them (8–10).

To the degree that Atwill also positions postmodernism in opposition to these universal notions, we could say that *techne* becomes a
postmodern concept in her work and that her work, in turn, is an indirect response to the critiques of the new classicist definition of art.[31]
Another way to put this would be to say that Atwill makes *techne*
compatible with postmodernism by revealing the ways in which it is
incompatible with humanism.[32] We encountered this incompatibility
between *techne* and humanism earlier in chapter 1, where I explained
that Atwill defines *techne* as an art of invention and intervention. In
short, this definition means that the knowledge associated with *techne*
cannot claim to be a disinterested representation of truth or a means to
the political and social ends a particular group associates with eudaimonia, or "the good life" ("Refiguring" 27). In contrast, *techne* as an
art of invention and intervention is concerned with transgressing and
redefining boundaries, that is, with "seizing the advantage" in order
to effect some change in the status quo (*Rhetoric Reclaimed* 210). For
Atwill, it is this emphasis on producing change that makes *techne* incompatible with humanism. Knowledge that is valued for its ability to
seize the advantage, she argues, is too dependent on time and circumstance to promote or perpetuate universal notions about anything, especially subjectivity, knowledge, and value. As I explain below, Atwill
demonstrates this dependence on time and circumstance throughout
Rhetoric Reclaimed by highligting *techne*'s relationships to concepts
like *kairos*, *tuche*, and *metis*, among others.

Echoing definitions offered by rhetoricians like James Kinneavy
and John Poulakos, Atwill identifies *kairos* with the critical or opportune moment an artist must seize if she is to successfully achieve her
goal (*Rhetoric Reclaimed* 57). The importance of *techne*'s relationship
to this kind of timing shouldn't be underestimated because it distinguishes the "rational intellection" required by arts like rhetoric and
medicine from that which is required by more theoretical bodies of
knowledge, (e.g., metaphysics and mathematics) (57). As she points
out, the Greek term "logos," which can mean "reasoned account,"
applies to both *episteme* and *techne*. But what distinguishes the logoi

associated with *techne* from those associated with *episteme* is their relationship to *kairos*. The reasoned accounts of *episteme* are expected to apply regardless or time or place, and, as a result, they can't help but to transform their subjects into static objects of study (98). The reasoned accounts of *techne*, on the other hand, are "provisional explanations" designed to enable some kind of invention or intervention in a particular place and at a particular time. In other words, they do not provide users with any kind of lasting knowledge about the objects or practices with which they deal. Thus Atwill concludes that "[t]emporality is not something to be excluded but rather is the 'work' of *techne*" (98).

Traditionally, we have also understood the work of *techne* in terms of its relationship to *tuche*, or luck. More specifically, we have understood *techne*'s work as the elimination or eradication of *tuche*. As Martha Nussbaum puts it, we rely on the rational intellection, planning, and foresight of *techne* to remove us from "blind dependence on what happens" (95). Although this opposition between *techne* and *tuche* does not completely go away in Atwill's work, it does become more complicated. Atwill acknowledges that *tuche* marks a boundary of *techne*, but she also points out that it provides the "indeterminacies" into which *techne* intervenes in order to create change. To illustrate this oppositional yet generative relationship between *techne* and *tuche*, Atwill turns to Detienne and Vernant's description of the art of sea navigation in *Cunning Intelligence in Greek Culture and Society*. While it's true the sea is an unpredictable force the helmsman must work against, Detienne and Vernant write, it's also true the sea provides him with opportunities to succeed. As they put it, the "art of the helmsman can only be exercised within the unpredictability of the sea. The play of the tiller cannot be dissociated from the movement of the waves" (223). In this case, then, *tuche* conditions and shapes the helmsman's work in such a way that his *techne* cannot be understood simply as a form of protection against the unpredictable. Instead the two act together in order to define the art of sea navigation.

Closely related to the concepts of *kairos* and *tuche* is the concept of *metis*. (In fact, Detienne and Vernant locate all three terms, along with *techne*, in the same "semantic field.") As we saw in chapter 1, *metis* typically refers to a kind of "cunning intelligence," that is, a resourcefulness or wily thought one uses to succeed in situations where readymade rules don't apply (Detienne and Vernant 21). In *Rhetoric Reclaimed*, Atwill explains that *metis* is "the intelligence identified with *techne,*" arguing that it enables the kinds of transformations that "disguise 'inner character' with deceptive artifice" (56). It is on account of this "cunning intelligence," then, that *techne* cannot produce the "static, normative" subjects Atwill associates with humanism (2). In other words, it is because of *metis* that *techne* operates in the world of appearances and Becoming, a world where identities have to shift in order to meet the constantly changing demands of a situation. As Atwill also explains, because something can both be and not be in this world of shifting identities, the binary logic of philosophical reasoning (as displayed, for example, in Aristotle's three laws of logic) does not apply (55, 99). Rather than "forcing situations [or subjects] into a predetermined calculus," *metis,* like the "fuzzy logic" Atwill also associates with *techne,* "work[s] *in* time and *with* time to response to shifting circumstances" (100). Thus *metis* both distances *techne* from the normative subjectivities of humanism and loosens its epistemological restrictiveness.

As I indicated earlier, there is much more to Atwill's recovered version of *techne* than its relationships with concepts like *kairos, tuche,* and *metis.* However, from her explanations of these relationships, we do get a clear sense of the ways in which Atwill understands *techne* as its own form of knowledge, distinct not only from theory and practice but also from the Western tradition of humanism. Although subsequent efforts to recover *techne* haven't focused on these distinctions to the degree that Atwill does, they have clearly been influenced by her work. In fact, it would be more accurate to say that subsequent efforts to recover *techne* have been made possible by Atwill's work. By that I mean that Atwill's investigation of *techne*'s pre-Aristotelian meanings loosened its association with the new classicist definition of art, thus allowing others to adopt the concept without also adopting (or dealing with) the composition theories and pedagogies so closely identified with it in the 1970s and 1980s. The case of invention serves to illustrate this point well since, as we saw in chapter 2, *techne* has been closely connected to invention from its first entrance into disciplinary conversations in rhetoric and composition. New classicists established this connection in the 1970s and 1980s by arguing that the field needed new arts of inventions, that is, new strategies for helping students generate questions, problems, or ideas to guide their writing. Earlier I acknowledged that the impetus for such arguments came from the belief that a research agenda informed by *techne* and focused on invention could put rhetoric and composition on the road to disciplinarity. It's important to point out, however, that this research agenda was conceived according to what some would refer to now as the "pedagogical imperative," that is, the idea that all composition research should originate with and attempt to solve pedagogical problems.[33] And for new classicists (as well as many others), the pressing pedagogical problem of the time was—to put it very simply—inadequate student writing. In this context, "inadequate" meant hollow, trite, predictable writing—the kind that came from what Janice M. Lauer described as a process of embalming, that is, a process of "pumping enough development into a thesis to preserve it until grading time" ("Writing for Insight" 5). Scholars like Lauer worried that if arts of invention were left out of the writing process, then students would have little investment in their work because they would have discovered nothing meaningful to say with it. However, if they could use a heuristic like the tagmemic discovery procedure or Burke's pentad to experience writing as an act of discovery or a search for insight, then they would have something meaningful to say and, as a result, the quality of their writing would improve.

Without question, the kind of writing new classicists hoped to see emerge from their efforts to return invention to composition represented a step forward in the field's definition of good writing. More specifically, their efforts to return invention to composition gave the field a broader, more substantial definition of good writing, one that wasn't so myopically focused on superficial features of correctness.[34] In contrast to the breadth of that definition, however, was the narrowness of the problem it tried to solve. By calling this problem narrow, I don't mean to suggest it was inconsequential. Predictable or hollow student writing was not (and is not) an inconsequential problem. But it is primarily a scholastic problem, one that appears narrow when compared to the political, social, and cultural problems that would come to dominate composition pedagogy in the 1990s. It's true, of course, that a student might use a heuristic in order to investigate a social, political, or cultural problem; but from the perspective of new classicism the goal of that investigation would be to produce better writing, not necessarily to intervene into the social, political, or cultural problem. Thus it's fair to say that the new classicist definition of art located invention primarily within the scene of the composition classroom.

In contrast, Atwill's work on *techne* locates invention in the much broader scene of political activism. Atwill herself never uses the phrase "political activism," and it's possible that she would object to my use of it here. However, to my mind it is an apt description of what happens to the art of invention when it is paired with the art of intervention: it begins referring less to a way of solving the problem of hollow student writing in the composition classroom and more to a way of solving the problems of injustice in the world at large. Atwill acknowledges this shift in the conclusion to *Rhetoric Reclaimed* where she explains that remaking rhetorical studies as an art of invention and intervention means focusing instruction on the forums needed to enable political agency (210). Thus rather than learning a particular body of knowledge, students try to renegotiate their symbolic capital by developing "a habit of vigilance that is alert for indeterminacies and points of intervention in existing systems of classification" (210). The purpose of such a habit, she explains, is to enable students to "be a part of constructing standards of value and advantage in their cultures" (210). Of course there is no reason to think students who develop this habit won't also become better writers. In other words, developing political agency in students and improving the quality of their writing by making it more inventive are not mutually exclusive pedagogical goals. Nevertheless, it's clear that Atwill moves *techne* beyond the mainly scholastic concerns that dominated new classicist scholarship in the 1970s and 1980s, thus making it more relevant to the shifting needs of the field and, importantly, making it available for additional recovery projects. Somewhat ironically, then, we could say that by returning to *techne*'s forgotten past, Atwill helped to secure its future.

There's probably no better place to look for evidence of this new relevance and "availability" than in *Technical Communication Quarterly*'s 2002 special issue on *techne*. Although their individual arguments differ, collectively the articles of this volume issue a statement of renewed interest in *techne* and its relationship to technical communication. In the late 1980s and early 1990s, this relationship came under fire from scholars like Carolyn R. Miller, Dale Sullivan, Thomas Miller, and Stephen Doheny-Farina, all of whom argued that technical communication was best understood not as a *techne* but instead as a form of praxis, that is, as a kind of practical knowledge concerned with right action. For them, the problem with *techne* was that it reduces technical communication to a set of skills for producing texts, thus exempting technical communicators from any ethical or political need to consider the ends their texts served. By relocating *techne* within the context of political activism, Atwill's work responded (at least indirectly) to these critiques, thus opening up a space within technical communication for recovering *techne*.[35] In "More Than a Knack: Teaching and Technical Communication," for example, James M. Dubinsky does something that would have seemed more than a little ironic ten years earlier: he argues that *techne* can solve the problem of prescriptive teaching in technical communication. When teachers rely on system-centered, formulaic pedagogy, says Dubinsky, they usually produce students who are tool-users rather than reflective practitioners. To change this trend, teachers themselves must learn to engage in reflective practice, that is, they must learn to teach according to the kind of knowledge Dubinsky describes as a "*knowing how*" rather than "*knowing how to*" (131).

According to Dubinsky, the difference between these two kinds of knowledge corresponds to the difference between a *techne* and a knack: the former requires the artist reflect on her work in order to determine the causes of success and failure, while the latter does not (131). The key to developing this ability to reflect, Dubinsky believes, lies in an often-overlooked feature of *techne:* collaboration. As he explains, in *De Paribus Animalum* Aristotle describes a master woodcarver, or *technites*, who explains why he struck the wood the way he did not to himself but rather "to someone else who is asking him questions" (134). For Dubinsky, this passage indicates that reflection is facilitated by collaboration, that is, "by hav[ing] someone present who can act as a vehicle to bring into language what might have lain dormant by experience only" (134). Far from a prescriptive set of rules, then, Dubinsky sees *techne* as a reflective, collaborative form of knowledge that, if applied to teacher training programs, could greatly improve pedagogy in technical communication.

Like Dubinsky, authors Ryan Moeller and Ken McAllister want to show that *techne* is more than the "inoffensive set of techniques" or "ethically void" concept that some in technical communication have made it out to be (185). To do this, they turn to ancient Greek and Roman texts, offering "historically-grounded, creative meditations" on *techne*'s "true range of connotations," (e.g., its identification with cunning intelligence, with ingenuity, and with trickery) (194, 189). The version of *techne* that emerges from these meditations is very similar to Dubinsky's—it's a more reflective, more collaborative, and all around more complex kind of knowledge. As Moeller and McAllister put it, this version of *techne* relies more on "human interaction," emphasizes "artistry and creativity," and is not bound by the "rational expediency" seen in more simplistic conceptions (192, 194).

However, in contrast to Dubinsky's recovered version of *techne,* which is aimed at helping us rethink teacher training in technical communication, Moeller and McAllister's version is aimed at helping us rethink the experience of becoming a technical communicator. In other words, Dubinsky is interested in what a more complex version of *techne* can do for teachers, while Moeller and McAllister are interested in what it can do for students, particularly those who are forced into workplace scenarios by textbooks that focus prematurely on "real-world" experiences (186). Moeller and McAllister find nothing wrong with "real-world" experiences per se, but they do believe that such experiences often come at the cost of what students should be doing in technical communication courses: "learning and playing with basic concepts, experimenting with them, and using one's imagination to form increasingly complex understandings of what is being practiced" (186). If technical communication curricula were designed around the concept of *techne,* they argue, then activities like these would receive more attention and, as a result, students would be encouraged to think more artistically, to see themselves as members of a society rather than as employees, and to understand that "ethics and ideologies" are an unavoidable part of their work as technical communicators (188). From an historical perspective, the irony of this argument is as striking as that of Dubinsky's: Moeller and McAllister recover *techne* in order to it offer it as a solution to the very problems in technical communication it was once accused of creating.

TECHNE REDEFINED

The difference between recovered versions of *techne* and redefined versions is not an absolute one. Recovering, after all, is a way of redefining. But when scholars try to recover *techne,* they usually turn to historical sources in order to retrieve one or more of *techne*'s forgotten features so that they can offer a richer, more complex version of the term. The features of instrumentality and teachability don't disappear in these more complex versions of *techne* but instead are complicated by their relationship to other features. Thus while it's true that recovered versions of *techne* mark a departure from the new classicist definition of art, they shouldn't be seen as a rejection of it. It would be considerably harder to make this claim about redefined versions of *techne*—or at least about the two examples that I discuss here, which are the only two examples I know of. When scholars try to redefine *techne,* they are less concerned with calling our attention to its forgotten features than they are with understanding and using it in a way that is new to rhetoric and composition.

Arguably, the most radical redefinition of *techne* within rhetoric and composition can be found in Barbara Biesecker's 1992 "Coming to Terms with Recent Attempts to Write Women into the History of Rhetoric." As its title indicates, this essay is not about *techne* per se, but instead about revisionist histories of rhetoric that try to "render the discipline more equitable" by adding great women rhetors to the canon (142). Although Biesecker appreciates the intention behind such efforts, she believes the criterion used for determining what goes into the canon is informed by an "ideology of individualism" that says the only discourse worthy of inclusion is discourse that results from "strategic choices made among available means of persuasion on the part of an autonomous individual" (144). In other words, historians make decisions about what goes into the canon according to a humanist theory of subjectivity that presumes human beings are autonomous, self-present agents capable of acting according to their own intentions and desires. The problem with this criterion (and the theory from which it derives), according to Biesecker, is that it maintains the binary between active and passive and in so doing "monumentalizes some acts and trivializes others" (147).

The challenge for Biesecker, then, is not just to offer readers a replacement for this criterion but, more fundamentally, to offer them a way of understanding rhetorical agency that does not participate in the ideology of individualism. In a move that would have surely seemed surprising then (and to some would still seem surprising now), she argues that the concept of *techne* can provide such an understanding. However, the particular version of *techne* she has in mind isn't one that already exists in the scholarship of rhetoric and composition. Rather, it's one she must fashion through a "strategic appropriation of post-structuralism" (147). To do this, Biesecker turns to two icons of post-structuralist thought, Foucault and Derrida, combining elements of their work into a theory of subjectivity that tries to avoid the pitfalls of both humanism (e.g., the idea that subjects are autonomous agents) and anti-humanism (e.g., the idea that subjects are discursive effects). From Foucault's work Biesecker borrows the concept of "discursive formations," which, she explains, highlights the discontinuity and heterogeneity of social space by characterizing it as "a nonstatic arena woven of dispersed 'I-slots'" (149). It's only by occupying one of these "I-slots" or subject positions, Foucault theorizes in *The Archeology of Knowledge & The Discourse on Language*, that human beings gain "enunciative modalities" and thus appear as the authors of discourse (54–5). For Biesecker, what makes this theory relevant to writing histories of rhetoric (and, of course, what characterizes so much of Foucault's work) is its focus on the cultural, social, political, and economic practices that create subject positions through discourse. Guided by such a theory, she argues, historians would be more likely to study *how* rhetors emerge as subjects rather *what* they say or *who* they are (148–9).

At this point Biesecker has only half of what she needs. While Foucault's work gives her a theory of subjectivity that avoids the pitfalls of humanism (and allows her to re-orient the focus of revisionist historiography in rhetoric), it does not, as many feminist critics have argued, give her one that avoids the pitfalls of anti-humanism. Within feminist scholarship, the most common charge leveled against Foucault's work (and perhaps against post-structuralism and postmodernism in general) is that it does not offer an adequate theory of agency or resistance.[36] Where does the possibility for social change or liberation come from if subjects are nothing more than "enunciative modalities" created by discursive formations? It's this question that, in another surprising move, sends Biesecker to the work of Derrida. I call this move surprising because Derrida himself has been the subject of many feminist critiques for failing to provide a theory of the subject based on the kind of "regulative ideal" or "normative vision" needed for the emancipatory politics called for by many feminists (Benhabib 214, 215). Importantly, though, Biesecker is after no such ideal or vision. To the contrary, she wants a theory of subjectivity that allows for the possibility of resistance but that does not understand this possibility as an inherent property of the subject (154). Thus what she combines with Foucault's concept of discursive formations is Derrida's "doubled morphology of the subject" (153). Following Gayatri Chakravorty Spivak, Biesecker argues that while, on the one hand, Derrida describes the subject's structure in terms similar to Foucault's (i.e., as an entity that is centered only by virtue of its location within a larger economy of discourses), on the other hand, he claims this discursively centered subject is also structured by *différance*, that is, by "a *temporality and a spacing* that always already exceeds it" and thus ensures that it will "forever be in process," never finished, never coincident with itself (154, 148). Although Biesecker insists this excess should not be understood as an "uncontaminated pocket" of resistance within the subject, she believes it can operate as "a force or structure of breaching" within the subject's actions that opens up the possibility of "an unforeseen and undesignated transgression" (155). In other words, she believes this excess creates a capacity—albeit one that is "non-intentional in the strictest sense of term"—within the action of the subject for disrupting the ways in which it is inscribed by and within discourse (154). At the risk of oversimplification, we could say, then, that what Biesecker's "strategic appropriation of poststructuralism" yields is a theory of subjectivity in which change and resistance are possible precisely (and only) because the subject is not identical to its intentions.

If my reasons for calling Biesecker's redefinition of *techne* "radical" were not apparent earlier, I assume they are becoming so now. None of the versions of *techne* we have seen so far—not even those that have been complicated by a forgotten feature or relationship—have explicitly questioned the subject's ability to achieve a particular objective through conscious, planned activity. Yes, the knowledge needed to carry out that activity might be provisional, embodied, and contingent. And yes, the objective toward which that activity aims might be unspecifiable, or at least subject to change as the process of making unfolds. But in every version we have seen so far, the result of that making can be linked (in varying degrees of directness) to the intentions of the subject.[37] Simply put, this is not the case for Biesecker. Using a theory of subjectivity forged from the work of Foucault and Derrida as a license to break away from *techne*'s "historically constituted semantic field," Biesecker argues that the term can now refer to "a brining-about in the doing-of on the part of an agent that does not necessarily take herself to by anything like a subject of historical or [. . .] cultural change" (156). In other words, the activity of making, according to this definition of *techne*, cannot be described in terms of art or cunning. As Biesecker makes clear, the artist here is not one who intervenes in a rhetorical situation in order to "throw off the mantle of her own self-perpetuated oppression" but rather one "whose enunciation, in always and already falling short of its intending subject," opens up the possibility that she might be inscribed within discourse differently (146, 155). Such a conception of *techne* could hardly be described as instrumental, much less teachable.

The other redefinition of *techne* I want to discuss here is Byron's Hawk's notion of a "post-*techne*"—a version of the term we are already somewhat familiar with.[38] In chapter 1, I explained that for Hawk the primary difference between the field's conventional understanding of *techne* (i.e., the new classicist definition of art) and his understanding of a post-*techne* is the source of the artist's agency. Whereas the former definition assumes writers are autonomous subjects who work through the power of their own agency to act *on* nature, the latter assumes they are embedded elements of complex ecologies who work through the power of that embeddedness to act *with* nature (379, 381). Hawk develops this redefined version of *techne* in both his 2004 essay "Toward a Post-*Techne*—Or, Inventing Pedagogies for Professional Writing" and his 2007 *A Counter-History of Composition,* moving easily in both texts from the discourses of classical rhetoric to those of continental philosophy and contemporary theories of complexity and posthumanism in order to explain the theoretical nuances and historical antecedents of a post-*techne*. In fact, we could say Hawk's work is performative in the sense that he uses this wide variety of sources to create an ecology of voices, arguments, and ideas from which the notion of a post-*techne* emerges. Trying to comprehensively summarize every element of this ecology would be a difficult (and probably counterproductive) task. What I want to do here instead, then, is focus a particular element—his reading of Aristotle's theory of entelechy—in order to get at the change he's after. As Hawk explains, Aristotle understands entelechy as "the process of development through having the goal within" (*Counter-History* 124). In other words, things that are entelechial have an inherent power to move from potentiality to actuality. A seed, for instance, requires no additional source of agency to come into being as a tree because it holds all four causes (material, efficient, formal, and final) within itself (124). What interests Hawk about this seed, however, are its "multiple potentialities," that is, everything else that it might eventually come into being *as* (e.g., a shelf, chair, or a house) and the "multiple factors" that can affect its movement from potentiality to these other actualities (125). When we consider the concept of entelechy from this perspective, he argues, we see that it is internal not only to the things of nature but also to the situations in which those things—and indeed all things—exist (125). As we can see in the following excerpt, it's according to this "more complex" understanding of entelechy that Hawk begins revising the concept of *techne* and, through it, the way we understand the process of producing rhetoric:

> The basic logic of entelechy is that the overall configuration of any situation, including both natural and human acts and forms, combines to create its own conditions of possibility that strive to be played out to completion. The combination of the four causes in nature is not just a push from behind but also a pull toward the future, the striving to develop potential. In more contemporary evolutionary terms, an ecological situation produces the structural conditions for certain types of plants or animals to develop and thrive and they strive to fill those gaps, to enact that potentiality. Humans as efficient cause cannot be abstracted from this larger contextual ground set up by the other causes and the ecology or potentiality they enact. A human might have an internal, psychological, or intellectual motive, but a huge variety of cultural, linguistic, and material factors help create and enact that motive. As part of nature, humans can help realize the situational potential via the *techne* available to them through the complex ecological arrangement, and it is in this larger movement that rhetoric operates. (126)

As this passage indicates, Hawk, unlike Biesecker, isn't redefining *techne* in order to "do away with intention" ("Post-*Techne*" 383). Rather, he wants to add "a layer of complexity beneath it," that is, he wants to situate human intention among the other three causes within complex ecologies so that we understand the process of making in terms of Heidegerrian co-responsibility rather than humanist instrumentality (383; *Counter-History* 176). We should note here that Hawk is not using the concepts of entelechy and co-responsibility to make the commonplace claim that rhetoric is situational. In other words, he is not simply trying to point out that the constraints of a particular situation shape rhetoric and are therefore co-responsible for it. According to this notion of rhetoric, situation is what the rhetor must take into account in order to produce effective discourse, and *techne* is what allows her to do that. In contrast, Hawk is using the concepts of entelechy and co-responsibility to refer to a notion of rhetoric in which the rhetor's ability to produce discourse is an internal function of the larger situation in which she works (165). When we understand rhetoric in these terms, he argues, our definition of *techne* shifts from the means by which a rhetor produces situationally appropriate discourse to the means by which she locates herself in a situation and helps create a "constellation [that] plays out its own potentiality" (177).

It's important to point out that for Hawk the implications of this shift extend beyond rhetorical theory into rhetorical practice. In other words, and more specifically, what's at stake here is not just a theoretically improved version of *techne* but also the higher level of "inventive open-endedness" that writers can achieve if the heuristics they use are designed to locate bodies within situations rather than to accomplish predetermined goals ("Post-*Techne*" 382; *Counter-History* 180). To illustrate the difference between these two categories of heuristics, Hawk turns to a number of concrete examples, among them a strategy for "seiz[ing] the advantage" from Janet M. Atwill's *Rhetoric Reclaimed* (210) and "a technique for mapping *kairos*" from Cythnia Haynes's 2003 essay "Writing Offshore: The Disappearing Coastline of Composition Theory." As Hawk explains, Atwill's strategy is a three-step heuristic that asks writers to (1) discern a point of indeterminacy in a situation, (2) try to overreach a boundary placed on them by the situation, and (3) intervene into the standards of value established by the situation ("Post-*Techne*" 381). Hawk sees the goal of Haynes's strategy as somewhat more open-ended (or, more precisely, he claims it is able to "achieve a certain level of inventive open-endedness") because it asks students to write about the imagined trajectory of a piece of writing left in a public place, directing them with broad questions like *Where will it go? Who will see it? What will they think* and *What would you like them to think?* (382). Although Hawk values both examples as heuristics that involve "a coresponsibility with *physis*," he believes that they "represent two kinds of doing"—action and enaction, respectively:

> Atwill's heuristic emphasizes the subject's power external to the situation that prompts the action—that is, the intervention. Haynes's technique seems to rely more on situating a body in a never-static context that prompts the enaction, the opening up of that constellation's possibilities. (382)

While Hawk acknowledges that Haynes's heuristic involves "conscious elements," he emphasizes that those elements are "created to enact unconscious, ambient coresponsibility" (382). In other words, they are based on the idea that writers can create a new potentiality just by being part of a situation (387). To link the term "heuristics" so closely to the power of situatedness in the way Hawk has is to give it a new meaning, one that goes against the grain of its new classicist meaning. As we saw in chapter 2, Young identified classroom practice as one of the primary sources of difference between new classicists and new romanticists, arguing that whereas the former taught writing directly through heuristics, the latter took a more indirect approach by trying to create situations in which it could be learned ("Arts, Crafts, Gifts, and Knacks" 55–6). By offering an understanding of heuristics that complicates this distinction, that is, by allowing us to "remember the past differently" through what we might call a new romanticist— or, rather, a vitalist—understanding of heuristics, Hawk's notion of a "post-*techne*" not only stretches the meaning of "*techne*," but it also plays an important role in the counter-history of composition he seeks to provide.

4 Closing Down and Opening Up: *Techne* and the Issue of Instrumentality

To be sure, we've covered a lot of ground in a relatively small amount of space here. Chapter 2 took us back not just to early work on heuristics but also to the mid-twentieth century changes in educational culture that created a need for solid foundations and intellectual rigor throughout the discipline of English. It was this need, I argued—not just Richard E. Young's personal "drive to disciplinarity"—that we saw reflected in the new classicist definition of art, particularly in its emphasis on research-based theories of writing and formal teaching methods. If scholars in the field devoted their energy to developing and testing such theories and methods, many composition teachers reasoned, then they would finally be able to answer some of those lingering questions about what writing was and how it should be taught. In short, then, the new classicist definition of art was a means of enlightenment, that is, a way of turning the ignorance and confusion of rhetoric and composition's pre-disciplinary period into the terra firma of a real academic discipline. Of course, the academic discipline imagined by Young and others was far from perfect, and thus the process of enlightenment in rhetoric and composition continued with critiques of the new classicist definition of art and the research agenda associated with it. I reviewed these critiques in the first part of chapter 3, beginning with Ann E. Berthoff's argument against heuristics and then moving to later critiques that used elements of postmodern theory (and continental philosophy) to challenge the new classicist emphasis on instrumentality and teachability. In the second part of chapter 3, I described the versions of *techne* that emerged from this postmodern challenge, pointing out the ways in which they broadened, complicated, or, in some cases, radically redefined the new classicist definition of art. For instance, we saw versions of *techne* that foster political agency, that emphasize reflection and collaboration, that promote experimentation, and that do not depend on the planning or the intentions of an autonomous subject. It's not just that *we* have come along way in only two chapters, then, but that *techne* itself has come along way, changing with the discipline in order to become less of a humanist concept and more of a postmodern one.

If we looked at this change from Stephen North's perspective in *The Making of Knowledge in Composition,* then we would almost certainly see it as a sign of progress, that is, as a sign that the dialectic of philosophical inquiry is doing its job by producing more robust, more synthetic arguments over time (111). That's not to say that all the work we've reviewed here should be understood exclusively as examples of philosophical inquiry. Atwill's, for instance, is historical as well as philosophical. But by defining the category of philosophical inquiry in terms of its method—dialectic—North made it broad enough to include any kind of argument that (1) moves inferentially from premise to conclusion and (2) interacts with other arguments dialogically to create ongoing conversations (96). The arguments about *techne* that we covered in the second half of chapter 3 easily fit this bill and, I would argue, effectively illustrate the kind of progress North believed philosophical inquiry could achieve through the give-and-take of dialectic. Although it's misleading to understand dialectic in terms of the very simple thesis-antithesis-synthesis scheme, we could employ it here to highlight this progress. Young's explanation of the new classicist definition of art in "Arts, Crafts, Gifts, and Knacks" would be our thesis, while Worsham's claim that this definition represents an instrumental approach to writing based on the kind of aggressive will-to-mastery at work within humanism could serve as our antithesis. (Other critiques of the new classicist definition could serve as our antithesis as well.) From the clash between these two positions, more complex versions of *techne* have emerged in rhetoric and composition, challenging and, in some cases, rejecting the idea that it can be defined primarily in terms of its instrumentality. In the case of Atwill's work, for example, we have a version of *techne* whose identification with instrumentality is complicated by its connection to concepts like *kairos, metis,* and *tuche.* We saw in chapter 3 that these concepts temporalize the knowledge associated with *techne,* making it impossible to understand the artist who uses that knowledge as the kind of static, normative subject of humanism. Moreover, while it's true that this artist will use her knowledge to achieve an external, predetermined end, that end is now explicitly anti-humanist (according to Atwill's definition of humanism) since, as an art of invention and intervention, *techne* is about developing "a habit of vigilance" that allows its users to intervene into existing systems of classification (*Rhetoric Reclaimed* 210). Hawk's notion of a post-*techne* provides another good example of a more complex understanding of *techne*. Here we have a version of the concept in which instrumentality is replaced by Heideggerian co-responsibility as the artist's agency is re-understood as a result of her embeddedness within a complex situation. While this artist hasn't given up on achieving external goals, according to Hawk, she now realizes those goals can be determined and accomplished *only* through the interaction among the elements of the situation in which she works (*Counter-History* 177). What *techne* provides, then, is a way for the artist to locate herself in that situation in order help enact *its* possibilities for invention, not a generic strategy for imposing her own pre-conceived plans (206).

We could move through this same kind of exercise for the issue of teachability, taking Young's claim that (some) knowledge about writing is rational and generic as our thesis, Vitanza's argument about the grand narrative of teachability as our antithesis, and the more complex versions of *techne* advocated by Atwill, Moeller and McAllister, and Hawk as our syntheses. In different ways and to varying degrees, all three of these versions of *techne* emphasize the important role embodied knowledge plays in the process of making. More specifically, they all acknowledge that because there is something experiential, ingrained, temporal, and intuitive about the knowledge associated with *techne*, the strategies one uses to apply that knowledge will sometimes be imprecise, ill-defined, and, in the case of Hawk's post-*techne*, non-transferable. These versions of *techne* do not perfectly synthesize Young's thesis with Vitanza's antithesis (just as they didn't perfectly synthesize Young's thesis with Worsham's antithesis), but perfect synthesis is not the kind of progress North had in mind. Through the dialectic of philosophical inquiry, he argued, arguments force adjustments in each other, producing more self-aware positions and, over time, creating a "potent force for change" (97–8). Without question, the arguments we've reviewed in the last two chapters have been a potent force for change in rhetoric and composition over the last thirty years, transforming not just our understanding of a particular concept but, more significantly, our understanding of what it means to practice, study, and teach the art of writing.

Even if we aren't satisfied with all—or any—of these transformations, it would be hard to deny the value of the arguments that initiated them. As I explained in the introduction, I find them valuable because, among other reasons, they give us a view of the discipline in which history, theory, pedagogy, and practice cannot be separated from each other. It's true that these arguments have often produced conflicting accounts of how we should understand *techne* and apply it to the study and teaching of writing. But we could argue that this conflict is just more grist to the mill, that is, more energy to keep the dialectic going so that it can produce better, more synthetic versions of *techne* over time. Besides, even if individual accounts are in conflict with each other, collectively they have demonstrated that *techne* cannot be reduced to its identification with instrumentality and teachability. For this reason alone I think we are justified in taking North's perspective in *The Making of Knowledge in Composition* and seeing the debate about *techne* as an example of the kind of progress than can be achieved in rhetoric and composition through dialectic.

Now, having said—*and meant*—all of that, I want to consider a troubling (perhaps even heretical) possibility. *What would happen if we didn't save* techne *from its identification with these two features?* In other words, what would happen if we accepted the critiques of *techne* but then choose *not* to revise or redefine it into a better concept? Would our only option be to get rid of it altogether? To declare that *techne* has outlived its purpose in rhetoric and composition and then replace it with some other concept, one that isn't weighed down by so much humanist baggage? Or could we find some way to hang on to it, recognizing that even though elements of *techne* are undeniably humanist, it can still play a valuable, even necessary, role in how we understand and teach writing?

To be clear, I am not asking these questions because I don't see the problems with the ways in which *techne* encourages us to use language as a tool and to reduce writing to rational causes of explanation. Rather, I am asking these questions because I believe that in an effort to update *techne,* that is, to make it as relevant to the increasingly sophisticated needs of our field as possible, recent scholarship has left important criticisms unanswered. Yes, this scholarship has successfully demonstrated why *techne* should not be reduced to its association with instrumentality and teachability. But it has not demonstrated why these two features do not necessarily make *techne* an inadequate or unethical approach to writing. Yet, if we consider the fact that definitions of *techne* exist on epistemological and axiological continua rather than in separate, self-contained spaces, then such a demonstration becomes necessary. In other words, if we consider the fact that there's no way to separate, once and for all, *techne*'s humanist traits from its postmodern traits, then we have to find a way of valuing it that isn't based only on revisions and redefinitions. My goal in this chapter and the next is to explain how we can do this, that is, I want to explain how we can affirm the value of a potentially problematic definition of *techne* (namely, the one embodied in the new classicist definition of art) without denying the legitimacy of the critiques that have been leveled against it. Although this explanation is not based (at least not primarily) on Heidegger's work, his description of the "goings on" of modern technics in "The Question Concerning Technology" does help us to understand the paradox at the center of it. However, as Samuel Weber points out in "Upsetting the Set Up," elements of this explanation have been lost in translations that prefer "conceptual univocity" to the contradictions present in the original German terminology (979). In order to restore these contradictions, Weber re-translates the essay's key concepts, starting with *Entbergung*, Heidegger's term for the goings-on of all technics.[39] Whereas most translations render the word as "revealing," Weber suggests "unsecuring" as a better fit since it refers both to the disclosure associated with "revealing" and to *Entbergung*'s root meaning—"harboring forth" (984). As Weber notes, "harboring forth" is an ambiguous phrase: "to harbor" is to protect, but "to harbor forth" is to respond to danger by moving from shelter into insecurity (984). Thus he concludes that the goings-on of technics should be understood as an unsecuring that is prompted by danger and that results in "a loss of shelter, an abandonment, a disclosure" (984).

The significance of this re-translation becomes clear when Weber turns his attention to *Ge-stell*, which, as we saw in chapter 1, is the name Heidegger gives to the way in which modern technics challenges nature forth into standing-reserve or *Bestand*. As Heidegger explains, the goal of this challenging-forth is not profit but control—*Ge-stell* is a way of securing nature, of putting it in its place as a ready-to-use resource ("The Question" 27). In this sense, then, we could say that *Ge-stell* gets at both *techne*'s axiological and epistemological problems, that is, its identification with instrumentality and teachability. In other words, it highlights the fact that *techne* sets language in place through rational causes of explanation and transferable strategies so that we can use it as a resource. In order to capture this "setting in place" function, most translators have used the word "Enframing," a choice William Lovitt justifies by describing *Ge-stell* as a challenge that "puts into a framework or configuration everything it summons forth" ("The Question" 19, n. 17). Weber, however, chooses "emplacement," a term he prefers not only because of its lexical accuracy (since "*stell*" can mean "to place") but also because it calls our attention to the strange combination of movement and stasis that characterizes modern technics (988). As he explains, in order for something to be "emplaced," a place must first be "staked out" (989). But, any place that must be staked out is one that "cannot stand on its own" and, therefore, must be continuously defended and re-established (989). Hence the mixture of movement and stasis: by securing in place, *Ge-stell* gives way to new settings that require continuous re-setting. Thus it is both a response to *and* a perpetuation of the movement of unsecuring it seeks to overcome. Or, to put it differently, Weber concludes that the "goings-on" of modern technics can "serve not just to close down but also to open up" (989).

Accepting the critiques of instrumentality and teachability as evidence of *techne*'s ability to "close down," I use Weber's re-translation of *Ge-stell* as Emplacement as an opportunity to demonstrate its ability to "open up." I do this in two ways. In this chapter, I focus on the issue of instrumentality, using Maurice Blanchot's understanding of negation in "Literature and the Right to Death" to argue that we can make language usable to us as an instrument only by simultaneously making it unusable to us as an object. In other words, I argue that by putting language to work through *techne*, we inevitably risk its ability to work. I then turn to the issue of teachability in chapter 5, relying primarily on Joseph Dunne's understanding of the relationship between *techne* and nature in *Back to the Rough Ground* to argue that the rational activity of *techne* both protects us from the possibility of losing control of writing and makes us vulnerable to that possibility. As I indicated earlier, my goal in making these arguments is not to stage some kind of final defense of *techne* by explaining—once and for all—why it's too complex to be identified with its most problematic features. To the contrary, what I want to do here is demonstrate how those features open up possibilities for experiencing writing as an inherently valuable, uncontrollable, and unpredictably creative activity.

MAKING VERSUS CREATING AND THE QUESTION ABOUT VALUE

What a strange, contradictory undertaking is this effort to act where immeasurable passivity reigns, this striving to maintain the rules, to impose measure, and to fix a goal in a movement that escapes all aims and resolutions.

—Maurice Blanchot

Run away from language and it will come after you. Go after language and it will run away from you.

—Jean Paulhan

In his 1936 essay, "The Origin of the Work of Art," Heidegger describes equipment as that which occupies "a peculiar position intermediate between the thing and the work [of art]" (29). Comparing a piece of equipment to a mere thing, (e.g., a granite boulder), he observes that both are "self-contained." But, unlike the granite boulder, a piece of equipment does not take shape by itself; rather, it is the result of human intervention and, in this regard, is similar to the work of art: both the piece of equipment and the work of art are "produced by the human hand," which is to say they are both the result of a process of bringing-forth out of concealedness into unconcealment (29, 59–60). However, the bringing-forth of art, which Heidegger calls "creation," is fundamentally different from the bringing-forth of equipment, which he calls "making" (59–60). Whereas the art work that results from creation affirms the material out of which it is made, allowing it to "shine forth," the equipment produced through making uses it up. In the case of equipment, then, the material "is all the better and more suitable the less it resists perishing in the equipmental being of the equipment" (46). That is, the more willingly it "disappears into usefulness," the better (46). According to Heidegger, when writing is brought forth as equipment the material that disappears into usefulness is language (48). Thus while poets certainly use words, he argues, they do not use them like "ordinary speakers and writers who have to use them up, but rather in a way that the word only now becomes and truly remains a word" (48).

Like the critiques of instrumentality we reviewed in the first part of chapter 3, Heidegger's comparison of art and equipment in "The Origin of the Work of Art" raises an important question about value for those of us who understand and teach writing as a *techne*: do our efforts to make language useful turn it into equipment whose value lies mainly in its usefulness? In other words, are we teaching processes of making instead of creating? And, if so, are we making it more difficult for students to experience and appreciate the ability of language to "shine forth" as something valuable in and of itself—or, worse, actually diminishing the ability of language to do that? As we saw earlier, scholars like Worsham, Vitanza, Davis, and Sirc have answered these questions affirmatively, arguing that when the bringing-forth of writing is guided by usefulness, something valuable is lost. While they don't necessarily agree on what this "something" is, they do agree that without it, writing becomes less pleasurable, less creative, and less disruptive. They also agree that since it is within these (and other similar) qualities that writing's inherent value lies, we should be teaching writing for their sake rather than for the sake of external goals like solving problems, raising political consciousness, building communities, or developing literacies.

That such arguments have not been met with unbridled enthusiasm should surprise no one. Definitions of rhetoric have come and gone over the past 2,500 years, focusing our attention on different canons, different genres, and different media, but the belief that it is language put in the service of an external goal has persisted. Gerard Hauser defines rhetoric explicitly in these terms in *Introduction to Rhetorical Theory*, claiming that rhetoric "is an *instrumental* use of language" in which "one person engages another in an exchange of symbols to accomplish some goal." Therefore rhetoric is not "communication for communication's sake" (2). Although Hauser does not use "*techne*" to describe this instrumental approach to rhetoric, we can certainly attribute some of its staying power to the term. In fact, we could argue that no other term highlights rhetoric's instrumental character as powerfully as *techne* does. After all, in chapter 6 of his *Nicomachean Ethics*, the locus classicus of *techne* definitions, Aristotle identifies *techne* with a reasoned state of capacity to make, arguing that it is always a means to some other end (EN II40a10). Thus it seems safe to apply Heidegger's distinction between making and creating here and conclude that when rhetoric is understood as a *techne*, it is more likely to make language disappear than to let it shine forth.

Of course my goal here is to explain why this isn't such a safe conclusion. I think in many cases we reach it by relying on broad criteria like genre or pedagogy to determine how language is functioning in a particular text and/or how students will experience the language of that text. For instance, we might reason that in a composition course taught as an introduction to academic inquiry and research, students won't produce anything that allows them to experience the pleasure of writing for writing's sake. Formal assignments in such a class would almost surely be limited to literature reviews, proposals, and other genres that value the work language accomplishes over language itself. And since students would have to control language in order for it to work effectively, they would need to learn conventional methods of invention, organization, and style. In other words, they would need to learn the *techne* of academic writing. Again, it seems safe to conclude that in this class students would be engaged in a process of making, not creating. But, if this were the case—that is, if we could turn writing into a process of making instruments by assigning certain genres or by teaching students how to control language—then there would be no writing at all. As I will argue here, our ability to use language in any capacity depends, paradoxically, on our inability to turn it into an instrument.

RHETORIC AND CONTRADICTION

Understanding rhetoric in terms of paradox or contradiction is nothing new. Since the fourth and fifth centuries, rhetoricians have maintained that discourse begins with a conflict, clash, or opposition. We see this clearly in classical concepts like *dissoi logoi*, *kairos*, and *stasis*. Drawing on such concepts, rhetorical theorists like Robert Scott, Michael Leff, Richard Cherwitz, and James W. Hikins argued in the 1960s, 1970s, and 1980s that rhetorical knowledge is born of uncertainty and antagonism.[40] Prominent compositionists of the mid and late twentieth century made similar arguments. For instance, new classicists like Richard E. Young and Janice M. Lauer claimed that writing should be understood and taught as a process of inquiry that begins with dissonance, while expressivists like Peter Elbow argued for a pedagogy of "embracing contraries" that employed binary thinking as an inventional strategy.[41] More recently, in his 2003 *Where Writing Begins: A Postmodern Reconstruction*, Michael P. Carter has argued not only that writing begins with contradiction but also that contradiction (understood as an opportunity for newness, change, and creativity) is the source of its intrinsic value.

At first glance, Carter's claim that writing is inherently valuable because it is inherently creative appears neither complicated nor controversial. And to some degree, it isn't. Teachers have been touting the creative power of writing for half a century now, arguing that it is a form of discovery and a means of generating new knowledge. But according to Carter, definitions like these have had the unfortunate effect of locating the value of writing outside the actual act of writing. His goal in *Where Writing Begins*, then, is to explain how we can define writing as a form of creativity that is valuable in and of itself. His first step toward this goal is to explain how writing's ability to bring opposing forces together (e.g., the known and the unknown) is a form of "archeological beginnings," an ontological (as opposed to temporal) concept of beginning as the "productive intersection of contradictory forces" (55).[42] Unlike most Western notions of creativity, which posit a subject-creator who produces an object in a singular, identifiable event, Carter agues that within archeological beginnings, creativity is on-going, each moment understood as a threshold point between the past and future that represents an opportunity for newness and change. Such a notion of creativity, he explains, is "utterly collaborative" in that it views *all* things as creative. Instead of unilateral, then, creativity in this archeological model is multilateral, flowing in all directions, erasing the border between creator-subject and derivative object (138). According to Carter, it is here, in the collaborative, multilateral nature of archeological creativity that we find its intrinsic value: "Because creation [in this model] is on-going and (dis)continuous, creativity is the chief source of the good, intrinsic to the ever-renewable creative moment, in and for itself, and available to all entities in the universe" (138). Thus it is also here (in the collaborative, multilateral nature of archeological creativity) that we find the intrinsic value of writing, an event through which Carter believes we not only participate in this creativity but can also become highly aware of that participation.[43]

Agreeing with scholars like Worsham, Vitanza, Sirc, and especially Davis, Carter then argues that writing should be taught for this intrinsic value rather than for an extrinsic value like self-actualization or cultural critique. However, Carter does not suggest that the presence of such a value turns writing to an instrument. Take, for example, his discussion of one of the most instrumental forms of writing students produce: notes. Carter suggests that the divergence that often exists between a student's notes and the actual content of a lecture isn't just evidence of error or misrepresentation but also evidence of how that student has shaped knowledge to meet her own needs and thus participated in the creativity and learning that happens in—and, according to him, defines—writing (144–5). In his view, then, genres that serve a purpose beyond writing don't diminish the intrinsic value of writing; rather they invite students to experience that value in different ways (145).

Carter's argument about writing, contradiction, and creativity goes a long way in responding to calls for a non-instrumental definition of writing, and it does so without suggesting that the value of writing can be determined by criteria like pedagogy or genre. Despite this important accomplishment, however, it doesn't address a key component of the critique behind those calls. As we saw in chapter 3, a—if not *the*—major problem with so many theories and pedagogies of rhetoric according to scholars like Worsham, Vitanza, Davis, and Sirc isn't just their failure to recognize the intrinsic value of writing in general but also the consequences of this failure for writers in particular: teaching writing as a means to an end limits the ways in which we can experience—and, indeed, perhaps our ability *to* experience—the non-resourceful, material properties of language[44]; and it is within these properties that they see the possibility for positive ethical, political, and aesthetic change. While I also believe such possibilities reside within language, I do not believe we can anticipate how or within which types of writing they will be realized or experienced. Writing is much *too* contradictory for such knowledge—contradictory not only because, as Carter puts it, it is what happens in the "creative space of the threshold" where opposing forces collide, but also (and more so) because language itself is contradictory (142).

When I say language itself is contradictory, I'm not referring (not directly, at least) to the way words can convey multiple, contradictory meanings but rather to the power that allows them to convey any meaning at all: the power of negation. As post-structuralist theory has taught us, language communicates meaning by negating the specificity of its objects. For example, when I use the word "tree," I might be referring to a specific tree with specific traits, yet the word "tree" communicates only the general idea of a tree. What the word represents, then, is not the object but rather the absence of the object. Yet it is through this ability to negate—to turn presence into absence—that language gives rise to the conceptual and thus to communication and understanding. It is also through this power, then, that language becomes useful to us. Language couldn't work for us at all if it couldn't communicate meaning. Instrumentality (and thus *techne*) depends on negation. Or, to borrow Heidegger's terminology, we might say that negation is at the heart of the equipmental being of linguistic equipment.[45]

However, as French writer, critic, and theorist Maurice Blanchot argues in "Literature and the Right to Death," the role negation plays in writing is not nearly as straightforward as this explanation suggests. On the one hand, Blanchot appreciates the products of negation in the world: meaning, identity, art, and understanding. But on the other, he is keenly aware of and interested in the de-stabilizing effect negation has on these products. What does it mean if every linguistic construction is based on nothing but absence? If the words that give our work being are themselves deprived of being? (379). If that when we speak, "a nothing demands to speak, [. . . that] nothing finds its being in speech and the being of speech is nothing?" (381). These are the kinds of questions that Blanchot asks in "Literature and the Right to Death"; he wants to understand the consequences of negation for literature at the level of writing, that is, to know what it is that a writer is doing when she attempts to create one kind of reality by destroying another. By drawing on Blanchot's responses to these questions in the remainder of this chapter, I hope to begin explaining not only how *techne*'s emplacements perpetuate the insecurity they seek to overcome but also how its ability to do this—or, more precisely, its inability *not* to—challenges conventional perceptions of what it means to write for the sake of writing.

THE DEVIL IS IN THE DETAILS

Like other important twentieth-century French intellectuals, Blanchot was heavily influenced by the lectures that Alexandre Kojève gave on Hegel's *Phenomenology of Spirit* at the *Ecole Pratique des Hautes Etudes* from 1933 to 1939. Credited by some for the post-WWII dominance of Hegelianism in Europe, Kojève's lectures did not merely translate Hegel's work for his francophone audience; they re-interpreted it through the lens of Marx. The predominance of this perspective is nowhere more apparent than in Kojève's emphasis on the master/slave dialectic, which comes from the well-known "Lordship and Bondage" section of *Phenomenology*. There Hegel describes a confrontation between two persons or "consciousnesses," both of whom want to dominate the other in order to receive "recognition." A fight ensues, and, as Kojève explains, the one willing to fight until death for that recognition becomes the Master, while the one who surrenders out of fear without it becomes the Slave (224). The Master then dominates the Slave, forcing him to work so that his "animal" desires can be satisfied without exerting any effort (228). Through this forced labor, however, the Slave, or as Kojève refers to him, the Worker, learns to negate his own animal desires, eventually replacing his "given" or natural self with a more civilized self. Paradoxically, then, the Slave gains freedom through servitude: his "auto-negating" work is also "auto-creative" in that it grants him a degree of autonomy and humanity that the Master cannot attain since he does not negate his "animal nature" (228, 225). What's more, Kojève adds, the products of the Slave's labor transform the natural world by bringing into it something that did not previously exist (e.g., an artifact) and by destroying something that did (e.g., natural resources) (228). As the Slave becomes conscious of these changes, he gains not only understanding of the world but also a desire to "keep up with progress," that is, to adapt himself to his evolving environment (230). Thus while the Master simply undergoes history, the Slave, through his work, creates it.

Like the Slave's forced labor in Kojève's materialist reading of *Phenomenology*, writing, according to Blanchot, is also a self- and world-transforming form of work ("Literature" 370). In fact, he argues that the writer's activity is paradigmatic of work: when a man works, he produces an object that is the "affirmation of a reality different from the elements that constitute it and [. . .] the future of new objects to the degree that it becomes a tool capable of creating other objects" (370). This object "affirms the presence in the world of something that was not there before, and in doing so, denies something which was there before" (371). "But what is a writer doing when he writes?" Blanchot asks.

Everything a man does when he works, but to an outstanding degree. The writer, too, produces something—a work in the highest sense of the word. He produces this work by transforming human and natural realities. When he writes, his starting point is a certain state of language, a certain form of culture, certain books, and also certain objective realities—ink, paper, printing presses. In order to write, he must destroy language in its present form and create it in another form, denying books as he forms books out of what other books are not. (371)

To emphasize the violent nature of this process, Blanchot (following Hegel) refers to it as a kind of death: death speaks in language, destroying its objects, and yet it is only through this death that the writer approaches the possibility of creation, communication, and understanding; it is only through death, in other words, that she "forms and produces history" (372).

One way, then, for Blanchot to understand what a writer is doing when she attempts to create reality by destroying it is through Kojève's Hegelian-cum-Marxist conception of work: writing is a way of putting the power of negation to work in the world for the sake of progress. For Blanchot, however, negation is not only the motor of history, and writing is not only a means of creation, communication, and understanding. Negation and writing are also the means through which the writer approaches the *im*possibility of creation, communication, and understanding, that is, the point at which language is no longer experienced as transparent, communicative medium but rather as opaque thing: sound, rhythm, weight, and shape. As we have established, negation creates meaning by denying the real existence of its objects, by sacrificing "flesh and blood" reality for the sake of the idea (379). According to Blanchot, however, sometimes negation goes so far that it reaches something that cannot be converted into meaning.[46] In the case of writing, this "something" is the materiality of language. Like the "accursed shares" of Georges Bataille's general economy, this materiality possesses a kind of surplus energy—an unemployable excess that is revealed *through* negation but cannot be converted into something positive *by* it. Once this materiality is revealed, Blanchot, like Worsham, Vitanza, Davis, and Sirc, believes that writing ceases to be only a means of representation, becoming also an experience of "a powerful universe of words, where relations, configurations, forces are affirmed through sound, figure, rhythmic mobility" ("Approaching" 42). And it is when this happens that language, dislodged from its meaning, begins to shine forth, "playing its own game, without man, who created it" ("Literature" 384).

Negation, then, is both the means through which a text manifests its objectness and the means through which that objectness is concealed for the sake of usefulness. In other words, negation is what allows rhetoric (as a *techne*) to secure language in place with a particular meaning and what allows it to unsecure language from that meaning. But how do we know when it's doing the former and when it's doing the latter? That is, how do we know how negation is functioning? Answering this question will allow us to answer the other one I asked at the beginning of this essay: how do we distinguish language that has been unsecured from its meaning from language that hasn't? To know how negation is working is to be able to make this distinction, to be able to see when language is shining forth and when it's not. But again, how do we do that—or better yet, can we?

To answer this question, we will need to turn to Blanchot's two-slope theory of literature, a theory heavily influenced by the work of French Symbolist poet, Stéphane Mallarmé. As John Gregg explains, in "*Crise de vers*" ("Poetry Crisis") Mallarmé divides language into two kinds: *parole brute* (everyday language) and *parole essentielle* (literary language). Whereas the purpose of *parole brute* is the efficient exchange of information, *parole essentielle* serves no predetermined purpose; its emphasis is on the form and materiality of language, not the content (Gregg 18–19). The two slopes of Blanchot's theory don't correspond directly to Mallarmé's categories, but they are closely related. On the first slope of literature Blanchot says we find "meaningful prose," that is, writing whose goal is to "express things in a language that designates things according to what they mean" ("Literature" 388). On the second slope we find poetry, whose goal, predictably, is more complicated—and less instrumental—than that of prose. Language here doesn't want to represent objects—it wants to present them. In other words, it wants access to the real nature of the things that were negated for the sake of meaning. Structurally, though, this isn't possible. How could language "turn around and look at what comes *before*," Blanchot asks, if all of its power "consists in making it into what comes *after?*" (383). In other words, how could it "become the revelation of what revelation destroys"? (384). Language on this slope isn't doomed, however. While it cannot access pre-linguistic reality, it can access linguistic materiality. Thus Blanchot writes:

> My hope lies in the materiality of language, in the fact that words are things, too, are a kind of nature—this is given to me and gives me more than I can understand. Just now the reality of words was an obstacle. Now it is my only chance. A name ceases to be the ephemeral passing of non-existence and becomes a concrete ball, a solid mass of existence; language, abandoning the sense, the meaning which was all it wanted to be, tries to become senseless. (383)

So far, Blanchot's two-slope theory seems straightforward enough: the goal on slope one is to create meaning by putting language to work, while the goal on slope two is to access materiality by freeing language from work; the former operates via securing, the latter via unsecuring. However, if we look beyond this description of the two slopes and the obvious difference in their objectives, we see that there is a "problem" with their apparent incompatibility; we see, in other words, that there is no definitive answer to our question about how negation functions (388). As Blanchot explains, language on the first slope fills words with meaning by negating the concrete, singular reality of its objects. Through this process words become containers, and it's the content of those containers that matters, not the containers themselves. This content, however, is nothing but absence, literally, "a nonexistence made *word*" (382). Paradoxically, then, language can (and does) become meaningful on the first slope only by filling itself with nothing, by "nullifying what it encloses" and becoming, in effect, a contentless container, the embodiment of emptiness (382). Indeed, while negation operates here by suppressing the materiality of the word for the sake of the concept, it also—simultaneously—condemns the concept to the foundationlessness through which the materiality of the word can appear.

Of course literature on the second slope wants nothing to do with concepts; its goal is to free language from meaning. And, as we've seen, to the degree that the negative power of language fills words with emptiness, literature can achieve this goal; it can change language into a "written thing, a bit of bark, a sliver of rock, a fragment of clay in which the reality of the earth continues to exist" (384). And yet this written thing cannot completely stop being meaningful. While it is indeed true that it no longer refers to things in the world in order to communicate meaning, it's also true that it cannot simply become illegible or un-interpretable. "Literature has certainly triumphed over the meaning of words," Blanchot writes, but what it has found instead is "meaning detached from its conditions, separated from its moments [. . .] the aggravation of what one cannot prevent oneself from understanding" (387). And what this meaning represents is the very possibility of signifying: "the meaning of the name [. . .] is really destroyed but signification in general has appeared in its place, the meaning of the meaninglessness embedded in the word as the expression of the obscurity of existence" (385). Hence the paradox of language on the second slope of literature: it can become an opaque thing only when this thing appears as "the proper determination of indeterminate and meaningless existence" (387). In other words, it can become meaningless only when its meaninglessness coincides with language's inability to stop being meaningful.[47]

The problem, then, with the apparent incompatibility of the two slopes is that they aren't incompatible. In fact, not only are they *not* incompatible, they're also *not* independent: meaning couldn't exist on slope one if words weren't empty, meaningless things, while meaninglessness (pure materiality) couldn't exist on slope two unless those things possessed a kind of fundamental meaning. One kind of writing is, therefore, the inherent possibility—and indeed the necessary condition—of the other. So, to finally answer our question about negation—can we determine how it is functioning within language—no, we cannot. The mechanism by which negation secures language in place with meaning on the first slope is the very same one that unsecures it on the second. Moreover, in order to accomplish either objective, this mechanism necessarily creates the conditions of the other. This is why, in "Literature and the Right to Death," Blanchot claims that "an art which purports to follow one slope is already on the other" (388). All writing—regardless of its form and its content—has the potential to be (and to be experienced as) both an object and a tool. And, try as we might, there's no reliable way to distinguish one from the other. Negation is capable of "work[ing] substantial metamorphoses" in language, Blanchot writes, but it is also "capable of changing everything about it without changing anything" (397).[48]

THE CASE FOR "INSTRUMENTALITY"

Admittedly, the heading above is a troubling one. Even with the word "instrumentality" in scare quotes, it is unsettling to advocate something with such a bad reputation. It should be clear by now, though, that I don't believe rhetoric, when understood as a *techne,* can be defined as an instrumental use of language. Or, rather, I don't believe it can be defined *only* as an instrumental use of language. Thus this case for instrumentality is not a wholesale endorsement of every instrumental approach to rhetoric. It is, however, an attempt to explain why those approaches, like any that we might label "non-instrumental," have the potential to bring-forth inherently valuable writing that does not conceal the materiality of language. As Blanchot's analysis of negation demonstrates, language always has the potential to be more than its meaning, and, paradoxically, every time we try to imbue it with meaning, we unleash that potential. Contrary to Hauser's claim, then, rhetoric is always communication for the sake of communication, no matter how diligently or obsessively we work to make it otherwise.

Of course, this is one of the main reasons why scholars like Worsham, Vitanza, Davis, and Sirc have critiqued *techne* (and other instrumental approaches to rhetoric). They recognize this potential, and they want to call attention to all of the ways in which we in rhetorical studies try to ignore it. As I indicated earlier, I don't doubt that we try to ignore language's potential to be more than its meaning. When we understand rhetoric as a *techne,* we ask our students and ourselves to pay more attention to the work language can do than to language itself, and, obviously, there are times when we do that. There are times, that is, when we use language to accomplish predetermined, external goals, and our need to make it work efficiently toward those goals keeps us from noticing its materiality. But there are also times when we don't do that—times when we become too aware of how words sound and of how they look on the page to be satisfied by (or interested in) what we are trying to make them do or mean. And isn't it possible that the thing making us so aware is that very same need to make language work efficiently? Isn't it possible, in other words, that sometimes it's our need to secure language in place that forces us to recognize the loss of security that accompanies all of our emplacements?

This is the point that Jean Paulhan, a friend and contemporary of Blanchot's, makes in *The Flowers of Tarbes* when he warns that if we run away from language, it will come after us (82).[49] The more intent we are on keeping language quiet and transparent, he suggests, the more attentive to it we have to be. Yet the more attentive to it we are, the more likely we are to notice its noise and opacity. And while noticing those features might not always (or obviously) change how we write, I do think it changes why we write. I think it makes us write not just so that we can put language to work but also so that we can experience its resistance to working. We want to have an encounter with the materiality of language, to be engaged in what Blanchot describes as the "strange, contradictory [. . .] effort to act where immeasurable passivity reigns," ("The Work" 105) and, ironically, the instrumentality of *techne* becomes the means by which we do it.

Obviously, this isn't a common rationale for *techne* or any other instrumental approach to rhetoric. In other words, there aren't many (or any) theories of rhetoric or writing out there that suggest using language to accomplish external goals is a way to experience its non-resourceful, material properties. But, as I hope I have demonstrated here, it can be. Because of negation, the goings-on of rhetoric are nothing if not contradictory. Rhetoric insists that language work but in doing so inevitably risks its ability to work. Thus while it's true that there is always a possibility for language to be something other than a means to an end, it's also true that getting rid of the end or replacing it with one that is presumably less instrumental won't necessarily enhance this possibility. Such reasoning might sound like nothing more than a way to protect those instrumental ends and maintain status quo in rhetoric, but it's not. Like Worsham, Vitanza, Davis, and Sirc, I believe rhetoric should be about more than creating and communicating meaning. I believe it should be about undergoing an experience with language, about hearing its excesses, and about realizing the limits of literacy. But I don't think there's any way we can know which theories, pedagogies, and genres of rhetoric will make that experience happen. Ultimately, then, this case for instrumentality isn't a case for instrumentality at all. It's a case for indeterminacy—a case for recognizing the indeterminacy in all language that makes the question about value nearly impossible to answer.

5 Closing Down and Opening Up: *Techne* and the Issue of Teachability

> *. . . we huddle loquaciously at the edge of the abyss, we protect ourselves pragmatically from the abyss [. . .] with techne.*
>
> —Michelle Ballif

When Michelle Ballif claims, as she does in the above epigraph, that we use *techne* to protect ourselves pragmatically from the abyss, she has a particular kind of abyss in mind: that of sophistry (183). It's important to note, though, that "sophistry" has a broad meaning for Ballif, one that, overlapping with the meaning of the related term "woman," refers to those elements of rhetoric (or language) that cannot be contained within a rational explanation of causation. "Sophistry," in other words, refers to those things that elude the will-to-mastery at work in our efforts to make writing knowable and teachable. Given this broad meaning, then, we could say that Ballif's claim captures the essence of all of the critiques of teachability, not just her own. Whether they're focused on chance, the materiality of language, or more radical forms of questioning, many of the scholars whose work I reviewed in chapter 3 are concerned about what we're missing (or what we're protecting ourselves from) when we understand and practice writing as a *techne*. As I explained earlier, this concern isn't merely academic, which is to say it isn't simply the product of a theoretical disagreement about what writing is and how (or if) it should be taught. While such disagreement is no doubt at work in the debate about *techne*, it's clear the arguments made by critics like Worsham, Davis, Vitanza, and Ballif are meant to highlight the ethical implications of *techne*'s epistemological profile, that is, the ways in which its emphasis on teachability reduces writing to a rational activity aimed at controlling language.

As we saw in the second part of chapter 3, scholars like Atwill, Moeller and McAllister, Dubinsky, and Hawk have helped to mitigate these critiques by demonstrating that *techne* is too complex to be identified with a narrowly conceived version of teachability. In their view, such an identification ignores a number of *techne*'s most important defining features, (e.g., its dependence on time, circumstance, experience, the contingencies of human interaction, and the situational potential of rhetorical ecologies). Do these other features mean *techne* is no longer concerned with rational explanations of causation or teachable, transferable strategies? In most cases, no. However they do modify its epistemological profile, making it harder to claim that *techne* reduces writing to a rational activity of controlling language. My argument here is similar to these counterarguments in that I, too, am interested in how *techne*'s complexity might affect our understanding of its epistemological profile. Rather than looking for that complexity in features that exist beyond *techne*'s association with rational control, however, I want to look for it *in* rational control. In other words, what I want to consider here is the idea that *techne* is too complex to be defined primarily as a rational method of control because of the function of rational control, not in spite of it. Admittedly, this sounds like a strange idea. How could the function of rational control within *techne* be the reason why it should *not* be understood as a method of rational control?

In a sense, we already know the answer to this question—or, we at least know it involves Weber's re-translation of the goings-on of modern technics as emplacement. In chapter 4, I explained the implications of this re-translation for arguments about instrumentality and *techne* by way of Blanchot's understanding of the role of negation in writing. Here I am after a similar kind of explanation, but the context is different—we're dealing with arguments about teachability, not instrumentality—and it's not Blanchot's work I will turn to but rather Joseph Dunne's, namely his 1993 study of *techne* in Aristotle and modern philosophy, *Back to the Rough Ground*. Interestingly, the purpose of Dunne's book is not to defend *techne*'s epistemological profile. Rather, he began the project with the intention of critiquing *techne* as an instrumentalist form of reason that too easily degenerates into "ends justifies the means" logic. And, indeed, Dunne offers an in-depth critique of this form of technical reason, arguing that it places too high a premium on efficiency, economy, and rational control to be a guide for understanding (or engaging in) practical activities like teaching and politics (5–8). For an alternative, he suggests we look to *phronesis,* the form of practical reasoning Aristotle opposed to *techne* and defined as the reasoned state of capacity to act (EN II40b5–7). Whereas acting (*praxis*) has no end outside itself, Aristotle argued, making (*poiesis*) is always a means to some other end. But according to Dunne, this opposition between *techne* and *phronesis* does not hold when we take into account what he calls Aristotle's "unofficial" understanding of *techne*—an understanding that, as we will see, is very similar to the stochastic version of *techne* explained by James Allen and the new classicist definition of art advocated by Richard E. Young. While I find Dunne's overall argument about *techne* and *phronesis* very compelling, what I am interested in here is how he portrays the role of the artist's rational activity within this unofficial Aristotelian understanding of *techne* and, most importantly, what that portrayal suggests about the possibility of creating something new or unpredictable through an art like writing. In what follows, I outline Dunne's reading of *techne* in Aristotle, explaining both versions of the concept but focusing on the "unofficial" understanding. Then, turning to a perhaps unlikely source—an essay about the work of Georges Bataille by Joseph Libertson—I explain why, despite its identification with teachability, *techne* is too complex to be defined primarily as a rational method of control.

TECHNE IN ARISTOTLE

The Official Version

As I explained above, Dunne identifies two distinct (though unequally developed) concepts of *techne* in Aristotle's work: an "official" concept more or less inherited from Plato and an "unofficial" concept that must be read "obliquely" through Aristotle's actual use of the term. The official version, Dunne claims, can be found in *Metaphysics* 1.1 and *Nicomachean Ethics* 6.4—the two passages in which he believes we find the philosopher's most explicit treatment of the term.[50] As we saw in chapter 1, in *Metaphysics* 1.1 Aristotle distinguishes art from experience on the grounds that art deals with universal principles while experience is limited to individual cases: "Art arises," Aristotle writes, "when from many notions gained by experience one universal judgment about a class of objects is produced" (*Meta* I.5–6). According to Dunne, here Aristotle brings *techne* very close to theory (*episteme*), characterizing it as a "source of comprehensive explanatoriness" or as a "theoretical tool" with which the artist can provide a rational account of his procedures (251). And it is the artist's ability to provide this account—that is, "to trace his product back to the causes to which it owes its being"—that gives him some degree of control over his materials and protection against chance (250).[51] Dunne argues that here and elsewhere (e.g., *Meta* 7.7), Aristotle espouses an "unrelentingly formal" conception of *techne* that places it squarely within the mind of the artist's knowledge of the form he will impose on his materials and in his ability to explain how he will (or did) impose it (284).

In addition to its "closeness to theory," Dunne argues that Aristotle's official concept of *techne* is also characterized by its "essential reference to fabrication," that is, by its very clear identification with production (*poiesis*)—hence "*techne poietike.*" As we have already established, in *EN* 6.4 Aristotle writes that art is identical with a reasoned state of capacity to make (*Nicomachean Ethics*). And as Dunne explains, making is "an activity which is designed to bring about, and which terminates in, a product or outcome that is separable from it [the process of making] and provides it with its end or telos" (244). Thus according to the official version, within any given *techne,* means and ends are distinct, and it's the end that is valuable, not the means.

Echoing the critiques of instrumentality and teachability we reviewed in chapter 3, Dunne argues that this official version of *techne* has two main problems: (1) it reposes too much control in the mind of the artist, thereby failing to acknowledge the important role of experience in the process of making; and (2) as a model of practical reasoning, it is dangerously instrumental in that it separates the end from the means, places all value in the end, and thus treats the means as value-neutral. While Dunne finds this potential degeneration into an "ends justifies the means" logic very troubling, he argues that the first charge is just as pressing, since, as he points out, it essentially means that *techne* represents a unilateral process of production. Rightly, then, Dunne maintains that when *techne* is understood this way, it appears "aloof from experience, abstracted from it" (283).

In order to understand Dunne's argument about *techne,* we need to clarify what is meant by "experience" here: rather than the accumulated experience that helped the artist form her *techne,* Dunne is using "experience" to refer to a singular instance or event of making. For him, a conception of *techne* that does not account for experience is one that does not account for unexpected situations in which the artist's ability to impose a preconceived form onto the materials is compromised by certain contingencies, for instance, the "feedback" she might receive from those materials (285). According to Dunne, this is a serious shortcoming since this feedback is essential to what he deems the "the most interesting aspect of production" —the creation of new or unpredictable forms and products. Thus what is "strikingly absent" from Aristotle's official treatment of *techne* is any account of creativity or experimentation, in other words, any account of a kind of making "that is itself intelligent" (284–5). The artist's thinking here, he concludes, "is strictly architectonic or 'ruling' and so remains invulnerable to any modification suggested in the actual process of material construction" (285). The official version of *techne* we are left with, then, is one in which the artist devises, initiates, and controls the changes that will turn the presumably inert materials into a predictable final product.

The Unofficial Version

Dunne's understanding of Aristotle's unofficial version of *techne* is based not on the philosopher's explicit comments about the concept but instead on how he actually uses it (254). Specifically, Dunne points to Aristotle's use of "*techne*" to describe activities that are not "straightforwardly productive" and that do not leave behind tangible, reified products. For instance, in *Magna Moralia,* Aristotle describes flute-playing as a *techne* in which the "the activity and the end are the same (for to play the flute is both [the artist's] end and his activity)" (*MM* 2.12.1211b26–31). He similarly describes harp-playing, maintaining that it is a *techne* but not a productive *techne* since beyond playing the harp "there is no other end apart from the action or process itself" (*MM* 1.34.1197a4–11). Dunne argues that by speaking of *technai* that are performative and intrinsically valuable, Aristotle "loosens the essential connection" between *techne* and *poietike* that he establishes in *EN* 6. He suggests the same is true for Aristotle's references to the *technai* of sea navigation, military strategy, and medicine. While such *technai* do produce "a definite result which is achieved by, and endures after, the exercise of the *techne,*" Dunne maintains they cannot be understood as productive in the same sense that house building or carpentry is productive. Dunne clarifies the nature of this difference when he states that within Aristotle's unofficial understanding of *techne,* the artist should be more readily thought of as "intervening into a field of forces, or as immersing himself in a medium" than as simply imposing a preconceived form upon "disposable materials " (254).

Although this distinction Dunne makes between, on the one hand, a "field of forces" or "medium" and, on the other, "disposable materials" is not new (we saw it in chapter 1 when I reviewed Allen's understanding of the stochastic *techne*), it is significant in that it allows him to explain why the relationship between the artist's thinking and the "actual process of material construction" in Aristotle's unofficial version of *techne* is different than in the official version. Whereas the "straightforwardly productive" *technai* are able to achieve their ends "by confining their sphere of operations to domains where chance has little or no foothold," Dunne argues that the non-traditional *technai* are "involved in areas where, since they are circumscribed by no fixed limit (*peras*), the play of chance is ineliminable" (255). Therefore, no matter how well the artist understands the causes of his previous successes and no matter how well he plans for future successes, his thinking cannot be the "architectonic" or "ruling" force in production that he intends it to be. If he wants to succeed, Dunne explains, he must do more than devise forms, prepare plans, and enact strategies; he must also react swiftly to the feedback he receives from the "polyvalent materials" of his art so that he can seize the opportune moment whenever it presents itself (256). In other words, he must be sensitive to *kairos* (256).

As we already know from chapter 3, Dunne is not the first or only person to call attention to the important relationship between *techne* and *kairos.* However, he does add something new to our understanding of this relationship when he argues that in addition to being "quick and decisive," the artist's actions must also "arise within a pattern of a certain kind of passivity" and that this passivity "should be conceived as an element in his very *techne*" (256, 354). On the one hand, then, successfully working with and responding to these "polyvalent materials" requires the swiftness or quick thinking associated with *kairos.* But on the other, it requires "a certain kind of passivity." Unfortunately, Dunne never directly says what this "certain kind of passivity" is. And on account of that, it would be easy to write it off as nothing more than a qualification of what it means for the artist to act quickly and decisively. Imagine, for instance, a ship's captain who decides to wait patiently for the auspicious moment when he can quickly change the direction of his sails, or, to use a more relevant example, a writer who decides to wait patiently for that bolt of inspiration to strike before she can hurriedly put pen to paper. If this is the case, then we can reasonably conclude that by "certain kind of passivity" Dunne is referring to the artist's choice to cease being active, that is, to give up rational control of her art and temporarily put its fate in the hands of some uncontrollable force in order to create something new or disrupt the status quo. While there's no way to rule out this reading of Dunne's comments, I want to argue for a different reading here—one in which the artist's passivity exists not as an alternative to her rational activity but rather as a consequence of it. What I want to argue for, in other words, is that the "certain kind of passivity" Dunne claims should be understood as an element of *techne* happens when the artist tries to gain control of the process of making, not when she decides to relinquish it.

If we look deeper into Dunne's investigation of Aristotle's understanding of *techne*, we find support for this reading of passivity. As Dunne explains, this investigation isn't so much a search for Aristotle's unofficial concept of *techne* as it is a search for "chinks" in his work where an "experiential element" of it might appear.[52] He finds this support in, among other places,[53] Aristotle's discussion of nature and art—two concepts that appear often in his corpus, usually opposed to one another as two ways in which change can happen. What interests Dunne about these two key concepts, however, isn't this "commonplace disjunction" (their obvious difference) but rather the fact that Aristotle "analyzes both of them so unproblematically in terms of the same conceptual structure," that is, in terms of (or in reference to) each other (335). Obviously referring to Aristotle's famous dictum, "art imitates nature," Dunne speculates about the possibility that by being compared to nature, so that it is even said to imitate it, *techne* might "undergo subtle modifications," taking on a less formal, more experiential quality (336). Immediately, however, he acknowledges a problem with this line of thinking. While the "art imitates nature" analogy is the most famous, it isn't the most common. Within Aristotle's work, the analogy usually works the other way, with *techne* as primary analogate used to elucidate nature. Hence the problem: if Aristotle's concept of nature is one that has been developed in terms of his concept of *techne,* how can it shed new light on *techne?* In other words, what in nature could warrant a different understanding of *techne* if it is through *techne* that Aristotle has already understood nature? (336).

The answer to this question, Dunne argues, lies in the recognition that within the two analogies, two different kinds of analysis are happening. When Aristotle says nature imitates art, Dunne believes he is making a pedagogical point, relying on our "homely familiarity with craft activities" to explain something more removed and mysterious: nature (336). But when the analogy is turned the other way, Dunne believes Aristotle is making an ontological point, indicating that nature is ontologically prior, that "its order and purposiveness [are] primordially established" (336). Citing evidence from, among other places, the *Politics* ("the deficiencies of nature are what *techne* and education seek to fill up")[54] and the *Protrepticus* ("nature does not imitate *techne,* but vice versa; *techne* exists to aid nature and to fill up its deficiencies"),[55] Dunne argues that, at least in some contexts, Aristotle understood *techne* as the artificial counterpart of nature, that is, as a secondary means of generation that carried to completion what nature could not (336). Such an understanding, he reasons, suggests that there are, in fact, grounds for attributing to nature some trait— "something primordial"—that remains hidden "even when the pedagogical efficacy of '*techne*' has been fully exploited" (336). In other words, he believes that for Aristotle, there is something about nature, some "opaque quality," that is not explained by or accounted for in the "nature imitates art" analogy. And it is this opaque quality, he maintains, that can supply an independent basis for saying "art imitates nature" and thereby save the analogy from the circularity of claiming that art imitates nature when nature has already been understood in terms of art (337).

To identify this quality, Dunne looks to passages where Aristotle, rather than simply extrapolating from *techne* to develop a concept of nature, draws parallels between the two concepts. In chapter 2 of the *Physics,* for instance, Aristotle claims that if a house had been a thing made by nature, "it would have been made in the same way as it is now by *techne*; and if things made by nature were made not only by nature but also by *techne,* then they would come to be in the same way as by nature" (2.8.199a12–15). Later in the same chapter he writes:

when an event takes places always or for the most part, it is not accident or by chance. In natural products the sequence is invariable, if there is no impediment. It is absurd to suppose that purpose is not present because we do not see the agent deliberating. *Techne* does not deliberate. If the ship-building *techne* were in the wood, it would produce the same results by nature. If therefore purpose is present in *techne*, it is also present in nature. The best illustration is a doctor doctoring himself: nature is like this. (2.8.199a24–32)

Focusing on Aristotle's suggestion that art and nature produce things in the same way, Dunne argues that in these passages, there is "as much encouragement to think of *techne* as naturelike as there is to think of nature as technical" (337). But what specifically does it mean to think of *techne* as naturelike? For Dunne, it means entertaining the idea that the material of a particular *techne,* like the material of nature, "might somehow be able to assemble itself into the finished *ergon*" (337). In other words, it means entertaining the idea that the *techne* is also in the materials, that *techne* is "an immanent potentiality of the material" (337). Thus the opaque or primordial quality (as well as the "experiential element") he's been searching for—the one that can save the "art imitates nature" analogy from circularity—is a kind of immanent creative agency or intelligence. Dunne is claiming that according to Aristotle's unofficial understanding of *techne,* the products of art, like those of nature, happen in and of their own accord.[56]

In light of Aristotle's official understanding of *techne,* this is an extraordinary claim to make. After all, it weakens if not collapses the fundamental difference Aristotle establishes between art and nature in the *Physics.* There he explains that the products of nature have within themselves their own innate principle of change and rest, while products of art must rely on an external force to initiate change or production (192b8–15). Dunne knows this, of course, and admits that the problem it presents for his interpretation of *techne* cannot entirely be overcome: "*techne* and *phusis* are different," he writes, "and the difference resides precisely in the fact that things of nature have their *arche* in themselves (*en hautois*), while things of *techne* have their *arche* in another (*en alloi*), viz., the *technites*" (337–8). Strictly speaking, then, art and nature *do not* produce things in the same way. And yet Dunne is unwilling to ignore Aristotle's suggestions to the contrary. A "force still remains in the two passages," he maintains, and even if they do not justify an understanding of *techne as* nature, they do

> encourage us not to be so impressed by the intervention of the *technites* as to suppose that it inaugurates a new realm that is entirely different from *phusis*. For we would not be too far from the truth if we were to imagine the craftsman's activity itself as but a *strategic detour* through which nature goes (and in which it surrenders its own name) in order to bring about a new class of beings (artefacts) which it can neither produce nor reproduce through its own channels." (338, emphasis added)

Faced with the clarity and absoluteness of Aristotle's distinction between art and nature, Dunne has had to temper his earlier position. He's no longer claiming the materials can assemble themselves into the final product but instead admitting that they do, in fact, depend on the artist's activity. By describing that activity as a "strategic detour," however, he minimizes its impact on the process of making. Although Dunne doesn't explicitly connect this description to his claim that a "certain kind" of passivity should be conceived as an element of *techne,* I believe that it can help us understand that passivity and, more specifically, that it can help us see how that passivity exists alongside the artist's rational activity, not as an alternative to it.

Combined, the words "strategic" and "detour" make an odd, oxymoronic phrase. Whereas "strategic" describes an action that is deliberate and essential, "detour" refers to something unplanned, unnecessary and aberrant, for instance (and most commonly) a circuitous route that interrupts a driver's pre-existing plan, sometimes to the degree that the final destination can't be reached. In this context, the phrase suggests that even though the artist's rational activity (e.g., her thinking, planning and strategizing) is a definitive, necessary element of her art, it doesn't necessarily "take" her where she believes it will. Pursuing the driving analogy suggested by "detour" further, we could say that the artist's activity is what gets her in the car and on the road, but—unbeknownst to her—it doesn't determine her route or even her destination, which is to say that it doesn't give her the control she thought it would. In fact, not only does her activity fail to give her control, but it also puts her in a position to lose control—to be *detoured,* so to speak. In this sense, then, the artist's activity prepares the possibility of her passivity. In other words, her activity pre-conditions her passivity, making it difficult to determine where one ends and the other begins. Thus while we are justified in recognizing a difference between the artist's rational activity and the kind of passivity she experiences when receiving feedback from her materials (or any other uncontrollable force), we should not assume, based on that difference, that the latter is more closely linked to the possibility of creating something new than the former. Such an assumption is problematic not only because it ignores the mutually constitutive relationship between activity and passivity but, more fundamentally, because it suggests that the way to get beyond the limitations of rational activity is to get rid of them. On the surface this suggestion makes sense. However, as Joseph Libertson demonstrates in "Bataille and Communication: *Savoir, Non-Savoir, Glissement,* Rire," such a move is just as likely to reinforce the humanist theory of subjectivity at work in the artist's rational activity as it is to challenge it.

"THE DECLINE IS FROM THE OUTSET INEVITABLE"

At the beginning of this chapter I admitted that Libertson's essay was an unlikely place to look for support in an argument about *techne* and teachability. And, to some degree, it is. Libertson is concerned with neither *techne* nor teachability but instead with the nature of opposition in the work of Georges Bataille. However, if we consider *why* Libertson is concerned with the nature of opposition in Bataille's work, then we can begin to see the connection between his argument and the one I am making here. Generally speaking, Libertson is reacting to a tendency among Bataille's readers to attribute what he sees as a "radical, violently subversive" quality to certain terms in the oppositions that pervade his work. According to this reading, the kind of rupture Bataille is after through something like inner experience would be achieved when the second term in a pair like prohibition/transgression (or homogeneity/heterogeneity) overcomes the first. While Libertson admits that such a reading is "proximate to the exuberance of Bataille's texts," he argues that ultimately it is untenable, unable to be "coherently posited within the context of [Bataille's] multiple demonstrations that 'the decline is from the outset inevitable' . . ." (219). Although Dunne is not after the same kind of rupture Bataille is, I would argue that his work creates a similar difficulty for anyone who argues that the process of making becomes more creative or inventive when the artist tries to diminish or relinquish her control over it. Or, to put it differently, I would argue that by understanding *techne* as a strategic detour, Dunne also demonstrates that "the decline is from the outset inevitable." What, though, does this enigmatic statement mean?

According to Libertson, in order for us to grasp what Bataille means when he says that "the decline is from the outset inevitable" we must first understand the nature of his dialectic, that is, "its sacrifice of a term of synthesis in favor of a space of tense contamination in which two modes of being invade each other, while paradoxically maintaining the integrity of their opposition" (210–212). Put differently, we have to understand that for Bataille oppposition is the complicated or dense relationship—what Libertson elsewhere calls the "compressed intimacy"—between two terms that keeps the ontological status of the issue they circumscribe in play. For example, in Bataille's work, together the terms "discontinuity" and "continuity" designate a form of subjectivity whose radical closure is in question, and the terms "savior" and "non-savoir" (knowledge and non-knowledge) designate a mode of cognition whose status as a reification is in question. As Libertson points out, the "space of tense contamination" circumscribed by the two opposed terms in pairs like these is the actual locus of subversive power in Bataille's work and, as such, has "strict priority" over the ostensibly subversive power of the second term. In fact, the triumph of the second term over the first term in a pair like discontinuity/continuity or savoir/non-savoir would be exactly the synthesis Bataille does not want since it would stabilize the ontological status of that space.

If we look closely at Libertson's analysis of a particularly important opposition in Bataille's work—the mastery/sovereignty opposition[57]—then we get a better sense of what he means by "compressed intimacy" and "space of tense contamination." Libertson compares his understanding of this opposition to the one offered by Derrida in "From Restricted to General Economy: A Hegelianism without Reserve." Among other things, Derrida's aim in this essay is to explain the effect of Bataille's categories on the Western philosophical tradition. A central part of this explanation is Derrida's belief that laughter (the *rire*) is an interruption of the "conservative, profane motivation of thought" associated with philosophical discourse (221). But Libertson wants to know what exactly is laughable about philosophical discourse. According to Derrida, what Bataille finds laughable is philosophy's submission to the imperative that there must always be meaning, "that a work must always be possible, which because it defers enjoyment, confers meaning, seriousness, and truth upon the 'putting at stake'" (Derrida 257). In other words, what's laughable about philosophical discourse is its submission to the self-evidence of meaning. Libertson disagrees, however, and reads the role of laughter in Bataille differently, arguing that this submission "takes its energy from, and is utterly conditioned by, the very desire which is its supposed opposite: "the desire for a questioning with no answer, desire for violent loss" (221). But because he is thinking in terms of a more clear cut opposition between mastery and sovereignty (an ironic charge, to be sure), Libertson believes Derrida fails to take into account this desire at the heart of knowledge. This is a significant failure, in Libertson's opinion, given his belief that this desire for infinite questioning or contestation, what he also calls an "awareness of the *putting at stake*," precedes the conferring of meaning. For Libertson this precedence is extremely important because it immediately "conditions and problematizes the transivity of the verb 'confer,'" which is to say that the transivity of the verb 'confer' is always already conditioned by a desire for infinite contestation—"it is already a *putting at stake* even though it appears to be the opposite" (222). Thus to confer meaning through philosophical discourse is to affirm contestation, that is, to open up a space or a possibility for philosophical discourse to problematize the self-evidence of meaning. Based on this understanding of the relationship between knowledge and contestation (or the conferring of meaning and the loss of meaning), Libertson argues that for Bataille, "the *rire* would not be an interruption of the servility of knowledge but rather an anguish at the heart of that servility, an anguish that immediately compromises the very term of servility" (222). In other words, laughter would be that which conditions not disrupts the "essence and element" of philosophy.

For Libertson, this "problematic of conditioning" challenges the idea that we can understand sovereignty as something that is opposed to mastery or the discourse of reason. "Sovereignty," he writes, "is far more than its difference with regard to mastery: it is an exigency so pervasive that, beyond the pseudo-opposition of its status as 'not-mastery,' it is part of mastery" (223). More specifically, he rejects the idea that sovereignty is somehow a loss of meaning, arguing instead that it is "a relation to the loss of meaning that exists within the project of conferring meaning itself" (223). On these grounds Libertson contends that sovereignty should not be understood as something that destroys the possibility of the discourse of reason but rather as something that contributes integrally to that discourse—as "the constant silent awareness that occupies the movement of reason itself" (223).[58]

Having established this alternative reading of the nature of opposition in Bataille's work, Libertson addresses what he views as one of the most pervasive problems associated with the more radical reading: the fact that it remains trapped within a classical philosophy of the subject. This problem, he believes, is evidenced by a "radical voluntarism" in which mastery and sovereignty are purely opposed, thus creating the impression that sovereignty is something that can be sought after by someone (224). Libertson turns again to "From Restricted to General Economy" to illustrate his point, focusing this time on Derrida's claim that mastery becomes sovereignty "when it ceases to fear failure and is lost as the absolute victim of its own sacrifice" (qtd. in Libertson 224). The problem here is that for Derrida, sovereignty begins when one *stops* fearing failure. But to stop fearing failure is to voluntarily give oneself over to the possibility of losing control. This voluntarism is the exact opposite of sovereignty in Bataille. Libertson writes: "The specificity of the sacrifice in Bataille is firstly, that the subject does *not* stop fearing failure, and secondly, that the sacrificer cannot lose himself as the victim of the sacrifice. The entire weight of the sacrifice and of sovereignty consists in their status as pre-voluntary conditions, problematizations of the concept of will" (225). Hence the specific meaning of Bataille's claim that "the decline is from the outset inevitable." The decline—that is, the loss of control that characterizes sovereignty for Bataille (and, I am suggesting, passivity for Dunne)—is inevitable *not* because it is guaranteed to disrupt our efforts to confer meaning but rather because it is already part of those efforts and, as a result, cannot be chosen as an alternative to them.[59]

Cultivating a Keatsian Negative Capability—Thirty Years Later

I realize it might be a stretch for some readers to associate Dunne's understanding of passivity in any way with Bataille's understanding of sovereignty (or any of the more subversive second terms in his oppositions, for that matter). After all, sovereignty refers to a break or disruption in subjectivity achieved through non-productive expenditures such as laughter, eroticism, and anguish. In contrast, Dunne uses the concept of passivity to highlight how the artist's control over the process of making is compromised by his rational activity. While such a compromise can make the process of making more "experiential" (in Dunne's particular sense of that term), Dunne is not claiming it radically changes the status or nature of the artist's subjectivity. Thus I am not suggesting that we understand passivity as a form of sovereignty. What I am suggesting, however, is that we understand the relationship between activity and passivity in Dunne's work—and in *techne,* more generally—according to the kind of dialectic Libertson sees operating in Bataille's oppositions. Among other things, such an understanding would require us to recognize that these two states condition each other to the degree that passivity cannot be chosen over activity for the sake of greater creativity. Moreover, we would need to recognize that when we make such a choice, that is, when we try to diminish or relinquish our control over the process of making, we are potentially reinscribing ourselves within a classical philosophy of the subject, not breaking free from it.

Importantly, my goal in making this argument about the nature of opposition and *techne* is not to align creativity and inventiveness on the side of rational control. That would be precisely the kind of synthesis, stabilization, or overcoming I have tried to avoid. However, my goal is to demonstrate why we can't understand rational control as an impediment to creativity and inventiveness—that is, as things that need to be diminished or eliminated in order to achieve a higher level of "inventive open-endedness," as Hawk would put it. As I've tried to show here, the artist's rational activity plays a contradictory role within *techne,* one that should not be understood primarily as a method of control since it jeopardizes the artist's status as subject even as it makes that status possible. To overlook this contradiction would be to overlook *techne*'s complexity and thus to miss why it remains such a fitting description of writing even 2,500 years after it was first introduced as such.

As I acknowledged at the beginning of this chapter, I know I am not the first of *techne*'s proponents to point to its complexity in order to mitigate the critiques of teachability and thus defend its value for writing theory and pedagogy. But as I have shown here, my reasons for doing this are different than those of the scholars who have come before me. Whereas others have encouraged us to think about *techne* beyond its association with the artist's rational activity, I am encouraging us to rethink what that association entails. Such a rethinking is necessary, I believe, if we are ever going to cultivate the kind of Keatsian negative capability Richard E. Young called for but could not fully implement in his own work. As we saw in chapter 2, when Young made this call almost thirty years ago, he was asking readers to accept and live with the idea that opposed sides of the debate about art (art as mysterious power and art as teachable strategy) were equally true ("Arts, Crafts, Gifts, and Knacks"). The argument about *techne* I've made here issues a similar call. That is, I also believe we need to recognize and live with contradiction. But, as I explained above, the contradiction I have in mind here is the productive contradiction within *techne,* the one that explains why getting beyond the limits of rational control is *not* primarily a matter of getting rid of them. Jean Paulhan, the French literary critic and writer who made a brief appearance in chapter 4, uses just the right analogy to illustrate this contradiction in his 1941 book, *The Flowers of Tarbes.* Taking issue with the anti-rhetorical aesthetics and polemics of writers like Victor Hugo and Arthur Rimbaud, Paulhan argues that rhetorical commonplaces can help, not just hinder, the writer's efforts to say something new or in a new way. To underscore his point, Paulhan draws the following comparison between the art of rhetoric and a safety rail placed at a dangerous precipice:

> The hand-rail that is erected at the edge of an abyss by a foresighted mayor could give a traveler the impression that his freedom is being infringed upon. The traveler is wrong, of course. All he would need to jump, if he really wants to, would be a little bit of energy. And in any case, the hand-rail allows him to get closer to the abyss, and to see every nook and cranny. Rhetoric is just the same. (85)

Like the safety rail that prevents travelers from falling into an abyss, the art of rhetoric gives writers something to hold on to; it lets them know that other writers have been in their place before them, and it assures them that that they have some degree of control over their fate. In this sense, it is a means of securing, of closing down—of limiting what can count as knowledge about writing. But also like that safety rail, the art of rhetoric allows writers to get closer to the abyss, to subject themselves—their plans, intentions, and goals—to the capriciousness and instability of their materials in a way more perilous, and

I believe, more promising than they otherwise could. In this sense, it is a means of unsecuring, of opening up. So, while I agree with those who would argue that we use *techne* to "protect ourselves pragmatically from the abyss," happily, I do not think we can count on that protection to reduce our risk of falling in.

6 Why *Techne?* Why Now?

Considering the two questions that comprise its title, it would seem that this chapter could introduce the arguments I have made in this book just as easily as it could conclude them. And, indeed, I began answering these two questions—*Why techne? Why now?*—in the introduction, explaining that a history of *techne*'s meanings in rhetoric and composition can also serve as a useful history of rhetoric and composition, as long as we recognize that it's a narrow history constructed from the perspective provided by a single concept. The advantage of this admittedly narrow perspective, I argued, is that it highlights some of the field's most complicated and controversial theoretical problems without losing sight of the classroom, since *techne* is inextricably tied to the issue of teachability. In other words, when we look at the history of rhetoric and composition from the perspective of *techne*—or, more precisely, from the perspective of the debates that have surrounded it—we see that some of the field's most taken-for-granted assumptions about what writing is and how (or that) it should be taught are actually quite problematic. To understand how and why these assumptions were first articulated, as well as how they have been critiqued and defended, is to understand, at least in part, why the relationship between theory and practice is not just one of rhetoric and composition's defining features but also one of its perennial sources of conflict.

As important as these explanations are, however, they don't fully answer the two questions that make up this chapter's title. If they did—that is, if they fully explained my reasons for writing this book—then it would be a book concerned only with the history of the debate about *techne*. But, as I hope chapters 4 and 5 have made clear, *Techne* is not just a history of the debate about *techne* within rhetoric and composition. It is also an argument about *techne*—one that doesn't offer a new or revised version of the term so much as it defends the value of an older one by explaining how it can serve not just to close down but also to open up. But why do this? Assuming my goal isn't just to make a theoretical point, it remains to be seen why this defense of *techne* matters. Why go to such lengths to explain how the instrumentality and teachability that are so closely associated with *techne* and that have rightly been understood as means of closing down can also serve to open up?

The most straightforward way for me to begin answering this question is to say that I believe the apparent opposition between closing down and opening up has marginalized writing in our field. Or, to put it in slightly different terms, I believe writing courses should be about writing, but, because of the opposition between closing down and opening up, often they are not. In this statement some readers will undoubtedly hear echoes of Stanley Fish's recent pronouncements—via his *New York Times* blog, "Think Again"—about what college composition courses should and should not do. Although I don't agree with everything Fish says about writing in his three posts on the topic (dated August 24, August 31, and September 7, 2009), I share his belief that "[w]riting is its own subject, and a deeper and more fascinating one than the content it makes available" ("What Should Colleges Teach? Part 2"). But what does this explicit focus on the subject of writing have to do with *techne*? In other words, what does my defense of *techne* have to do with teaching writing as writing? What does "teaching writing as writing" even mean? And how has it been marginalized by the apparent opposition between closing down and opening up?

Answering the two questions that make up this chapter's title means first answering these questions, beginning with the most formidable of them—*What does it mean to teach writing as writing?* What makes this question so difficult is the fact that it is, in essence, a question about the nature of writing. To teach writing *as* writing is to know what writing is. In other words, it is to define writing, and that is by no means an easy task, especially when one is attempting to conclude—not begin—a book. Rather than formulate my own definition of writing, then, I want to turn to the one offered by Michael P. Carter in his 2003 *Where Writing Begins: A Postmodern Reconstruction*. I discussed Carter's book earlier in chapter 4, explaining that for him, teaching writing *as* writing means teaching it as a form of creativity, specifically as a form of the archeological creativity or "beginnings" that he characterizes as "the productive intersection of contradictory forces" (55). According to Carter, writing not only allows us to participate in the disruptive, ongoing, and multilateral process of creativity that "underlies the universe," but it is also uniquely capable of heightening our awareness of that participation (177, 142). In other words, writing both locates us on the threshold between the known and the unknown and intensifies our experience of being there. From his perspective, then, all writing courses should be taught as creative writing courses, that is, as courses aimed at "promoting an awareness of being as creative being" (143). In practical terms, achieving this goal means we have to put more emphasis on invention—but not invention as it has commonly been understood in the field. According to Carter, this common understanding "has presupposed an anemic and externalized conception of creativity, [one] directed toward generating ready answers, finding something to say" (140). In contrast, Carter describes invention as an "archeological *topos*" that allows us to understand creativity as "embodying *the textual act of writing itself*" (142, emphasis added). Emphasizing invention, then, means emphasizing the act of writing; it means making writing itself the subject of the course, and structuring that course "in such a way that students are encouraged to develop, at least for a while, a hyperawareness of writing" (143). Such a course, Carter concludes, would be "a course in metawriting" (143).

To cut to the chase, my argument here—and my answer to that first question I asked earlier—is that teaching writing as a *techne* encourages us to teach writing *as* writing. In other words, my argument is that teaching writing as a *techne* encourages us to create the kind of "metawriting" course Carter describes. After all, when we understand writing as a *techne,* we are understanding it is a form of *poiesis,* that is, as a form of productive knowledge that engages its user in a process of making. It's true that by using the word "making" here, as I have done throughout this book, I am acknowledging (if not highlighting) the fact that *techne* is productive knowledge put in the service of some outside goal. Carter, on the other hand, never uses the word "making," preferring instead to define writing as a specific kind of creativity. This makes sense considering the fact that his main goal in *Where Writing Begins* is to offer us a way of understanding and teaching writing as something that has intrinsic rather than extrinsic value. In this sense, then, we could say that Carter's argument echoes the distinction Heidegger makes between creating and making in "The Origin of the Work of Art." Recall that for Heidegger, both creating and making are forms of bringing-forth, but whereas the former produces works of art, the latter produces equipment. To be clear, Carter doesn't use the term "creativity" in order to suggest that writing is always a form of bringing forth fine art. On the contrary, Carter is not at all concerned with the aesthetic qualities by which we usually define "good" writing.[60] But he does want to challenge the idea that the value of writing lies outside the act of doing it, and, by virtue of its opposition to terms like "making" and "equipment," the term "creativity" allows him to do that.

As I demonstrated in chapter 4, however, this opposition is not a stable one because the processes of making and creating cannot be separated in such a way that would allow us to associate the former with instrumentally valuable writing and the latter with inherently valuable writing. Because one kind of writing is both the inherent possibility and the necessary condition of the other, I argued, rhetoric is always communication for the sake of communication, no matter how hard we work to put it in the service of an external goal. Importantly, there's nothing in Carter's definition of writing as a form of archeological creativity that contradicts this argument. In other words, Carter never uses his definition of writing as an inherently valuable form of creativity to suggest that we should stop teaching instrumental genres. What he does suggest is that we should teach those genres as opportunities for students to experience the inherent creativity of writing in different ways (145). To my mind, this is precisely what *techne* does: by foregrounding the productive nature of writing, that is, its status as a form of *poiesis* or of bringing-forth, it creates opportunities for students to experience writing *as* writing even when they are using it to achieve an external goal. I am aware, of course, that this way of thinking about the meaning and value of *techne* goes against the grain of much (if not most) of what's been written about the term in our field. Historically, we have valued *techne* because it focuses our attention on external goals; or, to put it more precisely, we have valued *techne* because it allows us to align writing with particular kinds of external goals, (e.g., problem solving or political intervention).[61] As I made clear in chapter 4, I have no problem with external goals, which is to say I don't think we necessarily enhance the inherent value of writing when we get rid of them. Moreover, I think the goals we accomplish through writing are important and that they shouldn't be abandoned because some have interpreted the usefulness of rhetoric as a sign of our field's inferiority. But I also think that in our tendency to value *techne* because of its ability to align writing with particular goals, we have overlooked the ways in which it explicitly foregrounds the "thingness" of writing, that is, the ability of writing to engage us in a process—or, to use Debra Hawhee's term, a "manner"—of bringing-forth that is aimed more at doing something than at knowing something.[62] To return to Fish, I would argue that without this explicit foregrounding, we are less likely to teach writing for its own sake and more likely to teach it for the sake of the content it makes available. In other words, we are less likely to teach writing as a means of textual production and more likely to teach it as a means of textual interpretation.

Before I move on, responding to the other questions I asked earlier, I want to acknowledge that by promoting writing as a means of producing over writing as a means of interpreting I am buying into an opposition that has been productively complicated by a number of scholars in the field. For just two examples, we can turn to Julie Drew's 1999 "(Teaching) Writing: Composition, Cultural Studies, Production" and Steven Mailloux's 2002 "Re-Marking Slave Bodies: Rhetoric as Production and Reception." Although their arguments respond to different exigences (the former is defense of the value of cultural studies within composition and the latter a response to the disciplinary fragmentation of rhetoric), Drew and Mailloux both demonstrate that the productive and interpretive elements of writing can, to use Mailloux's terms, be "parts of the same integrated framework for understanding and participating in the cultural conversations of diverse public spheres" (97). Drew does this by first pointing out that cultural studies scholars aren't concerned only with deciphering the meaning of particular texts but also with analyzing the conditions in which those texts were produced. If we can incorporate this analysis of the conditions of textual production into the composition course, she argues, then chances are that our students will become not only more savvy readers but also better writers, that is, writers who understand the "economic, geographic, linguistic, political, technological, [and] social" conditions that both create and constrain them as authors (417–8). What Drew wants to do, then, is show us that interpretation can be put in the service of writing. In other words, she wants to demonstrate that in some versions of cultural studies composition pedagogy, interpretation can be a central *part* of the writing process, not just its objective.

Mailloux makes essentially this same point in "Re-Marking Slave Bodies," arguing that while rhetoric can indeed be used as an art for producing texts, "using it first to analyze past texts or present rhetorical situations can help the current production take place successfully" (101). In the case of rhetorical hermeneutics, for instance, students can use rhetoric (in the form of a "rhetorical vocabulary") to produce a reception history, that is, an interpretation of how a particular text was "understood, evaluated, and utilized" at a specific moment in history (100). While the knowledge that students garner through this interpretation isn't necessarily the same kind that emerges from the analysis described by Drew, it would be used to improve their writing process in a similar fashion—that is, by revealing to them the rhetorical strategies used by specific writers in specific historical and cultural situations. Thus in this model, as in Drew's, it is possible for interpretation and production to work together as "complementary events," giving us what Mailloux dubs a "reception-oriented take on production" (101, 98).

In principle, I agree with both Drew and Mailloux, which is to say I believe we can improve students' productive skills by teaching interpretive skills. However, I would argue that in practice the strategy of using interpretation to teach production—whether it's done under the auspices of cultural studies, rhetorical hermeneutics, or something else—more frequently leads to what we might call a "production-oriented take on reception" than to a "reception-oriented take on production." In other words, I think in the kinds of pedagogies described by Drew and Mailloux, interpretation becomes the primary concern of the course, leaving production to play a subordinate (if not epiphenomenal) role. Mailloux explicitly acknowledges this possibility when he defines rhetorical hermeneutics as "a version of cultural rhetoric studies," which is, first and foremost, "an interpretive project [that] attempts to establish meanings and values for texts and their results, analyzing the effects of cultural performances in general and language use in particular" (98–9). As I explained, Mailloux sees rhetorical hermeneutics as a "reception-oriented take on production," but, from the definition above, we get the sense that improved production skills are more or less a by-product of the larger, more important project of establishing meanings and values for texts. Importantly, we also get the sense that this isn't a problem for Mailloux—that he isn't trying to promote rhetoric as a productive art over rhetoric as an interpretive art but instead trying to show that rhetorical hermeneutics doesn't focus on the latter to the exclusion of the former. Drew, on the other hand, is after a more production-oriented pedagogy. She hopes that by emphasizing the conditions of textual production (rather than the meanings of texts), cultural studies composition pedagogies can avoid making writing a secondary concern. However, she also acknowledges that such an outcome is common in many courses (411, 417, 418). Citing trends in journal publications and conference presentations, Drew notes that composition instructors are typically more interested in "the objects of cultural studies analysis as texts for students to read and interpret" than as a means of incorporating "particular hermeneutics practices" into the writing process (418, 412). Thus she admits she shares Susan Miller's concern that it is "all too often the case" that reading, interpretation, and analysis replace writing in many composition courses (418).

Susan Miller expressed this concern about the over-emphasis on reading, interpretation, and analysis in composition courses in her 1997 essay, "Technologies of Self?-Formation." Along with other articles published in the same issue of *JAC,* the point of Miller's essay was to comment on the cultural studies-based composition pedagogy promoted by Jim Berlin. Despite what she described as their "mutual wish to learn how to use the active power of language," Miller took issue with Berlin's pedagogy, arguing that in courses where students are required to "reflect on or display their grasp of democratic consciousness," the content is typically reading rather than writing (498–9). More specifically, she argued that such courses direct students "not toward practice in manipulating genres, but to smart awareness of generic power, not toward guerilla stylistics, but to savvy about stylishness; not toward strength to withstand forces that prevent their critiques from wide acknowledgment, but to interpretations of those forces" (499). For Miller, the bottom line is that no matter how well students are taught to read culture, that ability "no more motivates active literate practices than reading great literature" (499). If we want to "teach the masses in the name of democratic virtue," she argued, then we must resist the turn toward "cultural hermeneutics" and "actually privilege a dose of vulgar composition—how to find and fulfill a textual purpose for a specific readership, in full awareness that safe purposes and already socialized results are waiting to choose us" (500, 499).[63]

Although Drew's goal in "(Teaching) Writing" wasn't to explain the forces responsible for this turn toward cultural hermeneutics, she did point to two possible explanations. First she argued that because the terrain of cultural studies is so vast, instructors often work with only a partial knowledge of its theories and methodologies (417). Thus production slips into interpretation because instructors don't know that there's more to cultural studies than analyzing texts. Second, and more significantly, Drew cited the perceived similarities between cultural studies analysis and literary interpretation, arguing that for those who have been trained to interpret literature, a cultural studies approach to composition feels familiar and comfortable (417). In other words, it allows them to apply the interpretive skills they've learned, albeit to a different set of texts (those produced in and by popular culture) and for different reasons (to improve students' writing and foster critical consciousness).[64]

Drew's explanations of why production slips so easily into interpretation in some writing courses make a lot of sense, particularly the second one. It seems obvious that instructors would want to use the training they already have to teach rather than go through the process of being re-trained. Presumably, though, more and more instructors are either being trained to teach writing *as* specialists in rhetoric and composition or they are being trained to teach writing *by* specialists in rhetoric and composition. To point this out is not to deny the fact that many composition instructors (especially those working as part-time or adjunct faculty) have no specialized training in rhetoric and composition. Nevertheless, it is less likely now than it was thirty, twenty, or even ten years ago that scholars working in rhetoric and composition—that is, those publishing research and/or administering writing programs—were originally trained as literature specialists. Thus I think it is also less likely that interpretation trumps production in their courses because they simply want to teach what they were trained to teach. Presumably, many of them were trained to teach writing. But then why don't they teach it *as* writing? That is, why is the kind of "metawriting" course described by Carter the exception in many composition programs, not the norm?

As I indicated at the outset of this chapter, I believe the answer to this question lies—at least in part—in the apparent opposition between closing down and opening up. More specifically, I believe that because of this opposition, many of us think that when we teach writ-

ing as production, that is, when we teach it as a *techne,* we are participating in—or forcing our students to participate in—a form of closing
down that does not count as actual writing or as writing *as* writing.
Actual writing, according to this line of thinking, is something else—
some form of opening up that stands in clear contrast to the seemingly
mundane activities that go on in the name of textual production. We
can see this belief reflected in the special status that the term "writing" has acquired in recent scholarship. Take, for example, three of the
scholars whose work I have already discussed here—D. Diane Davis,
Thomas Kent, and Michael P. Carter. All of these scholars take on the
difficult task of defining writing, but they do so from a wide range
theoretical perspectives, and, as a result, they produce quite different definitions of writing. What connects their work, however, is the
fact that all of their definitions distinguish the term "writing" and its
various opening up abilities from the related terms "composition" and
"scribing" and their various closing down abilities. As we saw in chapter 3, Davis makes this distinction in *Breaking Up [at] Totality* when
she claims writing teachers have sacrificed "genuine writing" for composition, which she defines as a set of teachable practices designed to
put language to work in the service of the university and its "prime di-
rective" of "Enlightenment, Enpowerment, and Emancipation" (229,
235, 211). Whereas composition must silence the laughter in language
in order to achieve these three goals, genuine writing exposes and cel-
ebrates that laughter, "blast[ing] open a passage to the excess, the im-
proper, the unaccountable, [and] the overflow" so that we might hear
the "Unheard," attend to inscription's exscriptions, and thus interrupt
the myth of common-being that so many composition pedagogies perpetuate (232, 234). When writing is understood in these terms, that
is, as a means of exposing our finitude, Davis reasons, we can assume
"there is a precious little bit of [. . . it] going on in comp classes today,
where students are commanded to 'know' their audience and their
(lone) purpose, where they are rewarded for grounding their inscriptions in 'common places' (the same), for pretending to have mastered
something, and for perpetuating the myths of community and identity via the strategies of clarity and linear presentation—for *effacing
inscription's exscriptions*" (238–9).

The distinction Davis makes here between writing as a way of
opening up and composition as a way of closing down is not a subtle
one. Many of the most common principles and strategies we associate

with writing as production (e.g., understanding audience, writing with a purpose, using commonplaces as aids to invention, and writing clear, linear prose) do *not* count as writing for her. In fact, these principles and strategies domesticate writing, turning it into a means of maintaining rather than challenging the status quo.

Although Thomas Kent is not necessarily interested in using writing to challenge the status quo, like Davis, he believes it should not (and, in fact, cannot) be reduced to the principles and strategies we typically teach under the rubric of textual production. Thus he also ascribes a special "opening up" status to writing, drawing (very loosely) on the work of Emmanuel Levinas in "Paralogic Rhetoric: An Overview" to argue that it is an "ongoing and open-ended communicative activity" that forces us to encounter the "singularity" and "strangeness" of other language users (147–8). Through this encounter, we "confront our assurance of our own selfhood," which is to say that we realize our sense of self exists only as a result of our interaction with others (147). "When we produce any kind of written text," Kent explains, "we cannot avoid responding to and interacting with others, and through this interaction, we define ourselves—including our ethics—by situating ourselves in some relation to others" (147–8). Thus for Kent, learning to write isn't just about learning the strategies necessary for expressing some kind of pre-given meaning (what he would call the *techne* of composition); rather, it's about learning how to engage others in order to figure out "who we are and what is important to us" (147).

To drive home this distinction between expressing pre-given meaning and engaging others—and thus to highlight writing's special status as a kind of ethical activity—Kent, like Davis, opposes it to the related term "composition." Understood "primarily and narrowly" to include knowledge about the composing process (i.e., knowledge about "semantics, style, cohesion, [and] genre"), he explains, composition "*is not the same as writing*" (149, emphasis added). As we saw in chapter 3, Kent defines writing as kind of communicative interaction that happens through the "hermeneutic guesswork" of two language users. Because this guesswork cannot be systematized and used across different situations, Kent believes writing is fundamentally unteachable. Composition, on the other hand, is teachable, and while Kent concedes that it should be a requirement in every student's curriculum, he warns us not to think that when we teach composition we are actually teaching writing (149). "Certainly we may employ heuristics and rules of thumb to help us in the written production of texts [. . .]," he writes, "but these rubrics, helpful as they might be, do not constitute a description of the writing act in any meaningful sense of the term" (148). Thus, we'd be better off if we "simply dropped the idea that writing can be taught as a codified body of knowledge" (149).

Michael P. Carter doesn't want us to drop the idea that writing can be taught, but he does want to reconceive our reasons for teaching it. Like Davis and Kent, then, he gives the term "writing" a special status, contrasting it not to "composition" but rather to "scribing." While both "writing" and "scribing" refer to forms of literate composition, the former is more like copying, which is to say it is characterized by "a way of knowing and being in the world marked by continuity, equilibrium, orientation to that which comes before" (*Where Writing Begins* 115). When we're engaged in the "modernist, humanistic" activity of scribing, Carter explains, we're generating text "without questioning, challenging, without upsetting" (115). To put it in the terms he used to describe the field's common understanding of invention, we could say that scribing is what happens when we use heuristics to generate "ready answers" or to find "something to say" (140). In other words, scribing is composition as a means of closing down, of securing into place what we already know. In contrast, the term "writing" refers to a form of literate composition characterized by creativity, "beginnings," or opening up. In other words, it refers to the kind of literate composition that locates writers in the archeological *topos* that Carter identifies with invention and describes as "the threshold between the known and the unknown, the familiar and unfamiliar" (141). In order to teach writing rather than scribing, Carter argues, we have to encourage our students "to extend their stay" on this threshold, focusing on "invention itself" and realizing that it's not "good writing" or "acceptable student texts" we're after, but rather "the good of writing"—that is, "the destabilizing experience of participating in beginnings" (142, 145).

To be clear, I find a tremendous amount of value in the work of Davis, Kent, Carter—and anyone else who doesn't just claim, as Fish does, that writing is a "deeper and more fascinating subject than the content it makes available" but also tries to explain why this is so. As Carter points out in the preface to *Where Writing Begins,* historically speaking, few scholars in rhetoric and composition have offered such explanations (ix).[65] Davis, Carter, and Kent all take on this challenge, providing compelling answers to the frequently overlooked but nonetheless central question *What is writing?* While it's true I find Carter's answer the most compelling of the three (which is to say I think it does the best job of describing the "thingness" of writing), I would argue that each helps us understand what it means to experience writing *as* writing. However, I would also argue that we don't necessarily increase the likelihood that students will have such an experience when we oppose it to the seemingly mundane activities that go on in the name of textual production—many of which would fit comfortably under the rubrics of "composition" and "scribing." Of course there are differences between those mundane activities and the experience of writing *as* writing. But we should not read these differences as evidence that these terms—and the activities to which they refer—exist in the kind of relationship that would allow us to more easily experience one by opposing it to the other. In other words, just as I argued in chapter 5 that we don't get closer to "the certain kind of passivity" that Dunne describes in *Back to the Rough Ground* by moving away from the artist's rational activity, I am arguing here that we don't get closer to writing *as* writing by moving away from composition or scribing. In chapter 5, I relied on Libertson's understanding of the Bataillean opposition to explain this contradiction, but we can also understand it in terms of Weber's re-translation of *Ge-stell* as Emplacement. As we saw, Weber characterizes Emplacement as "a strange combination" of securing in place and unsecuring. Although there is a clear difference between these two things—a difference Weber highlights by referring to the latter as "movement" and the former as "stasis"—separating them would be impossible since each prepares the possibility of the other. Weber makes this point himself when he explains that it's by securing in place that *Ge-stell* gives way to new settings that in turn require continuous re-setting. Put differently, we could say that it is by securing in place that we create the insecurity that necessitates our emplacements. This "problematic of conditioning," as Libertson would call it, shows us that even though we might prefer the movement of unsecuring and wish to engage in it without also securing in place, we can't. Simply put, there is no unsecuring without securing and, consequently, no securing without unsecuring.

Yet this is precisely what the opposition between these terms—on the one hand, writing *as* writing and, on the other, composition and scribing—suggests: if we can identify the mundane activities of textual production and then distance our courses from them, then we might be able to clear a space for something more special and more valuable, something more like real writing. My claim is that such distancing can indeed clear a space in our courses, but that what occupies this space is typically more reading, not more writing. To be sure—and despite the amount of theory used to support it—this argument is driven by a very practical concern for what happens in composition classes. When we define writing in opposition to the activities of textual production, we are implicitly suggesting (and, in some cases, explicitly claiming) that to teach those activities is to reduce writing to a version of itself so impoverished that it needs to be designated by another name. Yet, given the myriad demands and limitations imposed on most composition courses, these activities are precisely the ones that appear teachable. Thus to send the message that they don't count as writing—or, worse, that they debase writing—is to send the message that writing cannot (and perhaps should not) be taught. What can be taught, however, is the content that writing makes available, and so when faced with the equally unsatisfactory options of attempting the impossible (teaching writing *as* writing) or settling for the mundane (teaching writing as composition or scribing), many teachers choose, self-consciously or not, to focus their courses on interpretation. One way to reverse this trend, I think, is to stop sending the message that when we teach writing as textual production—that is, when we "actually privilege a dose of vulgar composition," as Susan Miller puts it—we aren't really teaching writing. Can those activities serve to close down? Yes, they absolutely can. But they can also serve to open up, and, for good or for ill, there's no way to separate these two possibilities.

Although I am reluctant to bring this book to a close with a caveat, I am going to do precisely that. I am going to conclude with a caveat because I want to make it clear that my claim about the inseparability of closing down and opening is not an argument for using only those composition pedagogies and practices that clearly meet *techne*'s definitional criteria—namely, teachability and instrumentality. In other words, my claim is not an endorsement of what we would (imprecisely, in my view) call the "traditional" over the "innovative."[66] Or, to put it yet another way, it is not a license to ignore those pedagogies and practices that are typically perceived as experimental or unconventional because they are designed to do something other than teach students to communicate effectively—something like celebrate the laughter-in-language, engage the singularity of others, or become aware of being as creative being. In fact, my claim is not an argument that we stop understanding the experience of writing *as* writing in these terms. What it is, however, is an attempt to complicate our understanding of how one actually comes to experience writing *as* writing. More specifically, it is a rejection of the idea that we can use a binary like closing down/opening up (or any of its cognates) to parcel out composition pedagogies and practices into categories and then, on the basis of those categories, know which ones are "better." Considering the prominence of Richard E. Young's work in this book and, more specifically, the role his own penchant for categorizing has played in creating the exigence to which it responds, there is more than a little irony in this call for us to resist evaluating pedagogies and practices on the basis of the categories to which we've assigned them. As I argued in chapter 5, however, what we need to take from Young's work is the way in which it tried—but sometimes failed—to cultivate the complementarity expressed in Keats's notion of negative capability. I've tried to cultivate that complementarity here by arguing that we can affirm the value of a potentially problematic definition of *techne* without denying the legitimacy of the critiques that have been leveled against it. More than just an attempt to "pick up" where Young left off, this argument is a response to the either/or mentality—*either we control language or we let it control us; either we use language to represent the world or we free it from representation; either we write for the sake of communication or we writing for the sake of writing itself*—that has obscured the contradictory nature of writing as a productive art and, to our detriment, diminished its presence in composition courses.

Notes

INTRODUCTION

1. Throughout this book, I use the words "rhetoric" and "writing" interchangeably, even though I recognize that they can, and often do, refer to different things. Arguably, though, all theories and pedagogies of writing (and of composition, for that matter) can be understood more generally as theories and pedagogies of rhetoric, and this is what I mean to suggest by interchanging them. I also interchange them in order to be consistent with the sources I use.

2. I've put quotation marks around the word "technical" in order to call attention to the fact that I am using it simply as the adjectival version of the word "*techne*." In other words, I don't mean to suggest, as the word "technical" often does in contemporary usage, that I am referring to the kinds of highly specialized knowledge associated with mechanical, technological, or industrial activities.

3. I am borrowing the phrase "*as* writing" from Michael P. Carter, who argues in his 2002 *Where Writing Begins* that when we teach writing "*as* writing," we are making writing itself the subject of the course in order to instill in students a hyperawareness of its creative nature (143). I elaborate on Carter's arguments about writing in chapter 4 and in chapter 6.

CHAPTER 1: WHAT IS *TECHNE*?

4. Gadamer's claim that the craftsman relies on his "design of the object and the rules for executing it" to apply his knowledge also suggests he has something like a handbook in mind when he uses the term "*techne*" (317–8).

5. The future of rhetoric and composition depended on the revitalization of invention, many scholars argued, because without this canon, rhetoric was reduced to a linguistic epiphenomenon—that is, a process of "dressing" the thought or knowledge created elsewhere or by other, non-rhetorical means, (e.g., science and philosophy). If rhetoric itself was understood as an epistemic process, however, then researchers could study (and teach) the

ways in which knowledge is created rhetorically. For more on the importance of invention in the mid-twentieth century revitalization of rhetoric, see *The Prospect of Rhetoric: Report of the National Developmental Project* edited by Lloyd Bitzer and Edwin Black; Elbert Harrington's "A Modern Approach to Invention" in *Quarterly Journal of Speech* 48 (1962): 373–78; Dudley Bailey's "A Plea for a Modern Set of Topoi" in *College English* 26 (1964): 111–117; *New Rhetorics* edited by Martin Steinmann; and *Roots for a New Rhetoric* by Daniel Fogarty.

6. Some would argue that this stochastic version of *techne* was first articulated (albeit indirectly) in Isocrates's critique of rhetoric handbooks (Roochnik 79). While it's true that Isocrates rejected the understanding of *techne* embodied in those handbooks, unlike Petraglia and Gadamer, he was not willing to reject the concept *in toto*. Not only did he use the term "*technikotatos*" in *Against the Sophists* to describe those speakers who had become "most skillfull," but he also implored teachers to "expound the principles of the art [of discourse] with the utmost possible exactness as to leave nothing out that can be taught" (Roochnik 75; *Against* 125). For scholars like David Roochnik, Isocrates's defense of these principles, combined with his insistence on the highly situational nature of rhetoric, indicates he was trying to offer a different version of *techne*, one that moved away from the mechanical teachability of handbooks without undermining the idea of teachability altogether (79). This second definition of *techne*—*techne* as a rational ability to effect a useful result—accomplishes this move, especially when the meaning of "result" is understood broadly to include both products and conditions. For other arguments that Isocrates understood rhetoric as a *techne*, see Takis Poulakos's "Isocrates' Use of *Doxa*" in *Philosophy and Rhetoric* 34.1 (2000): 61–78 and Terry Papillion's "Isocrates' *techne* and Rhetorical Pedagogy" in *Rhetoric Society Quarterly* 25 (1995): 149–162.

7. Saying that teachable principles and bodily knowledge work in concert suggests that Atwill sees these two things as completely distinct. However, she complicates this distinction in "Bodies and Art," arguing that art "socializes the bodies that enact it" (166).

8. I say that Hawk has done more to promote this non-instrumental version of *techne* because he deals with it extensively in his book, *A Counter-History of Composition*. However, Lynn Worsham was the first scholar in rhetoric and composition to challenge the field's prevailing instrumental conception of *techne* in her almost fifty-page article, "The Question Concerning Invention: Hermeneutics and the Genesis of Writing."

CHAPTER 2: THE NEW CLASSICIST DEFINITION OF ART

9. Specifically, Young and Becker argue that classical rhetoric cannot provide the foundation for a modern rhetoric because (1) the classical art

of invention "stresses authoritative confirmation of present beliefs"; (2) the art of arrangement in classical rhetoric "includes only patterns of persuasion and neglects considerations of form in other important rhetorical modes"; (3) "both the art of arrangement and the art of style divorce form from content, failing to consider the importance of the act of discovery in the shaping of form"; and (4) "the art of style is concerned primarily with embellishing, clarifying, and giving point to sentences, which neglects both the deeper roots of personal style and the ways in which style is manifested in patterns beyond the sentence" (454–5).

10. Young first made this connection between heuristics and the new classicist definition of art explicit in his 1976 "Invention: A Topographical Survey" when he argued that writers who used heuristics to deliberately guide the processes of invention had an art, while those who relied on habit had a knack (2). It is also worth pointing out that heuristics are the same kind of knowledge as *techne*: contingent, productive knowledge valued as a way of accomplishing something rather than knowing something.

11. See also David Harrington's "Encouraging Honest Inquiry in Student Writing" in *College Composition and Communication* 30.2 (1979): 182–6.

12. See Cynthia Selfe and Sue Rodi's "An Invention Heuristic for Expressive Writing" in *College Composition and Communication* 31.2 (1980): 169–74; Fred R. Pfister and Joanne F. Petrick's "A Heuristic Model for Creating a Writer's Audience" in *College Composition and Communication* 31.2 (1980): 213–20; Dorothy M. Guinn's "Composing an Abstract: A Practical Heuristic" in *College Composition and Communication* 30.4 (1979): 380–3; and Tommy J. Boley's "A Heuristic for Persuasion" in *College Composition and Communication* 30.2 (1979): 187–91.

13. Winterowd's chapter on invention (from which this heuristic comes) was over thirty pages long and included extensive discussion of not only the pentadic heuristic but also journaling, problem solving techniques, brainstorming, and a revised version of the tagmemic discovery procedure.

14. See Burke's "Questions and Answers about the Pentad" in *College Composition and Communication* 29.4 (1978): 330–5.

15. As Hawk explains, this conflation of romanticism and vitalism came from Hal Weidner's 1975 dissertation, "Three Models of Rhetoric: Traditional, Mechanical, and Vital," which was directed by Young (*Counter-History* 18–19).

16. See, for instance, Joseph A. Harris's *A Teaching Subject: Composition Since 1966*; Martin Nystrand et al.'s "Where Did Composition Studies Come From? An Institutional History" in *Written Communication* 10.3 (1993): 267–333; and Donna Burns Phillips et al.'s "*College Composition and Communication*: Chronicling a Discipline's Genesis" in *College Composition and Communication* 44.4 (1993): 443–65.

17. For a discussion of the arguments made by those who did not favor turning rhetoric and composition into a discipline, see Maureen Daly Goggin's *Authoring a Discipline: Scholarly Journals and the Post-World War II Emergence of Rhetoric and Composition,* particularly chapter 2, "Preparing the Ground: 1950–1965."

18. For more on Project English, see "Project English: The First Year" by J. N. Hook in *PMLA* 78.4.2 (1963): 33–5; "Research on the Teaching of English Under Project English" by Erwin R. Steinberg in *PMLA* 79.4.2 (1964): 50–76; "A Report on Project English" by Robert C. Slack in *College English* 26.1 (1964): 43–7; and "College English Departments and Professional Efforts to Improve English Teaching" by James R. Squire in *PMLA* 78.4.2 (1963): 36–8.

19. Kitzhaber makes this point in "4C, Freshman English, and the Future," explaining that at a four-day seminar held at NYU, Project English participants set out to identify research topics in English and ways of investigating them. Although they did not intend on ignoring literature and language, conversations focused on composition (132–3).

20. Those topics included (1) composition and the useable portions of classical rhetoric; (2) composition and the possibility of a new rhetoric; (3) composition and its relation to structural and transformational grammar; (4) composition and close reading, and the teaching of literature and its use as a rhetorical or structural model; (5) the construction of criteria and tests for the measurement of excellence in composition; (6) the analysis of levels of student maturity at which basic composition "habits" or "patterns of decision" are formed; and (7) the construction of criteria and tests for the correction of themes in the areas of syntax, logic, and persuasive strategy (Steinberg 69).

21. This was essentially Albert K. Kitzhaber's response to Warner Rice's claim that the course should be abolished. Kitzhaber agreed that as it stood, the composition course was not acceptable. However, he wanted to keep it under the condition that it would have to be improved after changes were made in high schools. In other words, he wanted to create a new course after the necessity of the first had been eliminated by the improvements happening at the secondary level ("Death—Or Transfiguration?" 372).

22. Virginia Burke also made a strong case for disciplinarity in her 1965 article, "The Composition-Rhetoric Pyramid," arguing that "the power of a discipline to maintain a field and to energize practice in it should be self-evident." "*Without a discipline,*" she continued, "arbitrary decisions to add or drop a composition course, to write a theme a week or a theme a month, to use this textbook or that, to feature one kind of writing or one kind of reading over another, to evaluate papers chiefly for content or for organization or for mechanics—all such arbitrary decisions are without rationale; no decision at all may do just as well as a decision one way or another. *With a discipline,* some reasonable sequence, moving *from* something identifiable *toward*

something identifiable is clearly suggested; [. . .] *Without a discipline,* under-graduate and graduate offerings in advanced composition and rhetoric can continue slight or nonexistent; and the preparation of teachers of high school and college composition can be treated in familiar, cavalier fashion; *with a discipline,* we must confront the peculiarities and gaps in our undergraduate and graduate offerings as well as our whole approach to English studies" (6).

23. What's striking about the way Hawk describes this turn is how much emphasis he puts on Young's individual agency. For instance, Hawk writes that "[i]n valuing scientific and ethnographic research—over and above his call for metarheorical, philosophical, and historical research—*Young is turning* rhetoric toward the scientific and the formal" (*Counter-History* 23–4, emphasis added). Although Young's work certainly contributed to the misun-derstanding of vitalism Hawk seeks to rectify, it's misleading to suggest that Young himself was turning the field toward "the scientific and the formal." The field—and not just rhetoric and composition but English more gener-ally—was turning away from its past toward the new theories and methods that (they hoped) could bring the discipline up to speed with changes hap-pening elsewhere. Young was certainly affected by these changes, but it's misleading to suggest, as Hawk's claim does, that if it weren't for his work, rhetoric and composition wouldn't have embraced those new theories and methods.

CHAPTER 3: POSTMODERN THEORY AND THE RE-TOOLING OF *TECHNE*

24. See also A. M. Tibbetts's "The Case Against Structural Linguistics in Composition" in *College English* 21.5 (1960): 280–5.

25 See Lyotard's *The Postmodern Condition: A Report on Knowledge* 60–67.

26. Sirc elaborated this notion of poetic writing via the work of 1960s avant-garde visual artists like Marcel Duchamp, Jackson Pollock, and Robert Raucshenberg in his 2002 *English Composition as a Happening.* Willing to "turn off expectation and be open to meaning, intensity, beauty," he argued, these artists refused to sacrifice personal vision for conventions and prede-termined, utilitarian purposes (21, 24). Sirc recognized the same attitude in teachers like Ken Macrorie and William Coles, both of whom he believes were ignored once scholars like Young set their sights on turning composi-tion into bona fide discipline. Once it took on the trappings of academia, Sirc argued, composition failed to develop "an idea of writing than fully reflects the splendor of the medium," embracing instead "a very limited notion of academic writing" (10). And the result of this choice, he lamented, has been less and less "expressivist or art-writing " (25).

27. Sirc's suggestion here that this non-utilitarian, poetic form of writing "simply becomes a rupture" and "cracks the mirror" so that it can reflect the "heart-breaking reality of humanity" is an incredibly humanistic reading of Bataille. Likewise, his claim that his student Mick's writing about an encounter with a homeless man is a "record of an inner experience" raises problems (551). As I explained in my brief discussion of inner experience, Bataille believes there is neither subject nor object in inner experience; it is a radical loss of self achieved through non-productive expenditures of energy (*Inner Experience* 42). To my mind, this not only problematizes the idea that "Bataillean writing" could ever reflect the reality of humanity but also any notion of a "Bataillean pedagogy." There's nothing wrong with Sirc's goal of "giv[ing] students a space to develop as sensitive people, able to communicate," but I don't think we can conflate this goal with Bataille's (553).

28. To clarify, Vitanza does not suggest that we should simply do away with invention/heuristics but instead that we need complementary theories of chance ("Invention" 137).

29. Although frequently used synonymously, here Vitanza differentiates "*techne*" from "art," identifying the former with method, systematized knowledge, and "means of production" and the latter with an avant-garde form of resistance that is neither codifiable nor teachable (160–161).

30. Bataille explains his understanding of the restricted and general economies in his 1933 essay, "The Notion of Expenditure" and in his three-volume *The Accursed Share* (1967, 1976). Generally speaking, the restricted economy, which dominates human life, is based on production and measures value in terms of utility. The general economy, however, is based on the notion of non-productive expenditures and excess. Although Bataille distinguishes between these two economies, and even promotes the general economy over the restricted economy, he sees them as inseparable, the latter being just a moment or phase in the former (*Accursed* I 37–43; "The Notion" 129).

31. We can see this positioning in Atwill's description of postmodern theory as "a large-scale assault" on the universal notions of subjectivity, knowledge, and value associated with humanism (*Rhetoric Reclaimed* 11).

32. We actually saw a version of this incompatibility earlier, when I reviewed Atwill and Lauer's 1995 "Refiguring Rhetoric as an Art" in chapter 1. *Techne* enables cultural critique, they argued, by exposing the indeterminate, arbitrary nature of social conditions and by making the values, subjectivities, and ideologies that operate in cultural practices explicit in teachable strategies. Atwill returned to this connection between *techne* and cultural critique in her 2006 "Bodies and Art," arguing that in order to construct an art, one must be able to decode social practices. Such decoding requires becoming an "expert outsider," that is, one who stands far enough outside of the practice to "observe its regularities" but also close enough to it to "sense its internal

logics" (169). If a minimal definition of critical perspective includes recognizing the contingent character of social conventions and identities, Atwill concluded, then art should both bear witness to and enable critical perspective" (169).

33. For more on the "pedagogical imperative," see Karen Kopelson's "Sp(l)itting Images; or, Back to the Future of (Rhetoric and?) Composition" in *College Composition and Communication* 59.4 (2008): 750–80.

34. In much current-traditional pedagogy, invention was considered unteachable, and, as a result, arragement, style, and mechanics took center stage in most textbooks and classrooms, allowing teachers to focus too narrowly on issues of correctness. The efforts of the new classicists (as well as others associated with the new rhetoric) to return invention to rhetoric were a reaction to this narrow focus on arrangement, style, and mechanics. For more on the lack of invention in current-traditional composition pedagogy, see Sharon Crowley's *Methodical Memory: Invention in Current-Traditional Rhetoric.* For alternative views on current-traditional pedagogy, see Charles Paine's *The Resistant Writer,* Robert J. Connors's *Composition-Rhetoric: Backgrounds, Theory, and Pedagogy,* and Sue Carter Simmon's "Constructing Writers: Barrett Wendell's Pedagogy at Harvard" in *College Composition and Communication* 46 (1995): 327–52.

35. Here I don't mean to suggest that all of the contributors to this issue of *Technical Communication Quarterly* explicitly endorsed Atwill's argument about *techne.* Instead I am arguing that the main claim of her argument—that *techne* is an art of invention and intervention—created the distance between *techne* and the new classicist definition of art that other scholars needed to understand and use the concept in new ways. Guest editors Tracy Bridgeford and Michael R. Moore make a similar point when they describe Atwill's work as one of the "underlying contexts" of the special issue on *techne* (125).

36. See, for instance, Nancy Fraser's *Unruly Practices: Power, Discourse, and Gender in Contemporary Social Theory.*

37. This is true even in the case of Atwill's re-understanding of *techne* as an art of invention and intervention. As I explained in chapter 3, Atwill turns to the concept of *metis* to distinguish the kind of reasoning at work in *techne* from strict philosophical reasoning. While *metis* is certainly more flexible than philosophical reason, it is still very much about premeditation, about making conscious choices in order to achieve predetermined goals. Marcel Detienne and Jean Pierre Vernant make this point in the following passage from *Cunning Intelligence in Greek Culture and Society*: "*Metis* is swift, as prompt as the opportunity that it must seize on the wing, not allowing it to pass. But in no way does it act lightly. With all the weight of acquired experience that it carries, it involves thought that is dense, rich, compressed. Instead of floating hither and tither at the whim of circumstance, it anchors

the mind securely in the project which it has devised in advance, thanks to the ability to look beyond the immediate present and foresee a more or less wide slice of the future (15).

38. Hawk uses the term "post-*techne*" in his *TCQ* article, "Toward a Post-*Techne*—Or, Inventing Pedagogies for Professional Writing" but not in *A Counter-History of Composition: Toward Methodologies of Complexity*. I would argue that the term describes his re-understanding of *techne* in the latter text just as effectively, though.

Chapter 4: Closing Down and Opening Up: Techne and the Issue of Instrumentality

39. It's actually more accurate to say that Weber's re-translations begin with the term "*technik*," from "*Die Frage nach der Technik*," the title of Heidegger's essay, which is usually translated as "The Question Concerning Technology." But according to Weber, "technology" is too narrow (it excludes the meanings technique, craft, skill) and too theoretical (it implies an applied science) to capture the sense of bringing-forth or unlocking present in *techne*, which is, in part, what Heidegger was referring to with the original "*technik*" (980). Thus Weber prefers "technic" to "technology." Weber also explains that it is normally assumed that the thing Heidegger is questioning (or, as he prefers, "questing") after is the *wesen* or essence of technics. But as Weber points out, later in the essay Heidegger argues that technics compels us to understand the meaning of *wesen* not as a kind of generic type but rather as the way in which things "hold sway, administer themselves, develop and decay" ("The Question" 30). Weber thus translates *wesen* as "goings-on" in order to capture this sense of movement he sees present in Heidegger's understanding of the term (983).

40. See, for instance, Robert Scott's "On Viewing Rhetoric as Epistemic" in *Central States Speech Journal* 18 (1967): 9–17; Michael Leff's "In Search of Ariadne's Thread: A Review of the Recent Literature on Rhetorical Theory" in *Central States Speech Journal* 29 (1978): 73–91; and Richard Cherwitz and James W. Hilkin's "Toward a Rhetorical Epistemology" in *Southern Speech Communication Journal* 47 (1982): 135–62.

41. For instance, see Young's "Arts, Crafts, Gifts and Knacks: Some Disharmonies in the New Rhetoric" in *Reinventing the Rhetorical Tradition*. Ed. Ian Pringle and Avia Freedman. Conway, AK: L and S Books, 1980. 53–60; Lauer's "Writing for Insight" in *Conversations in Composition, Proceedings of New Dimensions in Writing: The First Merrimack College Conference on Composition Instruction*. Ed. Albert C. DeCiccio and Michael J. Rossi. North Andover, MA: Merrimack College, 1987. 1–6; and Elbow's *Embracing Contraries: Explorations in Learning and Teaching*. New York: Oxford UP, 1986.

42. Carter develops the idea of archeological beginnings from the Greek term *arche,* which refers to a threshold point where the infinite enters the finite, the divine enters the human, and the spiritual enters the material. Characterized by the interpenetration of contradictory forces, *arche* evokes a kind of Janusian thinking that Carter describes as a state of "doubleness and betweeness—being neither in nor out but at once in and out; at once facing the past and future, the known and unknown" (25).

43. To elaborate, Carter argues that invention is an archeological *topos* where the known is juxtaposed against the unknown, the familiar against the unfamiliar (141). Not only does he then redefine writing, arguing that it is an event through which we engage in archeological beginnings, but he also re-values it, arguing that because writing is a form of archeological beginnings, it has intrinsic value. And what separates us as human beings who posses consciousness from entities that don't, he continues, is "our potential for awareness of that participation and thus the sharpened sense of intrinsic value that comes from the apprehension of a full partnership in creation" (138–9). As humans, in other words, we are capable of enjoying an awareness of participating in beginnings, something that Carter deems valuable in and for itself (138–9). For Carter, this awareness not only contributes integrally to the value of writing (allowing us to understand it as "one of the most powerful and accessible ways we have of heightening our consciousness of being creative and thus becoming full participants in creation") but also provides us with a powerful new rationale for teaching writing.

44. To clarify, critiques of instrumental approaches to rhetoric suggest that these approaches limit our experience of the non-resourceful, material properties of language in two ways: first, they suggest that under the auspices of instrumental approaches to rhetoric, writers experience language primarily as a tool and, as a result, encounters with the materiality of language are understood as failures to master language (i.e., as failures to efficiently use the tool); and second, they suggest that, through their demand for textual features like clarity and coherence and for pedagogical features like teachability and transferability, instrumental approaches to rhetoric actually suppress the materiality of language, thus presumably limiting writers' opportunities to experience that materiality. While the first suggestion is unequivocally considered a key component of the critique of instrumental approaches to rhetoric, there is some question regarding the status of the second one. Look, for instance, at the following three statements from D. Diane Davis's *Breaking Up [at] Totality:* (1) Writing is most threatening when it "opens the possibility for an/Other hearing, a hearing of that which has been drowned out by the workings of the [meaning-making] machine itself" (234); (2) What we need is "an/Other kind of writing, one that is interested at least as much in exscriptions as it is in inscriptions, an é*(x)criture* that zooms in on what the will to 'clarity' sheers off: what is laughable and laughing in language" (20);

(3) "What's at stake in the debate [about writing pedagogy] is the excess, the noise/static that gets 'let by' (silenced) in the name of a reproducible practice" (224). In these claims, Davis suggests that the need for meaningful, clear prose and for reproducible teaching practices suppresses the materiality (i.e., laughter, excess, or noise) of language. However, in the following two statements she suggests that nothing can ultimately suppress the materiality of language: (1) "The strategies of linguistic protection we teach students in comp courses [. . .] do battle perpetually with any text's own propensity to *crack up*" (100); (2) "And yet the philosophical impulse is relentless in its efforts to censor, to negate, to still the roaring laughter-in-language so that it might build epistemologies and establish ethics. It is relentless . . . but *unsuccessful*" (95). The message, then, is conflicted, as critics seem caught between the need to point out how instrumental approaches to rhetoric require (and, indeed, produce) a style of writing that does not allow the materiality of language to shine forth and the need to show that the materiality language shines forth no matter what we do to make it disappear into usefulness.

45. Negation, of course, is a central term in the philosophy of G. F. W. Hegel and is particularly important to his understanding of dialectic. To oversimplify, Hegel understood dialectic as progress or development through negativity: a thing (an idea, knowledge, society, etc.) develops, moving from potentiality to actuality, through opposition to its "other." Through this opposition, something new arises—a new determination of meaning that points beyond itself to a future determination, becoming both a result and a new beginning. Hence the idea that dialectic is positivity (i.e., progress, development) through negativity. But as many critics have pointed out, this progress comes at a price: every determination of meaning is also a denial of meaning. Or as Vitanza has aptly put it, negation is a process of inclusion through exclusion. In his 1997 *Negation, Subjectivity, and the History of Rhetoric,* Vitanza argued that the history of rhetoric as we know it is founded on the exclusion of sophistry. And in his 2000 "From Heuristics to Aleatory Procedures," he claimed that heuristics create meaning through negation, that is, by excluding the third alternatives or "monsters of thought" (193).

46. For more on this process of negation going "too far," see Derrida's "From Restricted to General Economy: A Hegelianism without Reserve," especially 259–260.

47. Blanchot also describes this paradox of language in the following: "If it [language] were to become as mute as a stone, as passive as the corpse enclosed behind that stone, its decision to lose the capacity for speech would still be legible on the stone and would be enough to wake that bogus corpse" ("Literature and the Right to Death" 384–385).

48. This quote comes from a larger passage in which Blanchot makes this point more clearly and emphatically: "Whether the work is obscure or clear, poetry or prose, insignificant or important, whether it speaks of a peb-

ble or of God, there is something in it that does not depend on its qualities that deep within itself is always in the process of changing the work from the ground up. It is as though at the very heart of literature and language, beyond the visible moments that transform them, a point of instability were reserved, a power to work substantial metamorphoses, a power capable of changing everything about it without changing anything" (397).

49. Blanchot reiterates Paulhan's point in "How Is Literature Possible?," arguing that anyone who "desire[s] not to take [words] into account, to leave thought its empire whole" provokes an excessive concern for language. In other words, the writer who "wants to be absent from words or to be present only to those he reinvents" is the one destined to be "endlessly occupied with them" (81).

CHAPTER 5: OPENING UP AND CLOSING DOWN: TECHNE AND THE ISSUE OF TEACHABILITY

50. Dunne believes EN 6.4 can actually be read two ways, more or less in line with Plato. Depending on the translation, he argues, it can be read in such a way that Aristotle stresses the process of making over knowledge or vice versa. Dunne acknowledges that it is strange and unlikely to read EN 6.4 the latter way (knowledge over making), but he does it to show that Aristotle does not really discriminate between the two meanings: (1) "*techne* as an excellence of knowledge that possesses explanatory power . . ." and (2) "*techne* as an excellence in bringing about an actual concrete effect" (318).

51. Martha Nussbaum describes *techne* primarily in terms of its opposition to chance, or *tuche*, in *The Fragility of Goodness*. There she argues that the best place to begin looking for the "ordinary conception" of *techne* is in the *techne-tuche* antithesis, "which both displays, and by its pervasiveness, shapes it" (94). The contrast between these two terms, she explains, is the contrast between "living at the mercy of *tuche* and a life made safer and more controlled by (some) *techne*" (95). Closely linked with practical judgment, forethought, wisdom, prediction, and planning, Nussbaum argues that *techne* afforded the Greeks this control over future contingencies by allowing them to apply reason and intelligence to a particular aspect of their lives (95).

52. Remember that by "experiential element," Dunne is referring to unexpected situations in which the artist's ability to impose a preconceived form onto the material is compromised by contingencies (e.g., "feedback" from the materials themselves).

53. See Dunne's discussion of Aristotle's understanding of matter (329–333) and of the soul (343–349).

54. Quoted in Dunne, p. 462, n71.

55. Quoted in Dunne, p. 462, n71.

56. Arguably, Dunne's understanding of Aristotle's unofficial understanding of *techne* is very similar to the one offered by Heidegger in both *An Introduction to Metaphysics* and "The Origin of the Work of Art." I would not argue, however, that this more Heideggerian version of *techne* that Dunne finds in Aristotle is the same as the Heideggerian version of *techne* outlined by Hawk in "Toward a Post-*Techne*—Or, Inventing Pedagogies for Professional Writing" and *A Counter-History of Composition.* Unlike Hawk, Dunne is not drawing on the work of contemporary thinkers like Deleuze, Mark C. Taylor, or Graham Harman to self-consciously push *techne* in a posthumanist direction. Moreover, while Dunne does make a distinction between the two versions of *techne* within Aristotle's work, that distinction is based on how they *account for* the role of nature in making, not whether or not nature actually plays a role. Hawk, on the other hand, seems to suggest that in the instrumentalist, non-Heideggerian version of *techne* that he sees operating in the work of people like Richard E. Young, nature doesn't play as significant a role in the process of making, if it plays any role. Thus he claims that in an instrumental model, *techne* "is under the control and will of the subject, which forecloses open-ended invention that emerges out of complex adaptive systems" (*Counter-History* 169).

57. Like the other binary pairs described here, the first term of this opposition (mastery) represents the integrity of the subject, particularly as it is revealed by—or, rather, created through—an individual's power to invest energy in projects. As I explained in chapter 3, sovereignty, too, is a power, but not a power exercised by a subject. Rather, it is a power that arises when the subject's knowledge and authority have been disrupted through non-productive expenditure.

58. Bataille makes a similar point when he describes inner experience. Recall the passage from *Inner Experience* I quoted in chapter 3, the passage in which Bataille plainly announces that inner experience is the opposite of project. Further down on the same page he qualifies this opposition, writing that the principle of inner experience is to "emerge through project from the realm of project" (46). And the only way to emerge from project, he continues, is through "discursive reason": "Reason alone has the power to undo its work, to hurl down what it has built up. Madness has no effect, allowing debris to subsist. . . . Natural exaltation or intoxication have [sic] a certain 'flash in the pan' quality. Without the support of reason, we don't reach 'dark incandescence'" (46–7). Maurice Blanchot addresses the paradoxical function of reason within Bataille's thinking by linking it to what he calls "the struggle between knowing and unknowing." Early in "Inner Experience," his first essay on Bataille's work, Blanchot describes inner experience as a state in which a man's "fact of existence" is called into question and as a state where "man meets unknowing as the expression of his supreme calling into play . . ." (38). He then elaborates the role "unknowing" plays in inner experience in

terms of its relationship to knowing: "Unknowing throws back into the night what a man knows about himself. This means two things: one, that fundamental knowing, which is linked to the fact of being, is left aside; second, that the fact of being itself is questioned, is no longer experienced or considered as possible" (38). Unknowing, then, is the absence of knowing. But how does one move from knowing to unknowing? According to Blanchot, this movement, this struggle between knowing and unknowing, begins with reason. Echoing Bataille, he writes: "Reason alone can unmake the stability that is reason's task. It alone is capable of enough continuity, order, and even passion to allow no refuge to remain" (38). What we have here, then, is not a situation in which reason and non-reason exist in a state of simple opposition but rather one in which reason plays an essential role in its own overcoming.

59. John Muckelbauer makes a similar point in the following passage from "Rhetoric, Asignification, and the Other: A Response to Diane Davis": "But if a discourse oriented toward irreducible otherness cannot avoid reduction, appropriation, and the return of the same, this is perhaps because it doesn't need to. If the irreducible other is not exterior to the same, then what follows is that the same is not simply a closed circle that returns to itself in a movement of self-identity. That is, perhaps one doesn't need to avoid appropriation because *the opening to the irreducible other may happen only with and through that very movement of appropriation.* The movement of the same may not be something that needs to be refused, *or even something that requires an 'other' dimension*; while appropriation may block access to the other, it might simultaneously enable that encounter as well. If this is the case, then knowledge, recognition, interpretation, all the tools in the arsenal of the same would necessarily harbor both appropriating and expropriating forces" (245).

CHAPTER 6: WHY *TECHNE?* WHY NOW?

60. This is obvious in Carter's discussion of lecture notes, a genre that often exhibits the traits we associate with "bad" writing but that, in his view, is capable of engaging students in the creative process of reshaping, interpreting, and generating knowledge (144–5).

61. I want to make it clear that Janet M. Atwill also uses the concept of *techne* to position rhetoric as an inventional form of knowledge over a hermeneutic form of knowledge. However, whereas her main goal in doing this is to challenge the theory/practice binary that enables foundational epistemologies, mine is to challenge the closing down/opening up binary that has marginalized the teaching of writing *as* writing in composition.

62. Hawhee uses this term, "manner," in her 2002 essay, "Bodily Pedagogies: Rhetoric, Athletics, and the Sophists' Three R's," to make a distinction between "the way one acquires artistic expertise" and the subject

matter about which one becomes expert (160). Her argument is that sophistic pedagogy focused on manner, that is, on "the materiality of learning," rather than the "material learned" (160). Although my argument about *techne* does not attend to issues of embodiment in writing in the way that Hawhee's does, I am also promoting a theory and pedagogy of writing that emphasizes the act of writing—that is, the fact that writing is way of doing something, of bringing something into being—over the knowledge or subject matter that writing makes available. I added Hawhee's term "manner" here because, more than the term "process," it gets at this emphasis on doing something over knowing something. See Janet M. Atwill's "Bodies and Art" for more on the connection between the concept of *techne* and embodiment.

63. In a 2004 issue of *Critical Inquiry*, J. Hillis Miller makes a similar argument about what activates literate practices more—reading or writing. Drawing on a comparison of "literary subjectivity" to what he calls "digital subjectivity," Miller argues that we can no longer assume that those who spend their time reading and interpreting are better off (intellectually) than those who spend it writing, even if that writing is happening by way of new media technologies like instant messaging. Of course Miller's point here is not to suggest that we should replace reading with writing—or that we should replace traditional forms of writing with newer forms—but, like Susan Miller, he is concerned that an emphasis on the interpretation of texts over the production of texts results in a more passive citizenry.

64. It's important to note that Drew believes cultural studies-based pedagogies cannot be justified only on the basis of this goal of raising critical consciousness. However, she also believes that "few would argue against the articulated aims of what is called libertory learning for students" (420). The reality is that many teachers would, in fact, argue against these aims—or at least question them. This is precisely what Victor Vitanza did in his 1998 Research Forum address at the Conference on College Composition and Communication. Drew responds to Vitanza's address in her essay but, by basing her argument on the claim that cultural studies-based pedagogies do not exclude production, manages to ignore Vitanza's main objective, which was to ask teachers to consider the possibility that pedagogies focused on critique produce not better student-citizens committed to social justice but instead cynics who, through their enlightened false consciousness, know that in doing what they are doing (buying Nike shoes, for instance) they are following an illusion but do it anyway. Vitanza's argument was based on Peter Sloterdijk's 1987 *Critique of Cynical Reason* and Slavoj Zizek's 1989 *The Sublime Object of Ideology*. Drew accused Vitanza of dismissing cultural studies in her essay but then went on to completely dismiss his reason for questioning the efficacy of cultural studies-based composition pedagogies. For other critiques of cultural studies-based pedagogies in rhetoric and composition see Marshall W. Alcorn Jr.'s 2002 *Changing the Subject in English*

Class: Discourse and the Constructions of Desire and Thomas Rickert's 2007 *Acts of Enjoyment: Rhetoric, Zizek, and the Return of the Subject.* The major points of Vitanza's address can be found in his response essay, "'The Wasteland Grows': Or, What is 'Cultural Studies for Composition' and Why Must We Always Speak Good of It?: ParaReponse to Julie Drew."

65. In making this point about a lack of scholarship that studies writing *as* writing, Carter was reiterating an argument made by Sidney I. Dobrin in a 2002 Conference on College Composition and Communication paper, "From Writing Process to Cultural (Re)production: Composition's Theoretical Shift."

66. John Muckelbauer complicates our understanding of these terms, "traditional" and "innovative," in his 2008 book, *The Future of Invention: Rhetoric, Postmodernism, and the Problem of Change.* Despite all of the persistent problematizing of binaries in our field, he argues, we've allowed this one—the traditional versus the innovative—to remain firmly intact. As a result of this neglect, we continue to be invested in a dialectical model of change that tries to achieve transformation through the negation of "particular others—outmoded concepts, oppressive social structures, limited subjectivities, or simply undesirable propositions" (4). In response to this problem, Muckelbauer offers an affirmative style of scholarly engagement through which we can bracket the content of those problematic "others," while still using them to move somewhere else, to other understandings, other readings, other strategies (45–8). Of particular relevance to my argument here is Muckelbauer's use of this style of engagement in chapter 6, "Situatedness and Singularities," to demonstrate that we can use "reasoned principles or generalized methods" to teach situatedness as long as we "inhabit them differently" as provocations—that is, as ways of being affected by actual situations—rather than as representations of the nature of writing (122).

Works Cited

Alcorn, Marshall W., Jr. *Changing the Subject in English Class: Discourse and the Constructions of Desire*. Carbondale: Southern Illinois UP, 2002. Print.

Allen, Harold B. "Counciletter: National Interest and the Teaching of English." *College English* 22.4 (1961): 265–283. Print.

—. "Linguistic Research Needed in Composition and Communication." *College Composition and Communication* 5.2 (1954): 55–9. Print.

—. "Will Project English Kill Freshman English?" *College Composition and Communication* 14.4 (1963): 228–33. Print.

Allen, James. "Failure and Expertise in the Ancient Conception of Art." *Scientific Failure*. Ed. A. Janis and T. Horowitz. Lanham, MD: Rowman and Littlefield, 1993. 83–110. Print.

Applebee, Arthur. *Tradition and Reform in the Teaching of English: A History*. Urbana, IL: NCTE, 1974. Print.

Arendt, Hannah. *The Human Condition*. Chicago: U of Chicago P, 1998. Print.

Aristotle. *Magna Moralia*. Trans. G. Cyril Armstrong. Cambridge, MA: Harvard UP, 1933. Print.

—. *Metaphysics*. Trans. W. D. Ross. *The Complete Works of Aristotle*. Vol. 2. Ed. Jonathan Barnes. Princeton, NJ: Princeton UP, 1984. 1552–1728. Print.

—. *Nicomachean Ethics*. Trans. David Ross. Oxford: Oxford UP, 1925. Print.

—. *On Rhetoric: A Theory of Civic Discourse*. Trans. George A. Kennedy. New York: Oxford UP, 1991. Print.

—. *On Sophistical Refutations*. Trans. E. S. Forster and David J. Furley. The Loeb Classical Library. Cambridge, MA: Harvard UP, 1965. Print.

—. *Physics*. *The Complete Works of Aristotle*. Ed. Jonathon Barnes. Princeton, NJ: Princeton UP, 1984. Print.

Atwill, Janet M. "Bodies and Art." *Rhetoric Society Quarterly* 36 (2006): 165–170. Print.

—. "Instituting the Art of Rhetoric: Theory, Practice, and Productive Knowledge in Interpretations of Aristotle's *Rhetoric*." *Rethinking the History of Rhetoric: Mutildisciplinary Essays on the Rhetorical Tradition*. Ed. Takis Poulakos. Boulder, CO: Westview Press, 1993. 91–117. Print.

—. "Introduction: Finding a Home or Making a Path." *Perspectives on Rhetorical Invention.* Ed. Janet M. Atwill and Janice M. Lauer. Knoxville: U of Tennessee P, 2002. xi-xxi. Print.

—. *Rhetoric Reclaimed: Aristotle and the Liberal Arts Tradition.* Ithaca, NY: Cornell UP, 1998. Print.

Atwill, Janet M. and Janice M. Lauer, eds. *Perspectives on Rhetorical Invention.* Knoxville: U of Tennessee P, 2002. Print.

—. "Refiguring Rhetoric as an Art: Aristotle's Concept of *Techne.*" *Discourse Studies in Honor of James L. Kinneavy.* Ed. Rosalind J. Gabin. Potomac, MD: Scripta Humanistica, 1995. 25–40. Print.

Bailey, Dudley. "A Plea for a Modern Set of Topoi." *College English* 26 (1964): 111- 17. Print.

Bailey, Dudley, et al. "Report of the Committee on Future Directions." *College Composition and Communication* 11.1 (1960): 3–7. Print.

Ballif, Michelle. *Seduction, Sophistry, and the Woman with the Rhetorical Figure.* Carbondale: Southern Illinois UP, 2001. Print.

Bataille, Georges. *The Accursed Share.* Trans. Robert Hurley. 3 vols. Cambridge, MA: Zone Books, 1991, 1993. Print.

—. *Inner Experience.* Trans. Leslie Anne Boldt. Albany: SUNY P, 1988. Print.

—. "The Notion of Expenditure." *Visions of Excess: Selected Writings 1927–1939.* Trans. Allan Stoekl. Minneapolis: U of Minnesota P, 1985. 116–129. Print.

Benhabib, Seyla. *Situating the Self: Gender, Community, and Postmodernism in Contemporary Ethics.* New York: Routledge, 1992. Print.

Berthoff, Ann E. "The Problem of Problem Solving." *College Composition and Communication* 22 (1971): 237–42. Rpt. in *Contemporary Rhetoric: A Conceptual Background with Readings.* Ed. W. Ross Winterowd. New York: Harcourt, Brace, Jovanovich, 1975. 90–7. Print.

—. "Response to Janice Lauer." *College Composition and Communication* 23 (1972): 414–5. Rpt. in *Contemporary Rhetoric: A Conceptual Background with Readings.* Ed. W. Ross Winterowd. New York: Harcourt, Brace, Jovanovich, 1975. 100–3. Print.

Biesecker, Barbara. "Coming to Terms with Recent Attempts to Write Women into the History of Rhetoric." *Philosophy and Rhetoric* 25.2 (1992): 140–161. Print.

Bitzer, Lloyd and Edwin Black, eds. *The Prospect of Rhetoric: Report of the National Developmental Project.* New York: Prentice Hall, 1971.

Blanchot, Maurice. "Approaching Literature's Space." *The Space of Literature.* Trans. Ann Smock. Lincoln: U of Nebraska P, 1982. 37–48. Print.

—. "How Is Literature Possible?" *Faux Pas.* Trans. Charlotte Mandel. Palo Alto, CA: Stanford UP, 2001. 76–84. Print.

—. "Inner Experience." *Faux Pas*. Trans. Charlotte Mandel. Palo Alto, CA: Stanford UP, 2001. 37–41. Print.

—. "Literature and the Right to Death." *The Station Hill Blanchot Reader*. Trans. Lydia Davis. Barrytown, NY: Station Hill Press, 1999. 359–399. Print.

—. "The Work and Death's Space." *The Space of Literature*. Trans. Ann Smock. Lincoln: U of Nebraska P, 1982. 87–107. Print.

Boldt, Leslie Ann. "Translator's Introduction." *Inner Experience*. Albany: SUNY P, 1988. ix-xxiv. Print.

Boley, Tommy J. "A Heuristic for Persuasion." *College Composition and Communication* 30.2 (1979): 187–91. Print.

Burke, Kenneth. "Questions and Answers about the Pentad." *College Composition and Communication* 29.4 (1978): 330–35. Print.

Burke, Virginia. "The Composition-Rhetoric Pyramid." *College Composition and Communication* 16.1 (1965): 3–7. Print.

Carter, Michael P. *Where Writing Begins: A Postmodern Reconstruction*. Carbondale: Southern Illinois UP, 2003. Print.

Cherwitz, Richard and James W. Hikins. "Toward a Rhetorical Epistemology." *Southern Speech Communication Journal* 47 (1982): 135–62. Print.

Connors, Robert J. "Composition History and Disciplinarity." *History, Reflection, and Narrative: The Professionalization of Composition, 1963–1983*. Ed. Mary Rosner, et al. Vol. 3. Perspectives on Writing: Theory, Research. New York: Ablex Publishing Corporation, 1999. 3–21. Print.

—. *Composition-Rhetoric: Backgrounds, Theory, and Pedagogy*. Pittsburgh, PA: U of Pittsburgh P, 1997. Print.

Counciletter. "The Report on Basic Issues." *College English* 21.1 (1959): 52. Print.

Crowley, Sharon. *Methodical Memory: Invention in Current-Traditional Rhetoric*. Carbondale: Southern Illinois UP, 1990. Print.

Cuomo, S. *Technology and Culture in Greek and Roman Antiquity*. Cambridge: Cambridge UP, 2007. Print.

Davis, D. Diane. *Breaking Up [at] Totality: A Rhetoric of Laughter*. Carbondale: Southern Illinois UP, 2000. Print.

de Romilly, Jacqueline. *Magic and Rhetoric in Ancient Greece*. Cambridge, MA: Harvard UP, 1975. Print.

Derrida, Jacques. "From Restricted to General Economy: A Hegelianism without Reserve." *Writing and Difference*. Trans. Alan Bass. Chicago: U of Chicago P, 1978. 251–277. Print.

Detienne, Marcel and Jean-Pierre Vernant. *Cunning Intelligence in Greek Culture and Society*. Trans. Janet Lloyd. Sussex: Harvester Press, 1978. Print.

Dobrin, Sidney I. "From Writing Process to Cultural (Re)production: Composition's Theoretical Shift." Conference on College Composition and Communication. 22 Mar. 2002.

Doheny-Farina, Stephen. *Rhetoric, Innovation, Technology: Case Studies of Technical Communication in Technology Transfers.* Cambridge: Massachusetts Institute of Technology, 1992. Print.

Donlan, Dan. "Project English (1961–1968): Conception—Birth—Life—Death—And Who Cared?" 1978. ERIC Document Reproduction Service ED 175016. Print.

Drew, Julie. "(Teaching) Writing: Composition, Cultural Studies, Production." *JAC* 19.3 (1999). 411-29. Print.

Dubinsky, James M. "More Than a Knack: Techne and Teaching Technical Communication." *Technical Communication Quarterly* 11.2 (2002): 129–145. Print.

Dunne, Jospeh. *Back to the Rough Ground: Phronesis and Techne in Modern Philosophy and in Aristotle.* Notre Dame, IN: U of Notre Dame P, 1993. Print.

Edbauer, Jenny. "Unframing Models of Public Distribution: From Rhetorical Situation to Rhetorical Ecologies." *Rhetoric Society Quarterly* 35.4 (2005): 5–24. Print.

Elbow, Peter. *Embracing Contraries: Explorations in Learning and Teaching.* New York: Oxford UP, 1986. Print.

Elbow, Peter. *Writing Without Teachers.* New York: Oxford UP, 1973. Print.

Faigley, Lester. *The Brief Penguin Handbook.* 2nd ed. New York: Pearson Education, Inc., 2007. Print.

Fish, Stanley. "What Should Colleges Teach? Part 2." [Weblog Entry.] Think Again. *The New York Times.* 31 Aug. 2009. Web. 27 Sept. 2009.

Fogarty, Daniel. *Roots for a New Rhetoric.* New York: Russell and Russell, 1959. Print.

Foucault, Michel. *The Archaeology of Knowledge & The Discourse on Language.* Trans. A. M. Sheridan Smith. New York: Pantheon Books, 1972. Print.

Fraser, Nancy. *Unruly Practices: Power, Discourse, and Gender in Contemporary Social Theory.* Minneapolis: U of Minnesota P, 1989. Print.

Gadamer, Hans-Georg. *Truth and Method.* 2nd ed. Trans. Joel Weinsheimer and Donald G. Marshall. New York: Continuum Publishing Company, 1993. Print.

Gleason, H. A., Jr. "What Is English?" *College Composition and Communication* 13.3 (1962): 1–10. Print.

Goggin, Maureen Daly. *Authoring a Discipline: Scholarly Journals and the Post-World War II Emergence of Rhetoric and Composition.* Mahwah, NJ: Lawrence Erlbaum Associates, 2000. Print.

Gregg, John. *Maurice Blanchot and the Literature of Transgression*. Princeton, NJ: Princeton UP, 1994. Print.

Guinn, Dorothy M. "Composing an Abstract: A Practical Heuristic." *College Composition and Communication* 30.4 (1979): 380–3. Print.

Hackett, Herbert. "A Discipline of the Communication Skills." *College Composition and Communication* 6.1 (1955): 10–4. Print.

Harrington, David. "Encouraging Honest Inquiry in Student Writing." *College Composition and Communication* 30.2 (1979): 182–6. Print.

Harrington, David, et al. "A Critical Survey of Resources for Teaching Rhetorical Invention: A Review Essay." *College English* 40 (1979): 641–661. Rpt. in *The Writing Teacher's Sourcebook*. Ed. Gary Tate and Edward P. J. Corbett. New York: Oxford UP, 1981. 187–206. Print.

Harrington, Elbert. "A Modern Approach to Invention." *Quarterly Journal of Speech* 48 (1962): 373–78. Print.

Harris, Joseph A. *A Teaching Subject: Composition Since 1966*. New York: Prentice Hall, 1996. Print.

Hauser, Gerard. *Introduction to Rhetorical Theory*. Prospect Heights, IL: Waveland Press, 1991. Print.

Hawhee, Debra. "Bodily Pedagogies: Rhetoric, Athletics, and the Sophists' Three Rs." *College English* 65.2 (2002): 142–161. Print.

Hawk, Byron. *A Counter-History of Composition: Toward Methodologies of Complexity*. Pittsburgh, PA: U of Pittsburgh P, 2007. Print.

—. Toward a Post-*Techne*—Or, Inventing Pedagogies for Professional Writing." *Technical Communication Quarterly* 13.4 (2004): 371–392. Print.

Haynes, Cynthia. "Writing Offshore: The Disappearing Coastline of Composition Theory." *JAC* 23.4 (2003): 667–724. Print.

Heidegger, Martin. "Building Dwelling Thinking." *Poetry, Language, Thought*. Trans. and Intro. Albert Hofstadter. New York: Harper and Row, 1971. 143–161. Print.

—. *An Introduction to Metaphysics*. Trans. Ralph Manheim. New Haven, CT: Yale UP, 1987. Print.

—. *On the Way to Language*. Trans. Peter D. Hertz. New York: Harper and Row, 1971. Print.

—. "The Origin of the Work of Art." *Poetry, Language, Thought*. Trans. and Intro. Albert Hofstadter. New York: Harper and Row, 1971. 17–78. Print.

—. "The Question Concerning Technology." *The Question Concerning Technology and Other Essays*. Trans. and Intro. William Lovitt. New York: Harper and Row, 1977. 3–35. Print.

Hook, J. N. "Project English: The First Year." *PMLA* 78.4.2 (1963): 33–5. Print.

Irmscher, William. *The Holt Guide to English: A Contemporary Handbook of Rhetoric, Language, and Literature*. New York: Holt, Rinehart, and Winston, 1972. Print.

Isocrates. *Against the Sophists.* Trans. George Norlin. The Loeb Classical Library. London: William Heinemann, 1929. 160–177. Print.

Jennings, E. M. "A Paradigm for Discovery." *College Composition and Communication* 19 (1968): 192–200. Print.

Kane, Thomas S. "Rhetoric and the 'Problem' of Composition." *College English* 22.7 (1961): 503–6. Print.

Keith, Philip M. "Burke for the Composition Class." *College Composition and Communication* 28 (1977): 348–51. Print.

—. "Burkeian Invention, from Pentad to Dialectic." *Rhetoric Society Quarterly* 9 (1979): 137–41. Print.

Kent, Thomas. "Introduction." *Post-Process Theory: Beyond the Writing-Process Paradigm.* Ed. Thomas Kent. Carbondale: Southern Illinois UP, 1999. 1–6. Print.

—. "Paralogic Rhetoric: An Overview." *Rhetoric and Composition as Intellectual Work.* Ed. Gary A. Olson. Carbondale: Southern Illinois UP, 2001. 143-153. Print.

—. *Paralogic Rhetoric: A Theory of Communicative Interaction.* Lewisburg, PA: Bucknell UP, 1993. Print.

Kitzhaber, Albert K. "4C, Freshman English, and the Future." *College Composition and Communication* 14.3 (1963): 129–138. Print.

—. "Death—or Transfiguration?" *College English* 21.7 (1960): 367–73. Print.

—. *Themes, Theories, and Therapy: The Teaching of Writing in College.* New York: McGraw Hill, 1963. Print.

Kneupper, Charles. "Dramatistic Invention: The Pentad as Heuristic Procedure." *Rhetoric Society Quarterly* 9 (1979): 130–36. Print.

—. "Revising the Tagmemic Heuristic: Theoretical and Pedagogical Considerations." *College Composition and Communication* 31 (1980): 160–8. Print.

Koestler, Arthur. *The Act of Creation.* New York: Macmiillan, 1964. Print.

Kojève, Alexandre. *Introduction to the Reading of Hegel.* Ed. Alan Bloom. Trans. Henry Nichols, Jr. New York: Basic Books, 1969. Print.

Kopelson, Karen. "Sp(l)itting Images; or, Back to the Future of (Rhetoric and?) Composition." *College Composition and Communication* 59.4 (2008): 750–80. Print.

Larson, Richard. "Discovery Through Questioning: A Plan for Teaching Rhetorical Invention." *College English* 30 (1968): 261–84. Print.

Lauer, Janice M. "Heuristics and Composition." *College Composition and Communication* 21.5 (1970): 396–404. Print.

—. "Invention in Contemporary Rhetoric: Heuristic Procedures." Diss. University of Michigan, 1967. Print.

—. "Rhetorical Invention: The Diaspora." *Perspectives on Rhetorical Invention.* Ed. Janet M. Atwill and Janice M. Lauer. Knoxville: U of Tennessee P, 2002. 1–15. Print.

—. "A Response to Ann E. Berthoff." *College Composition and Communication* 23 (1972): 208–211. Rpt. W. Ross Winterowd, ed. *Contemporary Rhetoric: A Conceptual Background with Readings.* New York: Harcourt, Brace, Jovanovich, 1975. 97–100. Print.

—. "The Teacher of Writing." *College Composition and Communication* 27.4 (1976): 341–3. Print.

—. "Toward A Meta-Theory of Heuristic Procedures." *College Composition and Communication* 30 (1979): 268–9. Print.

—. *"Writing for Insight." Conversations in Composition, Proceedings of New Dimensions in Writing: The First Merrimack College Conference on Composition Instruction.* Ed. Albert C. DeCiccio and Michael J. Rossi. North Andover, MA: Merrimack College, 1987. 1–6. Print.

Lauer, Janice M., et al. *Four Worlds of Writing.* New York: Harper and Row, 1981. Print.

Leff, Michael. "In Search of Ariadne's Thread: A Review of the Recent Literature on Rhetorical Theory." *Central States Speech Journal* 29 (1978): 73–91. Print.

Leggett, Glenn. "What Are Colleges and Universities Doing in Written Composition?" *College English* 23.1 (1961): 40–2. Print.

Libertson, Joseph. "Bataille and Communication: Savoir, Non-Savoir, Glissement, Rire." *On Bataille: Critical Essays.* Ed. Leslie Anne Boldt-Irons. Albany: SUNY P, 1995. 209–231.

Lunsford, Andrea and John J. Ruszkiewicz. *Everything's An Argument.* 3rd ed. Boston, MA: Bedford/St. Martin's, 2004. Print.

Lyotard, Jean-Francois. *The Postmodern Condition: A Report on Knowledge.* Trans. Geoff Bennington. Minneapolis: U of Minnesota P, 1984. Print.

Macrorie, Ken. *Telling Writing.* 2nd ed. Rochelle Park, NJ: Hayden Book Company, Inc., 1976. Print.

Mailloux, Steven. "Re-Marking Slave Bodies: Rhetoric as Production and Reception." *Philosophy & Rhetoric* 35 (2002): 96-119. Print.

Meagher, Robert. "Techne." *Perspecta* 24 (1988): 159–64. Print.

Miller, Carolyn R. "What's Practical about Technical Writing?" *Technical Writing: Theory and Practice.* Ed. Bertie E. Fearing and W. Keats Sparrow. New York: MLA, 1989. 14–26. Print.

Miller, J. Hillis. "Moving *Critical Inquiry* On." *Critical Inquiry* 30.2 (2004). Web. 23 September 2009.

Miller, Susan. "Technologies of Self?-Formation." *JAC* 17.3 (1997): 497-500. Print.

Miller, Thomas. "Professional Writing as Social Practice." *JAC* 11 (1991): 57–72. Print.

Modern Language Association of America, Members of the 1958 Conference. "The Basic Issues in the Teaching of English." *PMLA* 74.4.2 (1959): 1–12. Print.

Moeller, Ryan and Kenneth McAllister. "Playing with *Techne:* A Propaedeutic for Technical Communication." *Technical Communication Quarterly* 11.2 (2000): 185–206. Print.

Moore, Michael R., and Tracy Bridgeford, eds. *Technical Communication Quarterly: Special Issue on Techne and Technical Communication* 11 (2002). Print.

Muckelbauer, John. "Rhetoric, Asignification, and the Other: A Response to Diane Davis." *Philosophy and Rhetoric* 40.2 (2007): 238–47. Print.

—. *The Future of Invention: Rhetoric, Postmodernism, and the Problem of Change.* Albany: State UP of New York, 2008. Print.

National Council of Teachers of English, Committee on National Interest. *The National Interest and the Teaching of English: A Report on the Status of the Profession.* Urbana, IL: NCTE, 1961. Print.

North, Stephen. *The Making of Knowledge in Composition: Portrait of an Emerging Field.* Portsmouth, NH: Boynton/Cook Publishers, 1987. Print.

Nussbaum, Martha. *The Fragility of Goodness: Luck and Ethics in Greek Tragedy and Philosophy.* Cambridge: Cambridge UP, 1986. Print.

Nystrand, Martin, et al. "Where Did Composition Studies Come From? An Intellectual History." *Written Communication* 10.3 (1993): 267–333. Print.

Olson, David. *Jerome Bruner: The Cognitive Revolution in Educational Theory.* London: Continuum International Publishing Group, 2007. Print.

Paine, Charles. *The Resistant Writer: Rhetoric as Immunity, 1850 to the Present.* Albany: SUNY P, 1999. Print.

Papillion, Terry. "Isocrates' *techne* and Rhetorical Pedagogy." *Rhetoric Society Quarterly* 25 (1995): 149–163. Print.

Paulhan, Jean. *The Flowers of Tarbes Or, Terror in Literature.* Trans. Michael Syrontinski. Urbana, IL: U of Chicago P, 2006. Print.

Petraglia, Joseph. "Is There Life After Process? The Role of Social Scientism in a Changing Discipline." *Post-Process Theory: Beyond the Writing-Process Paradigm.* Ed. Thomas Kent. Carbondale: Southern Illinois UP, 1999: 49–64. Print.

—. "Shaping Sophisticates: Implications of the Rhetorical Turn." *Inventing a Discipline: Rhetoric Scholarship in Honor of Richard E. Young.* Ed. Maureen Daly Goggin. Urbana, IL: National Council of Teachers of English, 2000: 80–104. Print.

Phillips, Donna Burns, et al. "*College Composition and Communication:* Chronicling a Discipline's Genesis." *College Composition and Communication* 44.4 (1993): 443–65. Print.

Pike, Kenneth L. "A Linguistic Contribution to Composition: A Hypothesis." *College Composition and Communication* 15.2 (1964): 82–8. Print.

Pfister, Fred and Joanne F. Petrick. "A Heuristic Model for Creating a Writer's Audience." *College Composition and Communication* 31.2 (1980): 213–20. Print.

Plato. *The Gorgias*. Trans. Robin Waterfield. Oxford: Oxford UP, 1994. Print.

—. *The Phaedrus*. Trans. W. C. Hembold and W. G. Rabinowitz. Indianapolis, IN: The Library of Liberal Arts, 1956. Print.

—. *The Protagoras*. Trans. B. Jowett. Ed. Gregory Vlastos. New York: Liberal Arts Press, 1956. Print.

Poulakos, Takis. "Isocrates' Use of *Doxa*." *Philosophy and Rhetoric* 34.1 (2001): 61–78. Print.

Quintilian. *Institutio Oratoria*. Trans. H. E. Butler. The Loeb Classical Library. Cambridge, MA: Harvard UP, 1921. Print.

Rhetorica ad Herennium. Trans. Harry Caplan. The Loeb Classical Library. Cambridge, MA: Harvard UP, 1954. Print.

Rice, Warner. "A Proposal for the Abolition of Freshman English, As It Is Now Commonly Taught, from the College Curriculum." *College English* 21.7 (1960): 361–367. Print.

Rickert, Thomas. *Acts of Enjoyment: Rhetoric, Zizek, and the Return of the Subject*. Pittsburgh, PA: U of Pittsburgh P, 2007. Print.

Rohman, D. Gordon. "Pre-Writing: The Stage of Discovery in the Writing Process." *College Composition and Communication* 16 (1965): 106–12. Print.

Roochnik, David. *Of Art and Wisdom: Plato's Understanding of Techne*. University Park: Pennsylvania State UP, 1996. Print.

Sams, Henry W. "Fields of Research in Rhetoric." *College Composition and Communication* 5.2 (1954): 60–4. Print.

Schaedler, Louis C. "Call Me Scientist." *College Composition and Communication* 17.2 (1966): 110–14. Print.

Scott, Robert. "On Viewing Rhetoric as Epistemic." *Central States Speech Journal* 18 (1967): 9–17. Print.

Selfe, Cynthia and Sue Rodi. "An Invention Heuristic for Expressive Writing." *College Composition and Communication* 31.2 (1980): 169–74. Print.

Simmons, Sue Carter. "Constructing Writers: Barrett Wendell's Pedagogy at Harvard." *College Composition and Communication* 46 (1995): 327–352. Print.

Sirc, Geoffrey. *English Composition as a Happening*. Logan: Utah State UP, 2002. Print.

—. "Godless Composition, Tormented Writing." *JAC* 15. 3 (1995): 543–564. Print.

Slack, Robert C. "A Report on Project English." *College English* 26.1 (1964): 43–7. Print.

Sloterdijk, Peter. *Critique of Cynical Reason.* Minneapolis: Univerisity of Minnesota P, 1987. Print.

Squire, James R. "College English Departments and Efforts to Improve English Teaching." *PMLA* 78.4.2 (1963): 36–8. Print.

"Status in the Profession of the Composition Teacher." Report of Workshop No. 8. *College Composition and Communication* 4.3 (1953): 89–91. Print.

Steinberg, Erwin. "Research on the Teaching of English Under Project English." *PMLA* 79.4.2 (1964): 50–76. Print.

Steinmann, Martin, ed. *New Rhetorics.* New York: Scribner's, 1967. Print.

Stewart, Donald C. *The Authentic Voice: A Pre-Writing Approach to Student Writing.* Dubuque, IA: W. C. Brown Co., 1972. Print.

Sullivan, Dale. "Political-Ethical Implications of Defining Technical Communication as a Practice." *JAC* 10 (1990): 375–86. Print.

Tibbetts, A. M. "The Case Against Structural Linguistics in Composition." *College English* 21.5 (1960): 280–5. Print.

Vitanza, Victor. "From Heuristics to Aleatory Procedures; Or Toward Writing the Accident." *Inventing a Discipline.* Ed. Maureen Daly Goggin. Urbana, IL: NCTE, 2000. 185–206. Print.

—. "Invention, Serendipity, Catastrophe, and a Unified, Ironic Theory of Change: The Two Master and Two Mistress Tropes, with Attendant Offspring." *Visions of Rhetoric: History, Theory, and Criticism.* Ed. Charles Kneupper. Arlington, TX: Rhetoric Society of America, 1987. 132–45. Print.

—. *Negation, Subjectivity, and the History of Rhetoric.* Albany: SUNY P, 1997. Print.

—. "Three Countertheses: Or, A Critical In(ter)vention into Composition Theories and Pedagogies." *Contending with Words.* Ed. Patricia Harkin and John Schlib. New York: MLA, 1991. 139–172. Print.

—. "'The Wasteland Grows': Or, What is 'Cultural Studies for Composition' and Why Must We Always Speak Good of It?: ParaResponse to Julie Drew." *JAC* 19.4 (1999): 699–703. Print.

Warnick, Barbara. "Judgment, Probability, and Aristotle's *Rhetoric.*" *Quarterly Journal of Speech* 75.3 (1989): 299–311. Print.

Weber, Samuel. "Upsetting the Set Up: Remarks on Heidegger's Questing after Technics." *Modern Language Notes* 104.5 (1989): 977–992. Print.

Wild, John. "Plato's Theory of *Techne*: A Phenomenological Interpretation." *Philosophy and Phenomenological Research* 1.3 (1941): 255–93. Print.

Winterowd, W. Ross. *Composition/Rhetoric: A Synthesis.* Carbondale: Southern Illinois UP, 1986. Print.

—, ed. *Contemporary Rhetoric: A Conceptual Background with Readings.* New York: Harcourt, Brace, Jovanovich, 1975. Print.

—. *The Contemporary Writer: A Practical Rhetoric.* Chicago, IL: Harcourt Brace Jovanovich, 1975. Print.

Wilson, Gordon. "College Freshman Composition: How Can We Improve It?" *College Composition and Communication* 12.1 (1961): 27–32. Print.

Woolley, Edwin C. *Handbook of Composition: A Compendium of Rules.* Boston, MA: D. C. Heath and Co. Publishers, 1907. Print.

Worsham, Lynn. "The Question Concerning Invention: Hermeneutics and the Genesis of Writing." *PRE/TEXT* 8 (1987): 197–244. Print.

Wykoff, George S. "Toward Achieving the Objectives of Freshman Composition." *College English* 10.6 (1949): 319–323. Print.

Young, Richard E. "Arts, Crafts, Gifts, and Knacks: Some Disharmonies in the New Rhetoric." *Reinventing the Rhetorical Tradition.* Ed. Ian Pringle and Avia Freedman. Conway, AK: L and S Books, 1980. 53–60. Print.

—. "Invention: A Topographical Survey." *Teaching Composition: Ten Bibliographic Essays.* Ed. Gary Tate. Fort Worth: Texas Christian UP, 1976. 1–43. Print.

—. "Methodizing Nature: The Tagmemic Discovery Procedure." *Rhetoric and Change.* Ed. William E. Tanner and Jimmy Dean Bishop. Mesquite: Ide House, 1982. 126-132. Print.

—. "Recent Developments in Rhetorical Invention." *Teaching Composition: Twelve Bibliographic Essays.* Ed. Gary Tate. Fort Worth: Texas Christian UP, 1987. 1–38. Print.

—. "Working on the Margin: Rhetorical Studies and the New Self-Consciousness." *Rhetoric Society Quarterly* 20.4 (1990): 325–32. Print.

Young, Richard E. and Alton L. Becker. "Toward A Modern Theory of Rhetoric: A Tagmemic Contribution." *Harvard Educational Review* 35 (1965): 450–68. Print.

Young, Richard E., Alton L. Becker, and Kenneth L. Pike. *Rhetoric: Discovery and Change.* New York: Harcourt, Brace, and World, 1970. Print.

Zimmerman, Michael E. *Heidegger's Confrontation with Modernity: Technology, Poetry, Art.* Bloomington: Indiana UP, 1990. Print.

Index

Aeschylus, 29

aleatory procedures, 85, 86, 162n

Allen, Harold B, 62, 69

Allen, James, 25, 124

Applebee, Arthur, 64, 68; *Tradition and Reform in the Teaching of English*, 64

Arendt, Hannah, 33, 34, 36; *The Human Condition*, 33

Aristotelianism, 45

Aristotle, 4–6, 14- 17, 19, 21, 23, 25, 36, 45, 86, 88, 91, 94, 99, 110, 123–131, 163n–164n; *De Paribus Animalum*, 94; *Introduction to Metaphysics*, 23, 25, 45, 124; *Magna Moralia*, 15, 126; *Nicomachean Ethics*, 6, 15, 19, 21, 110, 124–125; *Physics*, 129, 130; *Rhetoric*, 21, 23, 27–30, 39, 45–52, 61, 69, 77, 79, 88, 89, 90, 93, 101, 105, 111, 121, 137, 143, 154n-156n, 158n, 159n-160n, 162n, 165n, 167n

art, 4. 9, 13, 15, 17, 21, 22, 23, 27, 28, 29, 30, 35, 38, 88, 89, 90, 91, 92, 93, 96, 98, 99, 125, 127, 137, 142, 144, 145, 152; critiques of, 83, 85, 86, 87; fine art, 109, 110, 114, 119; and nature, 128, 129, 130, 131; new classicist definition of, 26, 39-48, 50, 52, 54, 55, 60, 61, 67, 71, 72, 73, 74, 76, 77, 103-107, 124, 154n, 155n; new romanti-

cist definition of, 43, 44, 45, 57, 58, 59

Atwill, Janet, 13, 27, 28–30, 31, 37, 41, 73, 75, 88–94, 101, 104–105, 123, 154n, 158n-159n, 165n-166n; *Rhetoric Reclaimed; Aristotle and the Liberal Arts Tradition*, 88

axiology, 8, 11, 14–16, 18, 27, 31, 38, 73, 76–77, 103, 107–108, 114, 120, 160n

Ballif, Michelle, 13, 34, 86, 87, 122; *Seduction, Sophistry, and the Woman with the Rhetorical Figure*, 34, 86

Bataille, Georges, 11, 80–82, 85, 116, 124, 132–136, 158n, 164n, 165n; *Inner Experience*, 80–81, 158n, 164n

Becker, Alton, 24, 45, 46, 47, 49, 50, 51, 77, 154n; *Rhetoric; Discovery and Change*, 47, 49, 51, 77

Beisecker, Barbara, 96–98, 100

Berthoff, Ann, 47, 74–76, 103

Berlin, James, 145

Blanchot, Maurice, 11, 108- 109, 114–121, 123, 162n-165n

Bohr, Neils, 43, 58

Bordieu, Pierre, 30

Bruner, Jerome, 48–49, 55

Burke, Kenneth, 52–53

Burke, Virginia, 43, 156n

About the Author

Kelly Pender holds a PhD in English from Purdue University. She is an assistant professor of English at Virginia Tech, where she teaches courses in professional writing, public discourse, critical theory, and classical rhetoric. She has presented papers at numerous conferences, and her work has appeared in journals such as *Postmodern Culture*, *Composition Studies*, and *Rhetoric Society Quarterly*. Her research interests include the history and theory of rhetoric and composition, critical theory, and medical rhetoric, particularly rhetorics of genetic risk and disease prevention.

CPSIA information can be obtained
at www.ICGtesting.com
Printed in the USA
BVHW070741310120
570974BV00003B/413